Origins of Programming

A.P. Ershov

Origins of Programming
Discourses on Methodology

Translated by Robert H. Silverman

With 74 Illustrations

Springer-Verlag
New York Berlin Heidelberg
London Paris Tokyo Hong Kong

A.P. Ershov
Computation Center
U.S.S.R Academy of Sciences
Novosibirsk 630090
U.S.S.R

R.H. Silverman (*Translator*)
22 Trowbridge Street
Cambridge, MA 02138
U.S.A

Original Russian copyright held by Nauka 1977.

Library of Congress Cataloging in Publication Data
Ershov, A. P. (Andrei Petrovich)
    Origins of programming : discourses on methodology / Andrei P.
Ershov ; translated by Robert H. Silverman.
        p. cm.
    Translated from Russian.
    ISBN 0-387-97061-4
    1. Electronic digital computers—Programming. I. Title.
QA76.6.E77 1990
005.1—dc20   89-28493
                                                          CIP

Typeset by Macmillan India Ltd., Bangalore-25, India
Printed and bound by R.R. Donnelley & Sons, Harrisonburg, Virginia.
Printed in the United States of America.

9 8 7 6 5 4 3 2 1
ISBN 0-387-97061-4 Springer-Verlag New York Berlin Heidelberg
ISBN 3-540-97061-4 Springer-Verlag Berlin Heidelberg New York

Preface

This book represents a kind of experiment for the author. The experiment will have succeeded if it closes a gap in the mathematical literature. How important this effort will have been, only time will tell; in the meantime, I'd like to try to explain the reasons for undertaking such an experiment.

The book is intended primarily for readers who wish to study mathematics. A mathematics education has as its goals the acquisition of mathematical knowledge and the development of the ability to apply this knowledge in the solution of problems in the real world, or in the construction or modification of the unceasingly growing edifice of mathematics. Unfortunately, in that division of a mathematics education characterized by lesson plans and required assignments, there is a considerable gulf between mathematical knowledge and the creative component of mathematics itself. To a large extent, this gulf is unavoidable. The vast store of accumulated knowledge squeezed into the pages of a textbook or presented in a course of lectures leaves neither space nor time for learning about the nature and breadth of the creative efforts that went into the discovery of this knowledge. The faultless logic underlying the structure of a lecture and the polished delivery informing its presentation make the elements of mathematical structures, and the threads of reasoning that tie them together, invisible to the eyes of the students, and gives them a sense of confronting something ineffable that may not be tampered with (nezyblyaemost' ideal' nogo); students often think of themselves more as wayfarers in the temple of science rather than its inhabitants, let alone its true builders. And those areas in the curriculum that require a real effort on their part (exercises, applications) often seem contrived or like drills, and lack elements such as the statements of problems or searches for the methods of solution that are so essential in the development of the creative imagination.

It is generally agreed that the first three years of university study are critical for the formation of the student's professional orientation and, quite often, his or her general outlook as well. In the final two years, studies become more pragmatic, and are undertaken with a clear purpose in mind. This is why it is so necessary to accustom students early on to the creative principles underlying their fields of concentration. In mathematics education there is a further difficulty in that the majority of the various branches of mathematics now under development are highly advanced and cannot be studied in the lower grades.

The foregoing considerations have served as the motivation in the selection of material for the present book, as well as the method of presentation we have adopted.

*   *   *

Theoretical programming (in some translated works, it is also referred to as theoretical computational mathematics or mathematical computation theory) is a new branch of mathematics whose subject of study are mathematical abstractions of programs, i.e., sets of instructions expressed in special algorithmic languages that possess a designated logical structure and structure of knowledge, and moreover can be implemented on computers. Theoretical programming was created in part to meet practical demands, and in part from the desire to understand the nature of the new environment created by the computer. Once the new field had assimilated the tools and concepts of the fundamental mathematical disciplines of logic, theory of algorithms, algebra, and combinatorics, it began to build upon this initial foundation, gradually creating its own set of concepts and methods. To discuss some of these concepts and methods is one goal of the present work, though not the principal one.

We will start with a detailed discussion of two problems that have played an extremely important role in the emergence of theoretical programming as an independent discipline. Our principal goals in this book will be to explain the line of thought that was followed in solving these problems, to demonstrate the workings of the mathematical way of thinking, to analyze carefully the different stages of descriptive analysis and problem formulation, and to reveal the aesthetic component in the search for solutions—in other words, we will try to turn the reader into a true witness of the process of discovering mathematical results. This overall goal is also responsible for the mode of presentation we have chosen. The book is written in the form of a series of conversations, and is intended more for reading than for study.

In the first part of the book we consider the storage minimization, or storage packing, problem in program schemas. The constructions and concepts that became part of theoretical programming in the course of solving this problem not only constituted a major contribution to the development of the discipline itself, but also served as a foundation for a broad class of program transformations employed in computer-aided programming systems and in program testing. The problem of storage packing is treated as an example that illustrates how to solve a problem in applications by means of mathematical methods. The presentation is divided into chapters, each of which analyzes a single unified stage in the complete solution of the problem: descriptive statement of the problem, rigorous statement and general theory, search for a constructive method of solution followed by "algorithmization" of the search process, and, finally, the actual writing of programs in an algorithmic language.

In Part II, we present the theory of Yanov program schemas, a classical theory generally recognized as having served as a foundation of the mathematical theory of programming. Within the framework of a model of computer programs constructed by A.A. Lyapunov and Yu.I. Yanov, a formal calculus was developed (by Yanov) by means of which the recognition problem for the equivalence of program models was exhaustively solved. A system of independent transformations that may be used to convert one program into some other program equivalent to the original one, was also constructed. In the present book, the theory of Yanov program schemas is analyzed as a methodological example that illustrates how a fully developed mathematical theory (in this case, the formal propositional calculus) can be extended to a new class of phenomena and objects: program schemas and configurations of program schemas.

*   *   *

Some further remarks are in order if the reader is to understand the rationale for the mode of presentation adopted in the present book. The field of programming has now become a major professional occupation. Unfortunately, however, both in the teaching of programming and in its everyday practical use, a superficial and prescriptive approach to the study of the discipline itself and its applications is often dominant. In this approach, it is assumed that rudimentary literacy in the various algorithmic languages very nearly exhausts the scope of the entire profession of programming. Because of the gap between the high level of mathematics acquired by mathematicians who work as programmers, and the commonplace nature of their everyday duties in writing programs, some programmers come to feel that their mathematical skills are slighted in the very pursuit of their profession. It is our hope that the present book will help professional programmers discern the points where mathematical methods are applied to the objects and content of their everyday work.

Yet another convenient, so to speak, feature of theoretical programming is the fact that as a science it is being created right before our eyes. It is because of this feature that we are able to observe, in a very accurate and faithful manner, the mechanisms by which mathematical results are discovered and the different stages in the development of the discipline. Also, a science can be said to be in its infancy if direct methods of proof predominate and if many of its problems can be stated in an elementary way. This added feature makes for a more vivid and direct presentation of the discipline, and obviates the need for an advanced level of prerequisite knowledge. Last, but not least in importance, is the fact that theoretical programming happens to be the special scientific province of the present author, and this has made it possible to present material as it was first discovered, at "firsthand."

Because our presentation is elementary, the content of the book is complete in itself, i.e., no other books have to be read in advance. The absolute minimum of preliminary knowledge that is nevertheless useful, if not mandatory, is enumerated or briefly set forth in review sections inserted at appropriate spots in the text. While the presentation is elementary, the author must nevertheless forewarn the reader that successful comprehension of the substance of the book at just the reading level will require unstinting concentration and mental effort. Nevertheless, without feeling that there is some threshold of knowledge that must be attained at the outset, but simply following the thread of the presentation, by the end of the book the reader will have covered the full range of problems that constitutes the content of modern professional mathematics research, without any allowance ever having been made for his or her age or background.

*   *   *

As we have already remarked, the book is basically intended for independent reading by university students. It can also be used by mathematics clubs and in seminars at technical institutes, in classes in applied mathematics, and in the early grades of pedagogical institutes.

Material was gathered for the book over the course of many years and presented in part at the Far East Summer School for University Teachers (Vladivostok) in 1970, in a lecture course presented at Stanford University, also in 1970, and in a special course for freshman and sophomore mathematics students at Novosibirsk University in 1971–72.

While underscoring the experimental nature of the present book, the author can't help but mention a number of outstanding mathematical works that have inspired the present book. Undoubtedly, many contemporary mathematicians have experienced for themselves the effect of such remarkable books as *What is Mathematics?* by Richard Courant and Herbert Robbins, and *Mathematics and Plausible Reasoning* by George Polya. For a more direct influence, there is the small book by Aleksandr Ya. Khinchin, *Three Pearls of Number Theory* (available in English translation), which is an unsurpassed example illustrating how to reveal the content of a science through a discussion of actual problems, as well as the well-known memoir by René Baire, *On Discontinuous Functions* (*Leçons sur la théorie des fonctions discontinues*), a book that convincingly demonstrates the power of a step-by-step development of the solution of a problem, starting with an elementary statement of the problem and concluding with the complete solution in all its complexity. These works have made a strong impression on the author of the present work.

While I would hardly claim to be following in the footsteps of such illustrious predecessors, I nevertheless view the present book as a modest attempt at partially repaying the debt left us by our teachers— sparing no effort at revealing the utility, profundity, and beauty of mathematics to all those who wish to become familiar with this foundation stone of modern knowledge.

Akademgorod   A.P. Ershov
Novosibirsk

Contents

Part I Storage Allocation in Program Schemas

CHAPTER 1

Descriptive Analysis of the Problem

1.1. Brief Review of Computer Programming

The Electronic Computer

A computer is an automaton consisting of a memory and a control unit. The memory comprises *locations* numbered in sequence; the number of a location is referred to as the *address* of the location. Information is represented in the computer in the form of a binary number, i.e., as a sequence of zeros and ones, and is stored that way in the locations. And just as two sequences of dots and dashes in Morse code may denote very different pieces of information, so the zeros and ones stored in the memory locations may denote far more than just the digits of a binary number. To emphasize the great variety of interpretations of the content of a memory location, this content is referred to as a (*machine*) *word*; the number of binary digits in a word is called the *length* of the word.

The control unit executes individual *instructions*. The instruction set available is usually comparatively limited, and the instructions themselves quite simple. Here is a typical instruction. Take one or two words from given memory locations as arguments, transfer them to the control unit, execute a designated operation on them (add or multiply them or compare them in terms of magnitude), and transfer the result to a designated memory location.

Program

From the foregoing it is clear that to solve a problem of any degree of complexity, the computer must execute a very long sequence of instructions. Since a computer operates automatically, this sequence of instructions must be thought up in advance and placed into the computer's memory prior to starting the problem-solving process. Usually, one and only one instruction may be stored at any one memory location, and since the control unit operates continuously, this means that each instruction (provided it is not the computer's halt instruction) must deposit in the control unit the address of the location containing the next executable instruction. Thus, to create a *computer program* that will solve a given problem, it is necessary to write a sequence of computer instructions which will cause the control unit to implement a sequence of operations that lead to the solution, as these instructions are executed one after the other—once, that is, these instructions have been stored in the proper segment of the computer memory.

Each instruction induces the computer to perform a specified operation upon the contents of designated memory locations. This means that in writing a program it is necessary to determine which memory locations will be used when the computer is in operation and what will be stored in these locations. We usually proceed. in the following way. In the process of thinking up a method of solving some problem, a programmer decides which *variables* are likely to crop up and then used to solve the problem. Certain variables may already be specified in the conditions of the problem; these are usually the initial data and the desired results. Others arise in the course of solving the problem and are referred to as the *temporary variables*. These variables are computed by executing various instructions in the program (and are the "results" of these instructions), and are then used later on in other instructions as arguments.

Thus, in order to write a program a programmer needs two lists: a list of instructions and a list of program variables. These lists are associated directly with the computer memory (a location is correlated with each position in each of the lists) and with each other. The relation between the variables and the instructions may be described roughly as follows. Each instruction consists of two parts: an *operation code* indicating which operation the particular instruction invokes, and an *address part*. The address part specifies the addresses of locations used as either the *arguments* or the *results* of the instruction. In certain instructions, the address part specifies the addresses of instructions, rather than the addresses of locations containing the variables. This is particularly the case whenever the next executable instruction does not follow a given instruction in the program, but is located somewhere else, as indicated by its address. This may happen when a group of program instructions are to be repeated several times or when one or more directions of computation are to be selected depending upon the value of a variable used in the program.

Programming

Let us think a bit more about what we have just said. It is clear that there are similarities between programming on a computer and the high-school method of problem-solving in which a series of questions are posed. In this method, a student creates a plan of the solution that consists of a series of questions. In each of these questions, it is necessary to decide which problem variable is to be computed, further each question is framed in such a way that the computation can be performed in a single operation on variables whose values are already known. Bear in mind that a problem becomes quite intractable if its solution requires five or six operations. In programming real problems for a computer, by contrast, the plan of solution has to allow for tens of thousands of operations, (and sometimes even more) and for each such operation an instruction that causes the operation to be executed must be written out faultlessly. It is for this reason that from the very first appearance of the computer, programmers have devoted considerable effort in attempts to create methods that would facilitate the actual labor of programming.

One such strategy is to divide the process of writing a program for a computer into several stages. In the first stage, a programmer writes out the program in a form in which it can be easily conceptualized. In the next stage, an intermediate form of the program is converted—according to designated formal rules—into a machine–language program, i.e., a program that can be understood directly by the computer. These rules are formal in the sense that their application to the intermediate program requires punctilious exactitude on the part of the programmer without, however, any need to understand what the program really does. In other words, these rules are applicable in a universal way to the intermediate form of any program. For this reason, rules for the conversion of the intermediate program into its machine-language version can be described in the form of a general-purpose algorithm, which itself can be programmed. In the "supra-program" thus obtained, the input data will be any intermediate program, while the result will be a machine-language program that corresponds precisely to the intermediate form. In the specialized literature such supra-programs are called interpreters or compilers. If a compiler is available, the intermediate form of a program which a programmer feels most comfortable with becomes his final result, and all the other labor involved in creating the program is left for the computer to accomplish, by recourse to the compiler.

Understood as a field of applied science, programming consists in the development of "programming languages," that is, methods of expressing programs that programmers find convenient to use, and methods of translation or conversion from these programming languages into what may be called the *machine language.*

Symbolic Program

At the simplest level, a programmer can be taught how to write a *symbolic program* in place of a machine-language program. This he conceives of while keeping in mind the system of computer instructions. As before, he must write out a list of instructions and a list of program variables in such a way that each entry in these lists corresponds to a single memory location in the computer. However, a programmer usually has far less trouble working with such a program because of the way these lists are written out. Instead of addresses of memory locations for the program variables, he may use the ordinary notation these variables have in the statement of the problem, or some notation he himself may think up to help visualize the problem. In place of the numerical code of some operation, represented in the machine-language instruction by means of a combination of binary digits, he may use a *mnemonic code* which, by its very form, suggests the descriptive meaning of the instruction, for example, " + " for the addition instruction, " < " for the number comparison instruction, or the word **stop** for the machine's halt instruction. If a programmer must use the address of an instruction, all he has to do is insert any meaningfully appropriate word or letter, called the *instruction label*, next to this instruction in the symbolic program, and use this label in the address part as the address of the instruction.

A programmer may use any symbols, letters, or digits to denote values, mnemonic codes, and labels, provided that the resulting text of the symbolic program is suitable for input into the computer. To a first approximation, we may say that any text that may be printed on a typewriter without the need for special devices, i.e., without interlinear text, may be input into a computer.

The transformation, or, as is usually said, the *translation* of a symbolic program into a machine-language program occurs in the following way. The computer first reads in the symbolic program while it is under the control of the compiler. It then compiles a table of notation and labels for use in the program. The computer does not have to compile a table of mnemonic codes, since this table is the same for all symbolic programs and is stored permanently in the compiler. Memory is then allocated, i.e., a memory location is correlated with each variable and each instruction in the program. (This memory location is the actual place where the particular variable or instruction is to be stored.) Note that memory may be allocated trivially:

(a) The instructions of a machine-language program are distributed in precisely the same way they are distributed in the symbolic program. All the programmer then has to do is count how many instructions there are in the program, and assign in the memory as many locations as there are instructions beginning at some address A, correlating with the nth instruction (in the sequence of instructions) the location with address $A + n - 1$;

(b) Each variable is placed in a separate location; as many locations in memory are used as there are variables in the symbolic program.

After memory has been allocated, there remains the task of systematically substituting a binary code for the mnemonic code of the operations in each instruction of the symbolic program, likewise substituting the addresses of the locations correlated with the names of the variables and the instruction labels in the address parts of the instructions for these names and labels.

Algorithmic Languages

The invention of algorithmic languages was the next major advance in the effort to facilitate the work of the computer programmer.

A program written in an algorithmic language also consists of a list of instructions and a list of program variables. These instructions, however, are so different from the machine-language instructions that they are even called by a different name—*statements*.* Similarly, there does not have to be any direct relation between the program variables and the memory locations of the computer. For example, a programmer may use complex numbers in a program without having to remember every time how they are represented in the computer memory.

Computations by means of formulas is the basic operation of an algorithmic language. A computed value may be assigned to a variable or it may be used in some other way in accordance with the rules of the language. Operations used in formulas are either common mathematical operations or functions, or are dependent upon the rules of the language, or may invented by the programmer himself. Naturally, in the latter case the programmer must "describe" how the corresponding operation or function is to be executed by means of an appropriate computational procedure. Formulas used in algorithmic languages are called *expressions*, and the statements corresponding to them are called *assignment statements* or *arithmetic operators*.

In addition to these statements, algorithmic languages also make use of a special kind of "control" statement that does not so much compute as define the *order* of a computation. Among such statements are *if clauses*, or *branchings*, which select a particular type of computation depending upon whether a given condition is true, and *repetitive clauses* or *loops*, which cause certain computations to be repeated a designated number of times.

Finally, programs in algorithmic languages are not written in a rigid tabular format, as are machine-language and symbolic programs, but are structured like sentences, and moreover utilize (though, of course, within comparatively narrow limits) such generally understood words as **begin, end, integer, real, do, procedure, if, then, else,** and others (or abbreviations of these words). Because of these features, algorithmic languages resemble both natural human languages and the symbolic systems commonly used in mathematics.

ALGOL

In the present book we will restrict ourselves to one of the most well-known of the algorithmic languages—ALGOL-60. For beginning readers, we may note

---

* In the present translation, the term "statement" has been used to render the Russian word cognate to the English word "operator," in line with current usage in the world literature (except for explicitly mathematical discussion, such as the historical section 8.5). It should, however, be borne in mind that Russian research in computer science has aimed at a mathematical standpoint (as the author emphasizes in the preface), in contrast to the linguistic (more properly, "formal language") approach which largely dominates the field in the West; this difference in approach is reflected in the connotations of the two terms, "operator" and "statement." See also the author's footnote on page 168, as well as the English language references (especially, DiPaola, 1967), and also the translated references cited in Sections 5.2 and 8.5 (which generally, though not always, use "operator") (transl.).

in passing that the phrase, "the algorithmic language ALGOL," is almost like saying "black blackboard," since the name ALGOL was originally conceived of as an abbreviation for the very term, algorithmic language. For those beginning readers concerned about not having had a chance to become familiar with this language, we suggest the book by A. L. Brudno, entitled ALGOL (Moscow, Nauka, 1971).

Translating a program written in an algorithmic language into a machine-language program is already a substantially more complicated process than translating a symbolic program into a machine-language program. A minimal effort is to have the compiler likewise start by compiling a table of the symbolic names employed in the program as program variables, statement labels, and functions conceived of by the programmer. Next, the formulas used in the program are broken down into individual operations and functions, resulting in new temporary variables in the program. Notation used for the functions introduced by the programmer is replaced by references to procedures that compute these functions. Then, each elementary operation or function referred to in the program is replaced by a sequence of machine-language instructions that are said to *realize* or *implement* this operation or function. The "control" if clauses and repetitive clauses (loops) are treated in the same way. The correspondence between the elementary operations, functions, and statements of an algorithmic language and the "templates" of a machine-language program that implement them is permanent and is stored in the compiler.

By assembling these templates together, a symbolic program is created for which memory is then allocated, as described above. It is precisely the process of memory allocation that will be our principal topic of discussion in the first part of the book.

Before proceeding further, however, there is a technical point that ought to be made. Suppose an algorithmic-language program is written in such a way that each of its statements contains only a single operation. Then, if this algorithmic-language operation can be executed by a single computer instruction and if each program variable may be stored in a single memory cell, the correspondence between the algorithmic-language program and the symbolic program that implements it becomes literal, differing only in the mode of expression. It is for this reason that we will be using ALGOL exclusively in the present book, even though we will be dealing with examples that resemble symbolic programs in their degree of detail.

1.2. Some Facts About Linear Programs

Some Simple Examples

Let's imagine we are beginning programmers and try to calculate on a computer the value of $y = x^7$ without resorting to the operation of exponentiation.

After reading a review section on programming, applying the necessary rules of ALGOL and taking advantage of our high-school experience in solving problems by means of a series of questions, we may finally write out the following program:

EXAMPLE 1. Compute x^7.

```
begin real x, y, x2, x3, x4, x5, x6;
    input (x);
        x2:= x  × x;
        x3:= x2 × x;
        x4:= x3 × x;
        x5:= x4 × x;
        x6:= x5 × x;
         y:= x6 × x;
    output (y)
end
```

However, it is just as likely that the program will have the following form:

EXAMPLE 2. Compute x^7.

```
begin real x, y;
    input (x);
         y:= x × x;
         y:= y × x;
         y:= y × x;
         y:= y × x;
         y:= y × x;
         y:= y × x;
    output (y)
end
```

These two very simple examples already give us food for thought. We see, first, that both programs solve the problem. Further, the second program is much better than the first program: It requires only two memory locations and its final five instructions are all the same, which suggests an even further abbreviation of the program: simply repeat the single statement $y:= y*x$ five times (using a loop):

EXAMPLE 3. Compute x^7.

```
begin real x, y; int i;
    input (x);
         y:= x × x;
        for i:= 1 step 1 until 5 do y:= y × z;
    output (y)
end
```

First Conclusion. A problem may be programmed in more than one way; some ways are better, and some worse.

Second Conclusion. Programs may differ from each other to a greater or lesser extent; the first and second programs are more similar to each other than either is to the third.

Third Conclusion. The first two programs are so similar it is even more proper to say they are really the same program, except for different notation for the temporary variables; in the first program these variables are denoted differently, and in the second program they are denoted in the same way.

Fourth Conclusion. It thus makes sense to figure out a way of writing a program that uses the smallest number of notational symbols for the variables. Such a program would economize on storage allocation.

Note, however, that these conclusions are all purely observational in nature. There is nothing preventing the person who wrote the first program from asking his neighbor, "Do you really think the entire computation can be performed in terms of y alone?" If the author of the second program is no fool, such a question will scarcely baffle him, and after thinking a bit, he might respond by saying, "As soon as y is multiplied by x, I no longer need it, and therefore I can transfer the product to it." To justify his own approach, the first programmer could then respond, "But of course my program makes more sense; x raised to the fifth power, for example, will never equal x raised to the third power—I have called them by different names." The second programmer could then note, "On the other hand, I have used a loop and thereby shortened my program," and show his neighbor the third program.

If some reader thinks these examples are too elementary, consider the following: The discussion of the two programmers is taken from an actual class in programming, and each of the three remarks contains a grain of truth, which if allowed to "germinate," will lead us step-by-step to a solution of the problem. In particular, we may at once attempt to generalize the remarks of our two programmers in the form of a couple ground rules.

A. For the sake of convenience and logical rigor, in writing out a program different notation is introduced for the initial and temporary problem variables and for the results. If memory is allocated according to the principle, "to each variable a location of its own," once the symbolic program has been written out, it may be the case that more memory has been used than is "in fact" necessary. This circumstance may be expressed differently: A program may be rewritten in such a way that it solves the same problem as before, but contains fewer notational symbols.

B. The number of variables in a program may be reduced in the following way. If there is some result in an instruction (or statement), there is no need to rush and introduce a new symbol for it. Instead we need only consider whether there is some variable which is "free" at this moment, i.e., a variable whose current value is no longer needed. If there is such a variable, use it to denote the result.

New Examples

Let us consider several more examples. Suppose it is necessary to compute $y = x^{59}$, again without using the operation of exponentiation. Of course, with Example 3 in front of us it would hardly do to write out 58 multiplication instructions, one right after the other. Thus, a first approach gives us:

EXAMPLE 4. Compute x^{59}.

```
begin real x, y; int i;
    input (x);
        y := x × x;
        for i := 1 step 1 until 57 do y := y × x;
    output (y)
end
```

Though this program is very short, it nevertheless takes a very long time to run; at least 3×57 operations (multiplication, changing the value of i, and comparing this value to 57) are needed to solve the problem. In contrast, if we would like to compute 2^{64} ($64 = 2^6$), we would only need six operations:

$$y := x \times x \quad (x^2),$$
$$y := y \times y \quad (x^4),$$
$$y := y \times y \quad (x^8),$$
$$y := y \times y \quad (x^{16}),$$
$$y := y \times y \quad (x^{32}),$$
$$y := y \times y \quad (x^{64}).$$

This increasing sequence of powers of two in a geometric progression can help us also in the above problem (and the interested reader should now have no difficulty thinking up the rule for any integral exponent). We represent 59 in the form of a sum of powers of two: $59 = 32 + 16 + 8 + 2 + 1$. The program can then be set up in the following way: Compute and store powers of x with exponents equal to powers of two, one right after the other, so that the last power of two is still less than the initial exponent, while the next power is already greater. Then multiply together those powers of x whose exponents occur as terms in the representation of the initial exponent.

As a result we obtain

EXAMPLE 5. Compute x^{59}.

```
begin real x, y, x2, x4, x8, x16, x32;
   input (x);
      x2:= x × x;
      x4:= x2 × x2;
      x8:= x4 × x4;
    x16:= x8 × x8;
    x32:= x16 × x16;
       y:= x × x2;
       y:= y × x8;
       y:= y × x16;
       y:= y × x32;
   output (y)
end
```

In the concluding part of the program, we have used the experience gained in the first and second examples, and "performed the computation in terms of y," thereby minimizing the need for notation for the temporary values. However, Principle B encourages us to check the program more carefully and ask ourselves whether new variables were introduced only when they were needed, and not simply because we had initially wanted to compute x^{59}, and then just kept on going. Our reasoning goes something like this. We number the program statements

1. $x2:= x \times x$;
2. $x4:= x2 \times x2$;
3. $x8:= x4 \times x4$;
4. $x16:= x8 \times x8$;
5. $x32:= x16 \times x16$;
6. $y := x \times x2$;
7. $y := y \times x8$;
8. $y := y \times x16$;
9. $y := y \times x32$.

The result of statement 1 is not assigned to x, since the new x would then equal x^2, whereas the initial x is needed in statement 6. The result of statement 2 cannot be assigned to x nor to $x2$ for the same reason. However, after statement 3 has been executed, we no longer need $x4$ and can assign its result to this variable, naturally replacing $x8$ in instructions 4 and 7 by $x4$. Reading through the program to the very end, it's clear that there is no other way of reducing the number of program variables.

EXAMPLE 6. Compute x^{59}.

```
begin real x, y, x2, x4, x16, x32;
   input (x);
      x2 := x × x;
      x4 := x2 × x2;
      x4 := x4 × x4;
      x16 := x4 × x4;
      x32 := x16 × x16;
        y := x × x2;
        y := y × x4;
        y := y × x16;
        y := y × x32;
   output (y)
end
```

Our painstaking dicussion of the impossibility of reducing the number of variables in any of the first five statements (other than in the third one) nevertheless leads us to suggest why this is so: We have not organized our program very well. First we computed all the "powers of two," and only afterwards began to use these powers. Let us proceed a bit differently: Once a succeeding "power of two" has been obtained, we "thrust" it onto y if it is an addend of our exponent. But if it is not, we use it only to obtain the very next power of two. At the same time, we try to observe Principle B, obtaining the following:

EXAMPLE 7. Compute x^{59}.

```
begin real x, y, x2;
   input (x);
      x2 := x × x;
       y := x × x2;
       x := x2 × x2;
       x := x × x;
       y := y × x;
       x := x × x;
       y := y × x;
       x := x × x;
       y := y × x;
   output (y)
end
```

This result meets all our conditions, though you will never be a real programmer if you do not ask yourself whether it is possible to make do with even fewer variables. An affirmative answer may very well be a bit of a discovery for most:

EXAMPLE 8. Compute x^{59}.

```
begin real x, y;
  input (x);
    y := x × x;
    x := x × y;
    y := y × y;
    y := y × y;
    x := x × y;
    y := y × y;
    x := x × y;
    y := y × y;
    y := x × y;
  output (y)
end
```

Here is a second chance for anyone who has not been able to follow the reasoning in the last example: Prove why it is not possible to work with fewer variables in this program, i.e., with just a single variable.

A Moment for Reflection

With these eight examples, we have accumulated quite enough material to analyze before going any further. First, we have finally understood that the number of symbols used to denote the variables in any program and the number of memory locations needed are characteristics of this program and are directly related to each other. There is no real difference between the concept of a variable as used in a program written in an algorithmic language and the concept of a memory location as used in a machine-language program. As long as we are concerned with constructing a program, we may equate these two concepts, and in fact this will simplify the subsequent discussion. A variable in a program is not so much a physical or mathematical magnitude that enters a program from the initial statement of the problem, as it is a memory element in pure form, a unique compartment in computer memory that stores some value. But this value can get there only if it is the result obtained from the application of some statement or instruction. The old value of the variable magnitude then ceases to exist. Each value in a judiciously constructed program is created so that it can later be used as an argument elsewhere in the program. As long as it is not yet being used, a variable that stores some value is used only as "a last resort," and no new value may be assigned to it. Thus, how many variables are used in different versions of the same program, and the way they are denoted, are not so important as the fact that they must store all the data relations ("paths") in the program, i.e., all "data flow" of the results of certain statements to arguments of other statements.

A second conclusion is that there are different ways of constructing different versions of the same program, furthermore that this somehow influences the number of variables used in a program and the symbols that denote them. In the first method, we are essentially dealing with one and the same program, though with different sets of variables. Two programs are said to be the same if they consist of the same set of instructions and the same data flow between the arguments of certain statements and the results of other statements (Examples 1 and 2, 5 and 6, 7 and 8). The advantage of this method is that new variables are introduced only if they are really needed; our goal is to make do with variables already in use. The second method preserves the structure of the set of instructions and the data flow, but allows for moving the instructions in the program if this will help matters along (Examples 6 and 7). We are still far from a complete understanding of how memory is allocated in this method, apart from a number of vague generalities, such as: Arrange the computations in such a way that a result is used as soon as possible after it has been produced (so as to reduce the need for memory for storage of the values of variables). Finally, the third method is effective because it completely transforms the program. It is in general a better strategy to economize on the memory needed to store a program (which in Example 3 we achieved by means of a loop) rather than on memory needed to store program variables; in this example, we even introduced one more variable i. In some sense, however, the first method is the elementary method. By whatever method we create a program, however, if we wish to find the minimal storage allocation, we have to make certain that there are no redundant variables in the program and then try to find the best version of the program (as in Example 8).

Finally, it is quite obvious that we are still quite aways from a solution of the general problem of storage minimization (or packing). Principle B is the only working rule in our arsenal, and all the examples illustrate only the simplest forms of programs, what are known as *linear programs*, i.e., programs without any *if* clauses, loops, or function procedure calls (we are not counting Examples 3 and 4, as we have not analyzed them). Even for linear programs, Principle B is no longer of the nature of a formal rule, and instead requires further elaboration than we have time for here.

Data Paths. Cross Sections

Let us think a bit more about Principle B and try to turn the following thought into a systematic procedure: "Rather than being in any great hurry to introduce a new symbol for any one result, simply consider whether there is some variable that is 'free' at this point in the program, i.e., a variable whose current value is no longer needed." This remark would seem to indicate that any discussion of the strategy of storage packing must start by scanning the statement in a given program in the order in which they are to be executed. Then (in the case of a linear program written out in a column), the next statement to be scanned will be written below all the statements that have already been executed and that have already been taken care of somehow by a selection of variables, and will be written above instructions that have yet to be executed. Rather than rushing to introduce a new variable for the result of the next statement S, we glance at the variables that denote the results of statements preceding this statement, i.e., that occur higher up in the column. What does it mean to say that variable v, that is, the result of statement R, is not free? It means that below S there is yet one more statement T that has v as its argument.

Is this definition rigorous enough? It's easy to see that it is not. Combining all the possible cases yields the following alternative generations and applications of v relative to S (for the sake of clarity, suppose that there are no other applications of v in the program, other than those explicitly indicated):

Program	Program	Program	Program
$R:\quad v:=\ \ldots$	$R:\quad v:=\ \ldots$	$R:\ v:=\ \ldots$	$R:\quad v:=\ \ldots$
$S:\quad x:=\ \ldots$	$T':\quad z:=F'(v)$	$T':\ z:=F'(v)$	$T':\quad z:=F'(v)$
$T:\quad z:=F(v)$	$S:\quad x:=\ \ldots$	$S:\ x:=\ \ldots$	$S:\quad x:=$
	$T:\quad z:=F(v)$	$R':\ v:=\ \ldots$	
		$T:\ z:=F(v)$	
Case (a)	Case (b)	Case (c)	Case (d)

From these diagrams, we conclude that the only condition asserting that v is not free relative to S (is *bound* to S) is the situation in which S is between (in the sense of position in the program) a generation of v (statement R) and an application of v (statement T); in this case, there is no statement between S and T that generates v. We find that S seems to occur in the path along which the variable is transmitted from R to T. This situation may be made more graphic if the path of v is represented in the form of a line connecting the result of R and the argument of T:

$$
\begin{array}{ll}
R: & \textcircled{v}\quad :=\ \ldots \\[2mm]
S: & \quad x\ :=\ \ldots \\[2mm]
T: & \quad z\ :=\ F(\,\textcircled{v}\,)
\end{array}
$$

If it is possible for all the paths in the program, along which values of variables are transmitted from results to arguments, to be denoted in this way, Principle B can be greatly simplified: For a given statement S all variables whose paths "cross" this statement will be said to be bound.

We will not bother drawing this diagram for our examples, except for the fifth one (Figure 1.1). It is at once clear that x is the result of the entry statement and that y is the argument of the exit statement.

The program looks more unwieldy, though for our purposes it is nevertheless exceptionally clear. We have extended all the paths along which variable values are transmitted, from the results to the arguments. Let us at once refer

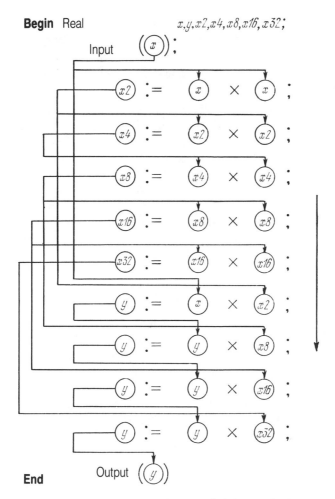

Figure 1.1. Program with extended data paths.

to them as the *data paths* between the arguments and results of statements. The paths are all oriented "in" the direction of execution of the program. By analyzing these paths, we can get a complete idea of how storage must be allocated in the program. In fact, let us mentally draw a horizontal line beneath each statement and extend it outwards; this line will indicate the moment of execution of the given statement. We call this line a program *cross section.* Then the number of data paths cut by a cross section will tell us how many variables are bound at the present time, i.e., how many variables are being used to store results generated earlier, but needed later on, while the symbols of variables that are associated with the end-points of these "routes" indicate which variables are actually in use at this time.

This observation at once suggests a systematic procedure for renaming the variables of a program to minimize the number of notational symbols. To emphasize its systematic nature, we purposely select entirely different notation: $t1$, $t2$, etc. The storage packing procedure in linear programs is then as follows:

1. *First Step.* Select the first statement. It contains only one result with which the variable $t1$ is associated. The name of this variable is associated with all the arguments of statements that data paths lead to from this result.
2. *Second Step.* Select the next statement S. Suppose that certain variables have been used by this time. Discard from this list of variables the bound ones, i.e., variables whose data paths cross S's cross section. If there are still variables in the list, select any one of them (say, the variable with least ordinal number) and associate it with S's result. If all the variables used so far are bound, augment the list with one more variable, and also associate it with the result. The name of the variable associated with S's result is associated with all the arguments of statements the data paths lead to from this result.

Obviously, if for each argument there is a result that specifies it, this will mean that all the program variables will have to be renamed, and in this case the number of variables will precisely equal the maximal *width* of all the program sections, i.e., the maximal number of intermediate values of variables that have to be stored at some point in the course of program execution. In fact, according to our procedure a new variable is added to the list of variables already in use only when all the variables are bound, and in that case the current width must be increased by one through the addition of a new data path. Applying this procedure to Figure 1.1, we obtain the following program:

```
begin real t1, t2, t3, t4, t5;
    input (t1);
        t2 := t1 × t1;
        t3 := t2 × t2;
        t3 := t3 × t3;
        t4 := t3 × t3;
        t5 := t4 × t4;
        t1 := t1 × t2;
        t1 := t1 × t3;
        t1 := t1 × t4;
        t1 := t1 × t5;
    output (t1)
end
```

This procedure is a major step forward. Moreover, it should now have dawned on us that it yields a complete solution of the storage packing problem for linear programs. Let us push forward and continue the analysis.

Program Schema

Some readers may have already noted that once the data paths in a program have been drawn in, the original names of variables used in the program are no longer needed. Moreover, they can even become a hindrance by taking up space needed in the procedure for the names of any new variables. We will find it more convenient to work with programs that have no variables, and are instead supplied with circles that mark the places of the arguments and results of statements (Figure 1.2).

As we glance over this graphic representation of a program, the irrelevance of the ALGOL style of programming becomes more and more striking, as does any other information which, though an integral part of the process of writing out a program, is not so important for solving our special storage

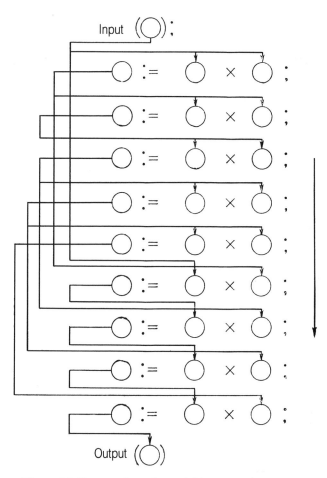

Figure 1.2. Data paths make variable names unnecessary.

packing problem. We have already dispensed with the list of variable declarations, and even the variables themselves once they have served their purpose in the construction of the data paths. What then do we really need? We have to know that the statements form a linear sequence; for each statement, we must also know how many arguments and results it has (an input statement, for example, can have several results). It is scarcely of any importance which function is executed by which statement. In other words, we do not have to know anything about the program itself, but only the program's schema, and this contains only the notation used for the statements, not their content, and indicates the order of execution of the statements and specifies in some way their arguments and results, moreover, in a way that makes it convenient to represent their data paths and assign variable names to them. And as we have already found the graphic representation so useful, it is natural to call it a *program schema*.

Leaving the reader in the dark as to the different kinds of diagrams that have been sketched out by different authors in the hunt for maximal clarity, we now present the schema for our program using what is now a generally accepted graphical form (Figure 1.3). Here statements are represented by means of rectangles; the designation of each rectangle is written inside the rectangle. The dark arrows indicate the order of execution of the statements. The small circles at the ends of the short branches are the arguments and results, with branches in the direction of the arrows being results, and in the opposite direction arguments. The names of the variables associated with the arguments and results are written alongside the circles (Figure 1.3(a)). Broken lines ending in arrows represent data paths. So as to simplify the diagrams (Figure 1.3(b)), wherever convenient broken lines emanating from the same result are merged together into a single *bundle*. Such a graphical confluence is even convenient in reality. If we wish to compute the width of a cross section, we count all the arrows emanating from the same result as one, i.e., they are at once thought of as a single bundle. To show the width of each data path more vividly, the paths are drawn as zigzag lines in the diagram rather than as straight lines.

The effect of transposing program statements in Example 7 becomes far more understandable through such a graphical representation of a program and its data paths (Figure 1.3(c)). By shortening the routes along which values are transmitted from results to arguments, we have "unloaded" the data paths and reduced their width down to two, which, incidently, is quite clear in this schema, unlike the program of Example 7.

Bundles. Width of a Cross Section

It would seem that all the useful information which the subject of linear programs can give us has now been covered exhaustively. Among our principal achievements is the discovery of the importance of analyzing the data paths of a program, and similarly the importance of extracting from a

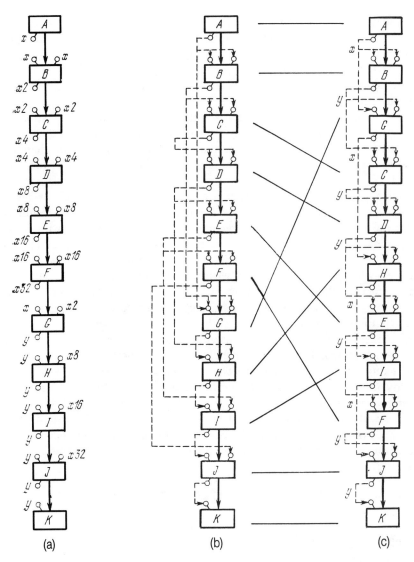

Figure 1.3. Program schemas: (a) Example 5; (b) data paths for Examples 5 and 6; (c) data paths for Examples 7 and 8.

program only those of its characteristics that can help in solving the storage packing problem and that can be depicted in the program schema. Now that we are fairly familiar with this finding, let us analyze in more detail the kinds of data paths that may be found in a given program and see how the data paths may be used to minimize on storage allocation. We lay out a path from the result of statement S to the argument of statement T if S has some variable x as its result, if T has x as its argument, and if T is executed after S, i.e., if there is a chain of statements from S to T, and, finally, if no statement in this chain has x as its result. To construct the data paths and, in general, minimize storage allocation, we only need a program schema that tells us which symbols are to be used for the statements, the arguments, and the results of the statements and the variable names associated with them, as well as the order of execution of the statements.

The initial storage allocation is no longer needed once all the data paths in a program have been constructed. Moreover, by means of the set of data paths we may construct any other storage allocation for a given program, including the allocation which is most economical in terms of the number of variables used.

Data paths in a program schema are grouped together into *bundles*. A single bundle will contain all the data paths emanating from some result. To allocate memory properly, the same variable must be associated with all the arguments and results of a particular bundle. The least economical storage allocation is one in which we associate with each result or —what is the same thing—with each bundle its own variable. Storage is economized whenever the same variable is associated with more than one bundle. However, so as not to disrupt the data paths, the same variable is not associated with competing data paths. In a linear program, those bundles —and only those bundles—are in competition which simultaneously "cut" a particular cross section in its program schema. There is a simple algorithm for finding a minimal storage allocation for a linear program. The number of variables used in this case turns out to equal the width of the cross sections, i.e., the maximal number of bundles cut by the cross sections.

We will now apply these conclusions as working hypotheses and verify them by means of more diversified examples in a quest for new results. Obviously, we must first complicate the structure of the programs.

1.3. Some Facts About the General Form of a Program

Program with Conditions

EXAMPLE 9. Solve the quadratic equation $ax^2 + bx + c = 0$ for the general case. Represent the complex solution in the form of values of the modulus and argument of complex conjugate roots. After representing the formula for the general solution

$$x_{1,2} = \frac{-b \pm \sqrt{b^2 - 4ac}}{2a}$$

in the form $p = -b/2a$ and $q = \sqrt{|b^2 - 4ac|}/2a$, we then find for the real case (depending upon the sign of the discriminant $b^2 - 4ac$) flag $= 1$, root1 $= p + q$ and root2 $= p - q$, while for the complex case flag $= -1$, root1 $= \sqrt{p^2 + q^2}$ and root2 = arcsin $(q/\sqrt{p^2+q^2})$. Introduce several more temporary variables to minimize the computations, but not trying to write out all the formulas down to the last detail, we finally obtain the following program:

```
begin real a, b, c, t1, t2, discr, p, q, root1, root2:
    integer flag;
    input (a, b, c);
        t1 := 2 × a;
        t2 := 2 × c;
        discr := b↑2 − t1 × t2;
        p := − b/t1;
        q := sqrt(abs(discr))/t1;
        if discr < 0 then
        begin
        t1 := p↑2 + q↑2;
        root1 := sqrt(t1);
        root2 := arcsin(q/root1)
        end      else
        begin root1 := p + q;
        root2 := p − q;
        end
    flag := sign(discr);
    output (flag, root1, root2)
end
```

Route

Let us now construct a schema for this program. We are no longer dealing with linear programs here, that is, the program schema now contains mutually exclusive computation branches (the case of a negative versus nonnegative discriminant). For the sake of convenience of the subsequent analysis, we denote each of the statements by the name of the variable associated with its result, making the obvious exception for **if** clauses and output statements. In the diagram (Figure 1.4) we draw the data paths using the same rule: A path is drawn from the result of statement S to the argument of statement T if the same variable x is associated with them and if there exists at least one path in the schema from S to T along which there is no statement other than S that generates x. It has already crossed our mind that such a path may be figuratively compared to a *route* along which the value of x is transmitted from S to T. Now seems like a good time to fix this image in the form of a term. One of the new situations we have found in this schema is that a value may be transmitted from a result to an argument, i.e., an existing data path realized along more than one route. For example, the value of discr may be transmitted to statement flag either along route (discr, p, q, $<$, $t1'$, root1, root2, flag) or along route (discr, p, q, $<$, root1', root2', flag).

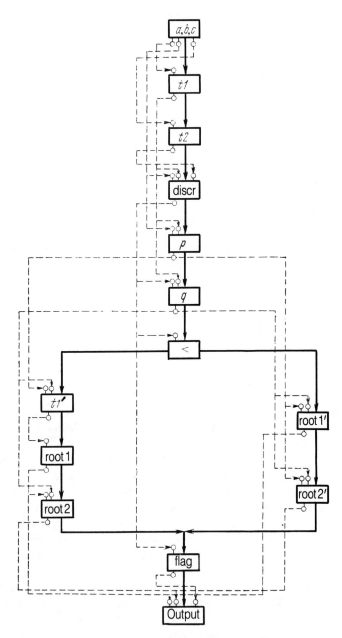

Figure 1.4. Program schema with condition.

The second observation has to do with bundles of data paths. Until now, each bundle has been treated as a beam of arrows emanating from one result to the several arguments using it. Now, however, the configuration of data paths is more complicated (Figure 1.5); the data paths for bundle root2 are joined together (converge) at the argument, while for bundle root2 the data paths are grouped together both at the argument and at the result. For the future (in fact, the very near future), it is therefore worth noting that once the name of a variable has been selected to denote a result, this name must be placed not only near the argument (or arguments) as we move with the arrows, but must also be transmitted from this argument to any other result against the direction of the arrow corresponding to the path.

The next step we wish to take is to construct cross sections of the sequence of executed statements to determine which are the competing data paths and how many variables there are in a minimal (economic) storage allocation. In constructing the cross sections, we must once again deal with new circumstances. As before, there is what may be called a dominant direction of computation as specified by the arrows between statements. In some segment, this direction divides into two branches which then converge again. We have already seen that our example represents the simplest case and that if we wish to get as much useful information out of it as possible, we will have to try to formulate every conceivable new rule in the most general form. The very concept of a cross section is independent of the degree of complexity of a schema. In drawing a cross section we always cut one arrow only from one statement to the next. The problem is to determine which data path a particular cross section cuts. Earlier there was a simple answer to this problem: Whatever begins above and ends below the given cross section. Why is this problem so simple for a linear program? Briefly, each statement in such a program is either below or above a particular cross section. Now this is no longer true. It doesn't make any sense to ask whether statement root1 is above or below statement root2, nor is there any answer to such a question. Recall,

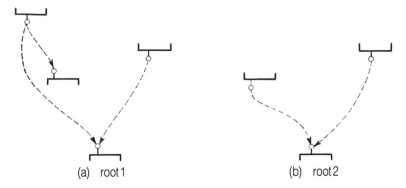

(a) root 1   (b)   root 2

Figure 1.5. New types of bundles for root1 and root2.

however, that we have made use of the cross sections by associating with each intersected data path a variable that stores a generated value and, in addition, asserted that these variables are bound at the time of execution of the intersected statement.* Therefore, the result of this statement cannot be assigned to any of the bound variables, and the data path that begins with this result is in competition with all the other crossed data paths. We may then say that, by definition, the cross section of any one statement crosses those data paths, and only those data paths, whose routes contain S; put differently, a data path that begins with the result of some statement S is in competition with those data paths, and only those data paths, whose routes contain S.

Though it may appear more complicated, this formulation nevertheless expresses the essentials (preservation of data paths) more directly and, what is most important, is no longer dependent upon the degree of complexity of the schema. Once we know all the data paths and the routes that realize them, we can then construct all the cross sections, since whether or not a particular statement belongs to a particular route can then be determined in a unique way.

Detailed Minimization Procedure

All 14 sections of Example 9 are depicted in Figure 1.6. As we will have to work with them further, we have numbered them. The width of each cross section, i.e., the number of mutually competing data paths, is indicated on the right. The maximal width is four.

Let us proceed to allocate storage in accordance with the procedure already developed for linear programs. We will find it useful to go through the process once again in all its detail. We suggest the reader redraw Figure 1.6 without the variable names, and then enter them in the course of traversing the schema.

Cross Section 1. Three results. Denote them a, b, and c, and transfer the names to the arguments in the direction of the data paths.

Cross Section 2. New result, b and c are bound, a is free. We denote them the result and the corresponding arguments.

Cross Section 3. New result, a and b are bound, c is free. We denote them the result and the (corresponding) arguments.

Cross Section 4. New result, a and b are bound, c is free. We denote them the result and the arguments.

Cross Section 5. New result, a and c are bound, b is free. We use it.

Cross Section 6. New result, b and c are bound, a is free. We use it.

Cross Section 7. No output.

---

* For the sake of brevity, we are using an undefined expression, since it is in fact not a statement that is intersected, but the shift arrow emanating from it.

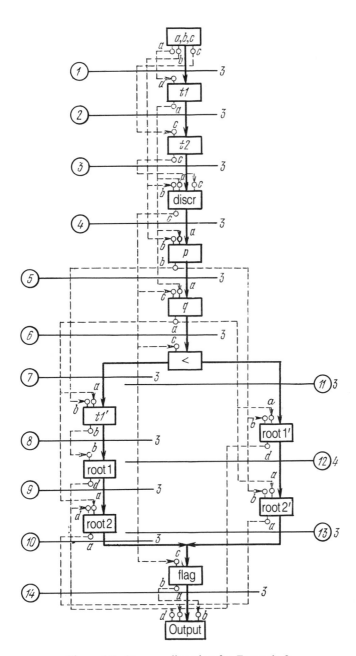

Figure 1.6. Storage allocation for Example 9.

Cross Section 8. New result, *a* and *c* are bound, *b* is free. We use it.

Cross Section 9. New result, *a* and *c* are bound, *b* is free. We use it. However, when we allocate *b* to the arguments of statements root2 and output, we see that *b* must also be allocated to the result of root1′. This cannot happen, however, since in cross section 12 this result is in competition with the data path from *p* to root2′ already associated with *b*. There is nothing else for us to do than assign a new variable *d* to bundle root1.

Cross Section 10. New result, *c* and *d* are bound, *a* and *b* are free. We make *a* the variable of the result and again find that it must also be allocated to the result of root2′. By analyzing the thirteenth cross section, however, we see that this can be done.

Cross Section 11. No result.

Cross Sections 12 and 13. The variables have already been allocated to the result.

Cross Section 14. New result, *a* and *d* are bound, *b* and *c* are free. We use *b*.

Let us analyze our conclusions. To a first approximation, our storage packing procedure works the way it's supposed to: The maximal width of the schema (the twelfth cross section) is four, which is precisely the number of variables we have used. As before, by analyzing the cross sections we learned which variables are bound when a particular statement is being executed. However, the situation encountered in the ninth cross section demonstrated that what happens in the twelfth cross section had to be checked by moving with (and against) the data path arrows forming the bundle to determine which were the competing bundles in the ninth cross section. That we were able to do so without much difficulty does not mean our position is any less tenable. It is not hard to see that here we are dealing with a very simple example that only suggests the real problems involved. There is one important conclusion to make. As before, to decide whether two data paths are in competition, all we need to know is whether or not the statement that begins one of the data paths belongs to a route of another path. It is, however, far more difficult to decide which bundles a given bundle is in competition with. The above "membership test" must now be undertaken for all the results of a given bundle. This is precisely what we have done in the ninth and tenth cross sections.

Fundamental Interpretation

If we think a bit about these conclusions and about the example as a whole, it becomes quite clear that our conception of the storage packing problem has expanded considerably. Let us put together a kind of preliminary conclusion to our discussion.

For each data path there exist *routes* that implement this path. These routes may be thought of as chains of statements, the first of which generates some variable as a result, and the last of which reads in this variable, further, no internal statement (i.e., one located between the initial and final statements) generates this variable. A single path may be implemented along several different routes.

The data paths form *bundles*, i.e., groups of paths linked together at their end-points (the arguments or results of the statements). For any storage allocation, the same variable is associated with all the arguments and results of statements in the same bundle.

(Reading this last paragraph over, it is apparent that our concept of a bundle is still somewhat informal. In the case of linear programs, it was defined more rigorously as the set of all the paths that begin with the same result. An even more rigorous formulation is needed for the general case.)

At first glance, we may understand a bundle to refer to all the data paths whose "end-points" are associated with the same variable in the initial schema. However, even in the example just considered we have seen in passing that the data paths implemented in the initial schema via the variable $t1$ divide quite clearly into bundles, the first with the two routes $(t1, t2, discr)$ and $(t1, t2, discr, p, q)$ and the second with the single route $(t1, root1)$. This in and of itself is nothing new. For example, each of the routes (G, H), (H, I), (I, J), and (J, K) in Figure 1.3(a) implements data paths that are in different bundles, though they share the same statements. What is new is that in applying a procedure that minimizes storage allocation, we have been led to associate two distinct variables a and b with these two bundles $(t1$ and $t1')$. We thereby see that the storage packing problem cannot be stated in what might be thought of as a naive formulation, i.e., "insert" as many of the initial program variables as possible into the same memory location. Example 9 suggests that the "unit" of storage allocation is not the entire "liveness domain" of an initial variable, but instead the individual bundles of data paths implemented through it.

Returning to our procedure for minimizing storage allocation, we see that, to begin with, it is now more complicated. First, the cross sections themselves have become more convoluted. A cross section may now be understood to result from intersecting those data paths—and only those data paths—at some statement S such that the routes that implement these paths contain S as an initial or internal statement.

Second, it is not enough to analyze just one cross section if we wish to determine which data paths a given path that begins with result r of statement S is in competition with. Instead, we have to check the cross sections constructed for all the statements that generate results that are in the same bundle as r. As before, a cross section tells us which variables are bound when a particular statement is executed, but it is no longer possible to then conclude that all the other variables are free at this point in the sense that they could store a new result.

Third, the procedure itself no longer serves a well-defined purpose. Since there are branches in the program, there are different ways of traversing the chain of statements. In Example 9, for example, we could have first traversed the right chain (cross sections 11–13), and only afterwards the left chain (cross sections 7–10). Though we obtain the same four variables here (the reader may use this as an exercise) as suggested by cross section 12, nevertheless in the general case (which may include branches) we can no longer prove that the procedure always yields the minimal number of variables.

Program with Loops

The next step in our descriptive analysis is to study programs that contain loops.

EXAMPLE 10. Compute the value of a using the recursive relation

$$a_n = \frac{b_{n-1} + \tan(a_{n-1})}{|\tan(a_{n-1})|} \qquad \text{where} \qquad b_n = \ln(|\tan(a_{n-1})|).$$

We are given the values of a_0 and b_0, and also a condition on the last value: $|b_n| < 0.1$. The program may be constructed literally from the initial formulas.

```
begin real a, b, c, d, e;
   input (a, b);
   repeat: c := tan(a);
          d := b + c;
          e := abs(c);
          a := d/e;
          b := ln(e);
       if abs (b) ≥ 0.1 then goto repeat;
   output (a)
end
```

Let us construct the program schema and draw the data paths. There are only a few cross sections and variables here, and to save space we insert them in the same diagram (Figure 1.7). As before, we advise the reader to redraw the diagram and data paths and then carry out the storage packing procedure on his own. Note that no cross section in the schema has width greater than two. Once again we will trace out the procedure in all its details, using a, b, etc. as the new variables.

Cross Section 1. Two new results a and b. We allocate these names to all the arguments and results of the corresponding bundles, a to the tangent argument, from it to the result of the division (/), and from the latter to the result argument of the result; b to the addition (+) argument, from it to the logarithm result, and from the latter to the comparison (<) argument.

Cross Section 2. New result. It competes with b. We use a, allocate it to the result, and assign it to the argument of the addition and also the computation of abs.

Cross Section 3. New result. It competes with a. We take b, allocating it to the result and insert it as the argument of the division.

Cross Section 4. New result. Its bundle competes with both a and b. We use

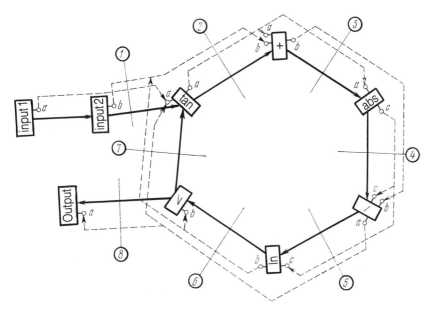

Figure 1.7. Program schema with loop.

c, allocating it to the result and assign it to the argument of the division and the computation of ln.

Now all the argument and result positions have had variables allocated to them, so that there is no point in glancing over the other sections.

Complications

At first glance, we have the same situation in the fourth cross section as in the ninth cross section of Example 9. There bundle root1 was in competition with bundles q (new name a), discr (new name c), and p (new name b), and we used yet another variable d. There is, however, a difference. In Example 7, all the bundles were also in competition with each other, so that whatever variable names we chose, we still needed four variables. In the example we are now considering, however, we find that the bundle of the result of statement abs is in competition with the bundles formed by the results of the addition (variable b) and division (variable a) operators (statements), though the latter two bundles are not in competition with each other. Thus, it now appears that we don't really have to introduce a third variable. With a different storage allocation procedure, it may happen that the same variables could be associated with these bundles, though we would still need two variables, which, as we have already noted, seems to be indicated by the width of the cross sections, which is never more than two. On the other hand, at any one point in our allocation of storage there can be no doubt that we are proceeding in the only way possible, and the reader is quite correct if he supposes there is no way we could make do with only two variables. The reader might even be able to find his own proof of this example, but we now have a different, and more general conclusion to make. The width of a cross section can no longer serve as a guide for determining the number of variables required in a minimal (economic) storage allocation. Together with what we have said above, these remarks finally put to rest our attempt to salvage the procedure as a method of optimal storage allocation. A storage allocation may be created by means of the procedure, but we can no longer claim it is the optimal (minimal) allocation.

Incompatibility

We do not wish to present our conclusion in such a negative light, however. Before leaving the storage packing procedure we have found for linear programs and adapted to the general case, we must consider more carefully what can be confidently claimed for it. Let us once again see what it involves. In traversing a program schema in which data paths have been drawn, we (a) determine which bundles are in competition, and which are not, and (b) assign to the bundles particular variable names, trying to make do with the least number of names. We have already seen that the actual variable names are not needed to determine which bundles are "in competition." It is now time to replace this chance expression by a special term—let us refer to two bundles which are "in competition" as being *incompatible*. Thus, two bundles are incompatible if the initial statement of some route that implements a data path belonging to one of the bundles is an initial or internal statement of some route that implements a data path belonging to the other bundle (please excuse such a lengthy sentence, a sentence which is nevertheless entirely rigorous). Thus, information about incompatibility in a program schema is uniquely defined and any arbitrariness or nonuniqueness of the results comes from our assignment of variables to bundles. In and of itself, there is nothing terribly wrong if there is a degree of ambiguity in a program schema; in fact, it is precisely because of this ambiguity that different storage allocations can be constructed. And in the case of linear programs it does not keep us from finding the optimal schema, as here we know in advance the least number of variables and how to achieve such an allocation. In attempting to preserve the algorithm for the general case, we have kept to the previously selected direction of motion through the schema and tried to assign a variable to a new result right after it has been generated. Because of the complicated structure of the bundles, we have, so to speak, gone ahead of ourselves and "scattered" variable names to segments of the schema that have yet to be traversed and, thereby, once we reach these segments, it turns out that we are very close to our previously made choices. Proceeding "in the small," in a neighborhood of a single cross section, we have used incomplete information about the incompatibility of a new result that has just been generated and those it is in competition with without knowing anything about the general pattern of incompatibility of bundles in the program as a whole.

Thus, we arrive at the notion of dividing the storage allocation procedure into two parts: (a) obtain general information about incompatibility, and (b) from an analysis of this information, select a particular storage allocation which, hopefully, is optimal.

Let us test this hypothesis right now on Example 10. We must represent information about incompatibility of bundles in some graphic way. Let us first put this information in a kind of literal form. We start by designating the bundles by the symbols used for statements whose results are at the beginning of these bundles. These are:

$$(\text{input1}, /), (\text{input2}, 1n), \tan, +, \text{abs}.$$

We have:

(input1, /) is incompatible with input2, 1n and abs
(input2, 1n) in incompatible with (input1, /) and tan
tan is incompatible with (input2, 1n) and +
+ is incompatible with tan and abs
abs is incompatible with + and (input1, /)

The table is not too graphic, but we have nevertheless captured a kind of loop structure in its outline and this we would like to represent in a form that is most easily discernible. A loop may be a circle, or a broken line. In turn, a broken line consists of vertices and edges. What are the vertices and what are the edges in our diagram? An edge connects two vertices, further the concept of incompatibility relates to a pair of bundles. Good! We denote the bundles by large circles, which become the vertices of a broken line, while the vertices of incompatible bundles are connected by a straight line. Figure 1.8 is the result.

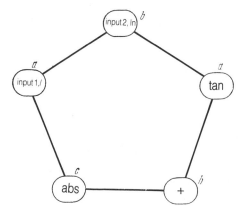

Figure 1.8. Graphic representation of information about bundle incompatibility.

Incompatibility Graph

We are assuming—hopefully with some justification—that most readers are familiar with the mathematical concept of a *graph*. We will introduce it formally in the next chapter, but for now state for the novice that a (undirected) graph consists of vertices and the edges that connect them. In a diagram the vertices are represented by points (or small circles), while the edges are represented by lines connecting the vertices. Vertices connected by edges are said to be *adjacent*.

Let us return to our problem. The graph in Figure 1.8 summarizes information about the compatibility and incompatibility of bundles of data paths. The graph itself may thus be referred to as an *incompatibility graph*. Bundles are the vertices of this graph. Incompatible bundles are the adjacent vertices in the graph, and, conversely, any pair of nonadjacent bundles are compatible. In a storage allocation in an incompatibility graph, a variable is associated with each vertex, and also no one variable is associated with any pair of adjacent vertices. A storage allocation is minimal if the same variable is associated with distinct nonadjacent vertices.

Again, we would expect that readers who have gone through the premise of the storage packing problem in this formulation will recognize a direct relation to a well-known problem of graph theory—the problem of coloring the vertices of a graph. In this problem, the vertices must be colored using the least number of colors in such a way that no pair of adjacent vertices have the same color. This result is of interest in and of itself, but we will not digress just how to discuss it and instead return to our example.

Let us allocate storage for our bundles. Since they form a loop in the incompatibility graph, it does not matter which vertex we begin with. Once variable *a* has been correlated with vertex (input1, /), variable *b* must inevitably be correlated with the adjacent vertex (input2, 1n), but *a* can again be correlated with the next bundle tan. The two variables *a* and *b* alternate as we move in the clockwise direction, and this continues until we reach vertex abs, which closes the loop. We see not only that the third variable must be correlated to it, but also understand at what point we could make do with just two variables. That is, if the last vertex *Z* is connected to a chain containing an even number of vertices, distinct variables are correlated to its end-points, and a third variable is needed for vertex *Z*; if the chain contains an odd number of vertices, the same variable may be correlated to both its end-points, in which case the second variable may be correlated to vertex *Z*.

It is easy to see that the introduction of this new construction (incompatibility graph) gives us a tool now related rather indirectly to the structure of the program. On the other hand, the incompatibility graph yields new information that may be used to allocate storage in a "pure" form without having to bother with minor details.

Now that we have this new form, we are naturally interested in seeing once again how it functions in the examples of storage packing analyzed above. We suggest that the reader independently construct incompatibility graphs for Examples 1–9, though, to be honest, we must caution the reader that to produce fine and graphic diagrams it would be a good idea to fuss over the constructions somewhat. For purposes of verification and brief discussion later on, all the graphs are depicted in Figure 1.9.

The bundles in Examples 1, 2, and 9 are denoted by the names of variables used in the first version of the program. Variables selected for the minimal storage allocation are placed next to the corresponding vertices of the graph. Examples 3 and 4 have been omitted, since it is still not clear how a program schema may be constructed for programs that contain loops. In Examples 5 and 6 and 7 and 8, the bundles are denoted by the names of the statements that generate the results of these bundles. In all the cases, it is self-evident that the number of variables used to "color" the vertices of the incompatibility graph is

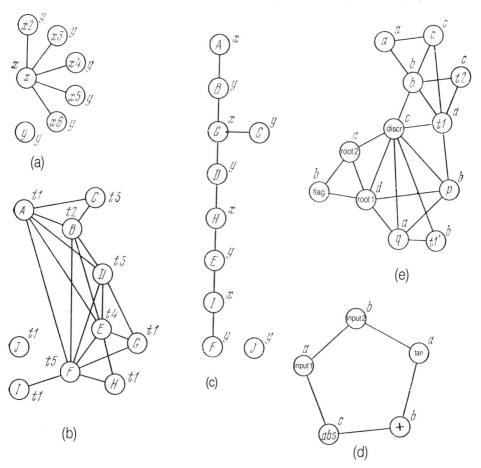

Figure 1.9. Incompatibility graphs: (a) Examples 1 and 2; (b) Examples 5 and 6; (c) Examples 7 and 8; (d) Example 9; (e) Example 10.

indeed the minimal number. Note the presence of a special kind of "nucleus" in the graphs of Examples 5 and 6, i.e., groups of vertices pairwise adjacent to each other, each of which therefore obviously requires distinct variables. All the other vertices are connected to each other by means of edges in a substantially "weaker" way and therefore require the greatest number of variables needed for the nucleus. The graph of Example 10 does not possess this property. Though it requires three "colors," it does not have three pairwise adjacent vertices. By now we should be quite accustomed to the fact that fine distinctions can be the source of major problems. This, in fact, is what has happened here. There is no getting around the fact that we will eventually have to treat the problem of coloring the vertices of an incompatibility graph as a major problem.

1.4. Summary

Program with Procedures

Now that we have treated such an important construction as the incompatibility graph, let's hurry on and complete our descriptive analysis by studying programs that contain functional notation expressed (in the case of ALGOL) by means of procedure declarations.

EXAMPLE 11. Compute

$$y = \begin{cases} \dfrac{x+b}{F(x)} & \text{if } x < 1; \\ (x-b)\,F(x) & \text{if } x \geq 1, \end{cases}$$

where $F(r) = r^2 + 1$. The computation of $F(x)$ is performed through a procedure declaration in accordance with the rules of ALGOL. We obtain the initial program:

```
begin real b, v, x, y, z;
    real proc F(r); real r;
    begin real f; f := r↑2; F := f + 1 end;
    input (b, x); if (x < 1), then begin z := x + b; y := z/F(x) end
        else begin v := x − b; y := v × F(x) end
    output (x)
end
```

In constructing a program schema, we must decide how to represent the relation between the body of a procedure and the points that call it to be executed, and also the relation between the actual and formal parameters. As we are not concerned with this question in its complete form, let us merely note that an actual parameter in a function's designator is called by name. Thus, the procedure body is executed with the name of variable x in place of r.

Control is transferred to the procedure body wherever the function's de-signators occur, and a "return statement" is assumed to be present at the end of the procedure body. It is by virtue of such a return statement that the computations continue on from the point where the procedure was invoked. As a result, we obtain the schema depicted in Figure 1.10(a).

The structure of the schema is simple enough, and as we are no longer concerned with cross sections that have outlived their usefulness, we will determine the relative compatibility and incompatibility of bundles of data paths. By analyzing a schema's statements and the routes of the data paths, we find that any one statement may be the initial statement on some routes, and an internal statement on other routes. Continuing on in a systematic fashion, we obtain the table shown in Figure 1.11. At each position in the table (*i*th row, *j*th column), we have entered the letter *I* (initial statement) if there is a route in the *j*th bundle that begins with the *i*th statement, and the letter *R* (internal statement) if there is a route in the *j*th bundle that by-passes the *i*th statement.

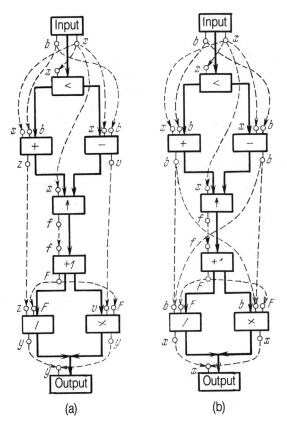

(a)   (b)

Figure 1.10. Program schema with procedure: (a) initial form; (b) schema with new data paths.

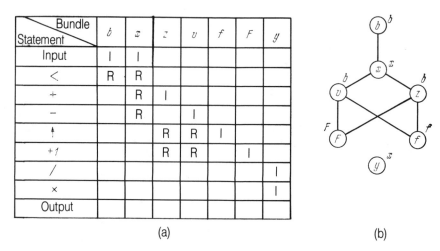

Bundle / Statement	b	x	z	v	f	F	y
Input	I	I					
$<$	R	R					
$+$		R	I				
$-$		R		I			
$\uparrow$			R	R	I		
$+1$			R	R		I	
$/$							I
$\times$							I
Output							

(a)   (b)

Figure 1.11. Construction of incompatibility graph for Example 11: (a) table; (b) graph.

By means of such a table it is possible to verify the pairwise incompatibility of bundles in a uniform way. Let us consider columns j_1 and j_2 and combine their contents. If as a result, I and I or I and R occur together at some position, the two bundles j_1 and j_2 are incompatible, since the joint occurrence of I and I or I and R indicates that the corresponding statement has both variables as its results or is, for some route, the initial statement of one of the bundles, and for another route a statement. This, as we have established, is at once a condition for the existence of competing data paths.

The resulting incompatibility graph is also shown next to the table in Figure 1.11. Coloring the graph presents no difficulty, and it is apparent that two variables suffice for proper running of the program. However, in this example it will be useful to rewrite the program using new notation for the variables and, so as not to violate the formal rules of ALGOL 60 (which do not permit the same name to be used to denote both a function and a variable), we use four variables b, x, f, and F, which thereby "colors" our graph.

As a result of minimizing the storage allocation, we obtain the following program:

```
begin real b, x;
    real proc F(r); real r;
    begin real f; f: = r↑2; F:=f+1 end;
    input (b, x); if (x < 1) then begin b:=x+b; x:=b/F(x) end
        else start b:=x−b; x:= b × F(x)
end;
    output (x)
end
```

Extending the Data Paths

Now that we are persuaded of the correctness of our storage minimization procedures, let us do something we have already done more than once: construct a schema for a program (Figure 10(b)) and draw the data paths in it. We have b as the result of operators $+$ and $-$ and also as the argument of operators $/$ and $\times$. Recalling the definition of a route, we find that the two chains of operators $(+, \uparrow, +1, \times)$ and $(-, \uparrow, +1, /)$ satisfy this definition in the same way as do the chains laid out in the program schema of Figure 1.10(a); that is, $(+, \uparrow, +1, /)$ and $(-, \uparrow, +1, \times)$. Finally, by virtue of what we believe is an entirely proper storage allocation, the set of data paths in the resulting program schema has been augmented with two new paths. Moreover, in the initial schema we had two bundles of data paths (each with one path)—z and v—whereas in the resulting schema there is only a single bundle (with four paths)—b. Until now all the different storage allocations had the same number of data paths (and also the same number of routes realizing them) as well as the same distribution of data paths into bundles. That is, if we were to use the schema of Figure 1.10(b) as the initial schema, we would never be able to select a storage allocation for it whose result would coincide with that of the schema of Figure 1.10(b), since according to our rules the same variable must be associated with all the arguments and results of bundle b. Thus, it turns out that our storage minimization procedure constitutes an irreversible transformation of the initial schema. The situation is so serious that a proper analysis cannot be avoided. As far as we can tell, the most important thing is that at each step we are proceeding properly. Let us once again enumerate the steps in the solution of the problem:

construct program schema;
draw routes and construct data paths;
construct incompatibility graph;
"color" incompatibility graph;
allocate storage in accordance with the coloring.

Recalling the rules for each of these steps, we can understand what underlies the procedure for laying out the routes. The chain of statements in the initial schema (Figure 1.10(a)) $(+, \uparrow, +1, \times)$ cannot happen, and in fact is not allowed by the sense of the problem. The only result that can be assigned to argument v of operator $\times$ is the result v of operator $-$. The procedure for computing $F(x)$ goes something like this. Rather than transferring control to either operator $/$ or $\times$, the return statement selects one of them strictly in accordance with the point at which the procedure is called. If it gets to $\uparrow$ from $+$ we will have to have $/$, and if it gets to $\uparrow$ from $-$, we will have to have $\times$, further there can be no intersecting paths from $-$ to $/$ or from $\times$. Thus, from the way we have introduced it, it is clear that the construction of a program schema does not take into account the fact that there are chains of statements in a real program which, through they may be formally constructed in accordance with the schema, nevertheless are not actually executed. A first response to this discovery might involve attempting to correct the definition of a schema so that chains that are, in some sense, impossible in the initial schema would necessarily be impossible in any resulting schema. For example, the chain $(+, \uparrow, +1, \times)$ is clearly impossible, if for no other reason than the fact that there can be no result along this path that operator $*$ could work with. We could require that this chain remain impossible and not permit any result produced along this chain to correlate this variable with variable v. As a result, bundles z and v turn out to be incompatible.

Still not knowing how greatly this complicates the rules for constructing incompatibility graphs, let us nevertheless try to see how it helps us. Indeed, the real problem is that variables z and v could both end up in the same location for no reason at all! These data paths will never be implemented simultaneously and therefore are not in competition. Actually, we need only take care not to disrupt any data path or any route. If as a result of a marked reduction in storage, new routes appear purely formally and if some of the bundles merge together, so much the better! Thus, we have a fundamentally new hypothesis: Consider storage allocations that preserve all the routes that implement a given data path to be proper without any stipulation as to whether or not new routes and new paths should arise.

Summary

Let us now summarize our descriptive analysis of the storage packing problem.

We have considered programming methods that have an effect upon the amount of storage needed for the variables in some program. We have learned how the choice of a problem-solving algorithm, as well as the order and choice of the individual statements in a program, can influence the number of variables required to solve a problem. In any event, however, a more restricted formulation of the problem makes sense. In this formulation, once the program statements and order of execution of these variables are established, an initial program, in which variable names have been selected for the sake of notational convenience, is replaced by a new program that has the least possible number of variables and preserves all the possible data paths of the initial program.

Further, we have found out what sort of information about a program is essential for the systematic solution of the storage packing problem. For this purpose, we had to have a list of program statements and, for each statement we had to know which statements may be executed immediately following it. We also had to know how many arguments and results each statement has and which variables are associated with it. All this information is specified in the form of the program schema, which may be visualized in the form of a graph (we have already used this word in referring to an incompatibility graph), where the vertices (represented as rectangles) denote statements and the arcs (arrows) indicate a possible sequence for passing control from one statement to the next. If we wish to refer to this construction as a graph, we ought to give it a name; the most natural name would be *control flow graph*. The arguments and results and the variables associated with them then become supplementary labels of such a control flow graph.

By means of a program schema, we construct data paths, which are special kinds of arcs that emanate from a result *a* to an argument *b*; the same variable *x* is associated with both *a* and *b*. For a data path to exist, it is necessary that there exist at least one route that implements it, i.e., a chain of statements that may be constructed in a control flow graph which starts from some statement with result *a* and ends at another statement with argument *b*, such that there is no statement (other than *a* and *b*) that generates *x*. The data paths are divided into bundles that group together paths having the same arguments or results.

The storage packing problem may be stated as follows. Find the storage allocation requiring the least number of variables from among all admissible storage allocations for a given program schema in which the data paths have already been constructed. Further, a storage allocation is admissible if it preserves all the routes implementing any data path.

Any storage allocation may be obtained by "coloring" the incompatibility graph of the bundles of data paths. In such a graph, the edges connect incompatible bundles, i.e., those in which the initial statement of an arbitrary route of a path in one bundle is the initial statement or an intermediate statement of an arbitrary route of a path from another bundle.

Focus of Future Work

After such a thorough review, we might wonder whether there is, in fact, anything left for us to do. We have considered a rather varied set of examples, described all the necessary constructions that can help in minimizing storage requirements, and have an idea of how to construct them. We may confidently claim that we are capable of handling any program whatsoever. But do not think that the question is purely rhetorical. Even in the professional literature it is possible to find many studies that conclude with such a purely descriptive or informal analysis of a problem. In fact, we are still only at the beginning of a rigorous analysis of the problem.

We must first give rigorous definitions of all the constructions in their full generality; as an example, the definition of a bundle requires such refinement. All the assertions must be subjected to logical analysis; assumptions must be separated from assertions, and the former must be tested for consistency and the latter proved. Analogously, from the set of all constructions we have to decide what are the initial constructions, and give rigorous rules for constructing them. By means of such an analysis—and only by means of such an analysis—can we become convinced that the problem has been solved in its entirety. Until then, our assertions are of the nature of plausible reasonings and definitions based on special cases. For example, we were unable to deal with Example 11 by assuming that the number of data paths was strictly preserved and could not be increased. For too long we held onto the concept of a cross section without distinguishing the procedure for constructing the incompatibility graph from direct allocation of storage and, without noticing it, thereby limited our freedom to choose variable names. In a word, we must now give a mathematical formulation of the storage packing problem and, on the basis of this formulation, present a rigorously described method of solution, after which we may resume our discussion of the practical application of the method. This topic will be the subject of subsequent chapters of the first part of the book.

Analyzing a Conjecture

In the present chapter we have tried to familiarize the reader with the creative effort that must be made to discern the nature of a problem and undertake a successful search for methods of solution. Naturally, such a demonstration is a kind of model that must be subordinated to the needs of the presentation, and the reader's time. In particular, we have not reproduced incorrect hypotheses and dead-ends in reasoning, nor trivial examples, and instead attempted to make the presentation gradual and "forward-looking." In this way, it is even possible to create in the reader the illusion of flexibility and simplicity in the implementation of each step. Running ahead of ourselves a bit, note that in none of the actual studies of storage packing were we able to guess at the complete theory involved all at once; in fact, it took 10 years to construct the theory. We will therefore try to give a rough idea of the "nontriviality" of the conjectures that led us to a rather complete conception of the essentials of the problem. Naturally, these judgments are subjective in nature and can serve only as guideposts for the reader.

It is quite natural to interpret the storage packing problem as a matter of renaming the arguments and results of a program's statements (instructions), but this requires a clear understanding of the nature of the programming process and, in particular, the function of storage. It may take quite some time to see that the concept of a variable value and the concept of a memory location are rather analogous in nature. A further requirement, more psychological than theoretical, is the capacity to "recognize" one and the same program in the guise of new notation for the variables.

Just guessing at the idea of introducing the program schema as the initial construction presupposes certain mathematical abilities, basically the ability to abstract and identify those properties of a program that are essential for minimizing storage as well as the capacity to discard all other properties. To motivate the introduction of the notion of a program schema, we could use the important concept of a program flow chart, which is in fact nothing other than a control flow graph; within the rectangles corresponding to the

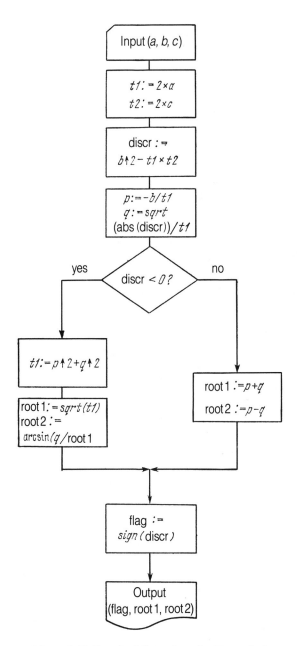

Figure 1.12. Standard flow chart for Example 9.

statement vertices in such a graph may be found information that gives the meaning of the particular statements. As an example, in Figure 1.12 we have given the standard representation of the flow chart of a program that solves quadratic equations (cf. Example 9).

The least trivial and, in general, the key findings in our solution of the problem are the distinctions we have made between the arguments and results of statements and the variables used to denote them, the introduction of the concept of a data path, and the creation of a graphic representation of the data paths in the form of arcs that emanate from results to arguments. We were able to get a thorough grasp of the problem quite rapidly by means of the naturally arising concept of a cross section in linear programs as well as the concept of a bundle as the "unit" of storage allocation in the general case. The set of data paths then became an important program invariant, which was, in fact, independent of the methods used to allocate storage.

Just as essential a logical step was the idea of severing the process of gathering complete information about bundle incompatibility via the incompatibility graph from the direct search for an optimal storage allocation, expressed as a process of "coloring" the vertices of a graph. This is extremely important from the standpoint of a concrete implementation of the storage packing procedure. That is, the straightforward process of obtaining unambiguous information about the pairwise incompatibility of bundles was severed from the highly nondeterministic, combinatorial search for an optimal coloring, which, moreover, is, in and of itself, a well-known mathematical problem. By its very nature, this finding is purely mathematical in nature. Note that we could have arrived at the idea of coloring the vertices of a graph as a means of minimizing storage in a rather offhanded way, without having to resort to the concept of a data path. As an example, let us interpret the storage packing problem as expressing the wish to place just a few more variables in the same memory location so as to minimize total storage consumption. Two variables are then incompatible if they cannot be placed in the same memory location, and are otherwise compatible. The relation of incompatibility can be represented in the form of a graph whose vertices are the variables and whose edges connect incompatible variables. An optimal coloring of a graph yields a minimal storage allocation. Clearly, this is "very nearly" an incompatibility graph with, however, two essential differences. First, we have no way of guessing that the arguments and results denoted by the same variable could belong to distinct bundles and therefore could be associated with distinct memory locations, and, second, at this level there is no way of reaching an actual definition of incompatibility.

Finally, the discovery of the need to enlarge the set of data paths was, to some degree, a matter of chance. It was at first very difficult to make any conjecture here, though it is also true that any analysis of the mathematical formulation of the problem would lead nearly inevitably to the need for such an assumption, if for no other reason than to "tie both ends of the theory together" without any loss in generality.

CHAPTER 2

Statement of the Problem and General Theory

2.1. Brief Review of Mathematical Foundations

Abstract Objects

A properly written mathematical work will always clearly distinguish what is defined or described in the work from what is assumed to be already known. In certain cases a rule of omission is in effect, according to which everything not explicitly defined or explained is assumed to be known. There is a degree of risk in such a rule of omission: The reader must be certain he understands the unexplained concepts in precisely the way in which they are used by the author. In view of the didactic nature of our presentation, we propose to help out our reader a bit, and will briefly describe those mathematical concepts we will be using in this book. Though all of them are, without exception, part of the lexicon of mathematics, we nevertheless will summarize them if for no other reason than to underscore how few in number are the concepts needed for the development of the theory underlying our problem.

The concept of an abstract object is among the most basic concepts. An understanding of this concept places in our hands a key to comprehending the universality of the mathematical method of investigation. An *abstract object* is understood to refer to the subject of a mathematical discourse, which may consist of definitions, assumptions, or postulates, and assertions derived from the definitions and assumptions in accordance with readily comprehensible, i.e., once again, *postulated*, rules of logical deduction. At the highest level of abstraction are the initial or primitive abstract objects, which are objects whose nature we can allow ourselves to ignore totally. In a mathematical discourse a primitive or, as is usually said, *arbitrary* abstract object is subordinated solely to the assumptions that may be "applied" to it and under which it may be "considered" in accordance with the notation assigned to it and by virtue of which it may be "distinguished" from all other objects. All other properties or manipulations with this object are outside the scope of the *given* discourse. We did not emphasize the word "given" by chance, since in some other discourse "the same" primitive object may have an entirely different form and possess additional properties or different internal structure

—after, that is, it has been specified in some way. For example, below we will be defining a graph as a construction whose vertices may be arbitrary abstract objects. Later on, however, once we have begun to speak of incompatibility graphs, vertices will be understood to refer to bundles, i.e., objects with an extremely complicated structure. The reader may even have to make a deliberate effort to associate in his mind the concept of a bundle with a mere point in the plane, which is the ordinary graphic representation of a vertex of a graph. The latitude and flexibility with which the mathematician changes the level of abstraction at which he considers objects, selecting the most appropriate kind of graphic representation of the object for each level, resembles the case of the experimental photographer who switches camera objectives, zooming from a panorama to a close-up. They are also the watchwords for the successful and effective solution of mathematical problems.

In considering abstract objects it is necessary to distinguish between the notation used for the object and the notation used for its representation. Notation is introduced in a discourse by means of a defining sentence, such as "Suppose that S is a statement of our program." Other sentences recall the object introduced by the defining sentence. Notation serves as a kind of bridge connecting the definition of a given object and its use. A rigorous presentation will indicate explicitly the defining sentences, and not leave the reader to *guess* from the context what object is under discussion. In certain languages the distinction between a definition and a discussion of a previously defined object is part of the grammar of the language, as, for example, the definite and indefinite articles in English. In ALGOL and certain other algorithmic languages, the role of defining statements is played by declarations, such as **integer** x, **proc** F, and so forth.

A representation of an object is a graphic visualization of some concrete object. By itself, it asserts what object is being considered and, in general, does not require a defining statement.

Besides the initial abstract objects, mathematical discourse also deals with secondary or derived objects, i.e., objects that may be obtained somehow from initial objects, for example, by constructing or computing a derived object from an initial object. This method presupposes the existence of an algorithm, or set of rules or instructions, that describe in a convincing manner the individual steps in a computational process that lead to the construction or generation of some arbitrary object. By a "convincing manner," we understand that, in any implementation of the algorithm, we can always execute the very next step, we always know precisely which step must be executed, and we always know that our process must terminate. In mathematics there are several rigorous definitions of what sort of computational rules may be considered algorithms. All of them describe one and the same group of computational processes; further, the method of expressing an algorithm is quite analogous to writing a program for a computer.

Another method of generating arbitrary objects from initial objects consists of grouping or combining together the initial objects into compound objects, called sequences (tuples) or sets.

A *tuple* is an abstract object that is known to consist of a definite and finite number of other objects, called the *components* of the tuple. If a tuple is given, so are its components, and conversely, by specifying the components we completely describe the tuple. A rational fraction is a tuple of two integers, a numerator and a denominator, a complex number is a tuple of two real numbers, its real part and its imaginary part, a vector is a tuple of its coordinates, and a polynomial is a tuple of its coefficients. The components of a vector may always be distinguished from each other; once a name is introduced for a tuple, so are names (here, distinct) introduced for its components. Two identically constructed tuples are equal if their corresponding components are the same (equal). We did not choose the words "identically constructed" by chance: the complex number $2 + 5i$ and the rational fraction $\frac{2}{5}$ are not equal, even though their components are equal.

There are two ways of denoting tuples. Either a simple symbolic notation is assigned to the ordered sequence as a whole and introduced in an ordinary way, or notation is introduced for the components of the tuple and at the same time the way the components are combined into the tuple (rules of composition) is indicated. Here are a number of well-known examples:

fraction	$r = p/q,$
complex number	$z = a + ib,$
vector	$a = (a_1, a_2, \ldots, a_n),$
polynomial	$P_4 = a_0 + a_1 x + a_2 x^2 + a_3 x^3 + a_4 x^4,$
matrix	$B = \|b_{ij}\|\ (i = 1, \ldots, n; j = 1, \ldots m),$
triangle	$\Delta = (a, b, c).$

If the expression of a tuple is given, its components may sometimes be denoted by means of an access function having the form $K(T)$, where T is the symbol (notation) for the tuple and K the name of the corresponding components, for example,

Re (z),
Im (z),
numerator (r),
denominator (r).

Obvious identities hold between rules of composition and access functions, for example:

$z \equiv (\mathrm{Re}(z), \mathrm{Im}(z)),$
$p \equiv$ numerator $(p/q),$
$q \equiv$ denominator $(p/q).$

In many cases where the components of a tuple are homogeneous terms, there is no need to introduce a name for each component individually; instead, the components are arranged in some order and enumerated. Each component is then assigned a number that also becomes the name of the component. In this case, the access function is specified differently. The number of the component is written as a subscript either next to the notation used for the tuple (as in the case of a vector) or next to the general symbol used for the component (as in the case of a matrix B).

Sets and Correspondences

The act of combining objects into *sets* is of exceptional importance in all mathematical constructions. The best explanation of the nature of a set is due to Georg Cantor, the founder of set theory. Cantor wrote that "by a 'set,' we understand any combination of designated and entirely distinguishable objects m drawn from our perception or imagination into a single whole M (these objects are called the 'elements' of M)." The assertion that an element m belongs to a set M is denoted $m \in M$ (m belongs to M).

All the different methods of combining elements into a set reduce ultimately to specifying either a method of "generating" the elements of the set or a characteristic property by means of which the elements of the set may be "distinguished" from all other elements. Since it makes sense to assume that a procedure for obtaining the elements of a set may turn out to be ineffective and that the characteristic property may never be fulfilled, we have to assume the existence of an empty set that does not contain any element. The symbol $\varnothing$ is the universal notation for the empty set.

The variety of general assertions also reduces ultimately to two types of assertions:

(a) an assertion that there exists an element with some property that belongs to a set;
(b) an assertion that some property holds for all elements of a set.

A proof of particular general assertions about the elements of certain sets is, in general, the ultimate goal of any mathematical discourse.

There is still one more fundamental concept associated with sets and elements of sets—the concept of a correspondence. A *correspondence* establishes a relation between the elements of two sets M and N of the same type such that if we are given some element of M, we are also given an element of N defined completely by this correspondence. The simplest type of correspondence is an identity, i.e., a correspondence in which we "recognize" for some element of M an element in N equal to it.

Once a correspondence S has been defined for any element of M, we may speak of a *mapping S* of M into a set N:

$$S: M \to N.$$

The corresponding element n of N is called the *image* of its *pre-image m* from M. This relation is represented by the equality $n = S(m)$.

A set M that may be identically mapped into a set N is called a *subset* of N ($M \subseteq N$), and it is said that N *includes* M.

By definition, the empty set is assumed to be the subset of any set. If each element of N is the image of some pre-image in M under the mapping S, we speak of a mapping of M *onto* N. In this case, the set N is also called the image of its pre-image M. If in a mapping S of M onto N, each element in N is the image of only one element in M, the inverse mapping S^{-1} of N onto M may be defined, such that with each image $S(m) \in N$ we may associate its pre-image $m \in M$. In this case, we speak of a one-to-one correspondence between the elements of M and N, and M and N themselves are said to be *equivalent*. If there is a one-to-one identity correspondence between the elements of two sets M and N, the sets are said to be *equal* ($M = N$).

We sometimes read that "sets are said to be equal if they consist of the same elements." In fact, this is an unwarranted formulation that demonstrates quite well the difference between everyday speech and rigorous mathematical language. By elucidating the meaning of the brief phrase, "one and the same," we are at once led to the concept of a correspondence and to the definitions just presented. This does not mean that mathematics is in contradiction with everyday speech. The punctilious repetition of every definition and transcribing of each and every logical stage of the reasoning in a proof would make any presentation cumbersome, tedious, and sterile. Using, however, "ordinary." words and abbreviations and reasoning by analogy, a mathematician is able to conceive an intellectual framework of faultless constructions, and make his presentation rigorous. It is this ability to combine the logic of mathematical reasoning with the structure of man's everyday language that is referred to as mathematical literacy.

The following simple assertion holds: If $M \subseteq N$ and $N \subseteq M$ simultaneously, then $M = N$. In fact, since $N \subseteq M$, for any $n \in N$ there is an element in M equal to it. This means that in any mapping of M into N, each element in N is an image of an element in M, moreover the image of only one element in M (since the correspondence is an identity). Thereby, the correspondence between M and N is an identity and one-to-one, i.e., $M = N$.

Virtually all the sets treated in mathematics are based on the series of natural numbers and subsets of this series, in particular, n-segments of the series of natural numbers, i.e., sets of all the natural numbers k such that $l \leq k \leq n$. A set M equivalent to some n-segment is called a *finite* set, and the number n (equal, naturally, to the number of elements in M) is the *cardinality* of M. The empty set is also assumed to be finite with cardinality zero. All other sets are said to be *infinite*. An infinite set which is equivalent to the natural series is said to be *countable*. If a correspondence between a finite or countable set M and an n-segment or series of natural numbers is defined, M is then said to be a *denumerable set*, and the correspondence is referred to as an *enumeration* of its elements, while the image of an element of M becomes the *ordinal number* of this element.

Denumerable sets are sometimes said to be ordered, though this is not entirely correct. A set M is said to be *ordered* if for any pair of distinct elements of this set m and m' an order relation $(m < m')$ may be defined which possesses the following properties:

(a) if $m < m'$, it is false that $m' < m$;
(b) if $m < m'$ and $m' < m''$, it is true that $m < m''$.

If M is a denumerable set $(M = \{m_j\})$, it is always possible to introduce an order relation between its elements if it is assumed that $m_i < m_j$ if and only if i is less than j in the ordinary sense. This order, however, reflects not so much particular intrinsic properties of the elements of M as the properties of its enumeration, and in fact there are other possible methods of ordering the elements. The concept of enumeration and the concept of order must therefore be distinguished.

As in the case of tuples, once a set M has been denoted, the symbols used for this set simultaneously introduces a notation for any element m of the set:

$$M = \{m\}$$

or (for countable denumerable sets)

$$M = \{m_j\} \qquad (j = 1, \ldots)$$

and (for finite sets)

$$M = \{m_1, \ldots, m_n\}.$$

At this point, it is also worth noting the difference between finite denumerable sets and tuples. An object which is a component of a tuple may be distinguished from an object of a set by the fact that, in the former case, the object is always perceived together with information that tells us which component of the tuple it is. In particular, a tuple may have several identical components, whereas it does not make sense to speak of a set containing several identical elements. These differences may be emphasized by examples of several sets related to a particular tuple, e.g., a vector

$$a = (a_1 = 1, a_2 = 3, a_3 = 1, a_4 = 2),$$

the set of names of its components

$$\{a_1, a_2, a_3, a_4\},$$

the set of names of its components together with the components themselves

$$\{(a_1, 1), (a_2, 3), (a_3, 1), (a_4, 2)\},$$

and the set of values of its components

$$\{1, 2, 3\}.$$

The second set is the one closest to the initial tuple. It may even be taken as the definition of an ordered sequence.

Variables and Functions

By means of the notion of a set, we are able to introduce yet another fundamental concept—the concept of a *variable*. Simplifying the treatment somewhat, we may say that the concept is used in two different senses. In the first sense, a variable is understood as the notation (symbol) x of an arbitrary (i.e., any) element of some set X ($X = \{x\}$). A particular element of X associated with this notation is called the *value* of the variable x. In the second sense, a variable is an abstract object such that at any moment it is being considered it may be associated with some element of a set X, called its *current value*. In this second interpretation, the meaning of a variable is quite close to that of a memory location in a computer, in which some object—the variable—serves as the "storehouse" of some other object—its current value. In this interpretation, there are three symbols associated with the concept of a variable—**x** for the variable itself; x, an arbitrary value of the variable which is also an element of a set X, called the *domain of definition* of the variable **x**.

The use of variables in the first sense is somewhat unwarranted whenever the notation for the variable and its values are not distinguished or may be distinguished only from the context. This happens in ALGOL 60. For example, in the program

begin real x; input (x); $x := x + 1$; output (x) **end**

the first, second, and third occurrences of the letter x denote a variable, the fourth and fifth occurrences denote its current value, while the keyword **real** describes the domain of definition (in computer science, the "liveness domain") of x.

If under the mapping

$$F: X \to Y$$

the set X is the domain of definition of some variable magnitude **x**, we may speak of the existence of a *function* $F(\mathbf{x})$ of the argument x. If x is the value of **x**, $F(x)$ is called the value of the function $F(\mathbf{x})$ corresponding to this value of the argument.

In certain cases it makes sense to speak of a mapping

$$S: M \to N$$

in which the correspondence between the elements of M and N does not hold for all elements of M. In this case, S is called a *partial mapping*. We may analogously speak of *partial functions*.

There are certain standard procedures for constructing new sets from given sets. Suppose that we are given a tuple of n nonempty sets $M_1 = \{m_1\}$, $M_2 = \{m_2\}, \ldots, M_n = \{m_n\}$. The set whose elements are arbitrary tuples of the form $(m_1, m_2, \ldots, m_n)$ is called a *direct product*, and denoted $M_1 \times M_2 \times \ldots \times M_n$.

If at least one of the sets M_i is empty, then by definition their direct product will consist of the empty set. Any subset B of the direct product of the two sets $M = \{m\}$ and $N = \{n\}$ is said to be a *binary relation* specified on the set $M \times N$. In this case, the elements (m, n) of B are referred to as pairs that satisfy the specified binary relation.

Suppose we are given two sets M and N. From M and N we may construct new sets, called the *union* $(M \cup N)$, *intersection* $(M \cap N)$, and *difference* $(M \backslash N)$. The following membership relations are the characteristic properties of the elements of these sets:

M or N for the union,
both M and N for the intersection,
M, but not N for the difference.

If $N \subseteq M$, then $M \backslash N$ is called the *complement* to N with respect to M.

Constructive Object

In mathematics we often distinguish objects, structures, and reasonings as being *constructive*. The use of this word is motivated by the fact that for these types of objects, structures, and reasonings, it is desirable to emphasize the further assumption that these objects may be used and considered, the constructions carried out, and the reasonings performed "effectively." To make this assumption more concrete, we may say that in the real world any "constructive" operation is one that may be carried out in finite time using a finite quantity of mathematical tools.

The only initial mathematical objects are those that may be indisputably asserted to be primitive and that can always be considered all at once. To test these properties of constructive objects, a representation of the objects may always be created, i.e., a representation by means of a limited ordered sequence of "self-evidently" primitive objects which may be thought of as the "atoms" of every object. In the constructive approach, these atoms are usually understood as the elements of some designated finite set, called an *alphabet*; the elements themselves are called *letters*. With each alphabet is associated its own set of words. Each *word* is a finite tuple of letters in which not just the initial letter and final letter are distinguished, but also—for each letter other than the initial letter—the letter's left neighbor, and for each letter other than the final letter—its right neighbor. There also exists the empty word—namely, the word without any letters. The number of letters in a word is called its *length*. Virtually any representation of a constructive object reduces to a representation of the object in the form of words in some alphabet. For example, natural numbers in a carefully written work in constructive mathematics will be represented by words in a one-letter alphabet, so that the number n is represented by a word of length n.

In the constructive approach, an arbitrary correspondence or construction is assumed to be given or implementable only if it may be described within the confines of one of the recognized rigorous definitions of an algorithm that implements operations on constructive objects.

Constructive mathematics considers infinite sets (for example, the natural numbers or the set of all words in some alphabet), though no operations or reasonings are allowed that make use of the principle of actual infinity. An element m of a set M is assumed given only if there exists an algorithm whose application to any other previously given constructive object yields this element. By means of the principle of potential infinity, we may consider any natural number or any word in a designated alphabet to a given object.

An assertion that some object exists is recognized as a constructive assertion if it depends upon an algorithm by means of which it may be explicitly constructed. Such a proof is in contrast with an indirect argument, in which the assumption that such an object does not exist leads to a contradiction (proof by contradiction).

Graph

We conclude our review section with a description of a construction that will be regularly used in what follows.

Suppose we are given a finite set $A = \{a_1, \ldots, a_n\}$. A *directed graph G = (A, Γ)* is understood to refer to a tuple consisting of A and any binary relation Γ defined on the direct product $A \times A = \{(a_i, a_j)\}$. The elements of A are called the *vertices* of the graph, while pairs (a_i, a_j) that satisfy the binary relation are called the *arcs* of the graph. In the arc (a_i, a_j) the vertex a_i is called the *predecessor* of its *successor* a_j.

The use of such words as "graph," "vertex," and "arc" is motivated by the geometric representation of binary relations in the plane or in space. In such a representation, the vertices are represented by points and the arcs by arrows that emanate from predecessors to successors. The reader should be already familiar with the use of directed graphs from the examples of program schemas given in the preceding chapter, where statements were the vertices and control transfers the arcs. Now suppose that A' is a subset of a set A. Then a *subgraph* of G is understood to be a graph $G' = (A', \Gamma')$ where the binary relation $\Gamma' = \Gamma \cup (A' \times A')$. It is clear that G' is a graph with vertices A' between any pair of which there is an arc if and only if these vertices are connected by an arc in G.

A binary relation Γ that possesses the property that if $(a_i, a_j) \in \Gamma$, then both $(a_j, a_i) \in \Gamma$ and $(a_i, a_i) \notin \Gamma$ (does not belong to Γ) is said to be *symmetric* and *antireflexive*. Any symmetric and antireflexive binary relation Γ defines an *undirected* graph. As before, the elements of A are called the vertices of the graph, and each pair (a_i, a_j) and (a_j, a_i) in Γ are together referred to as the *edge* connecting the two adjacent vertices a_i and a_j. In a geometric representation of an undirected graph in the plane or in space, the vertices are represented by points and the edges by lines connecting the representations of adjacent vertices.

Both directed and undirected graphs will be studied here at a substantially deeper level, so that it will make better sense to give the corresponding definitions in the course of the presentation, accompanied by explanatory examples.

*   *   *

We are running the risk that this brief review of the mathematical foundations will satisfy virtually no one on a first reading. The well-prepared reader may find it too superficial, and the beginning student may think it too compressed. While recognizing the legitimacy of this point of view, we would also like to mention that, in the course of preparing the present book, the temptation arose, on more than one occasion, to lay the book aside and write an entirely different one on the foundations of mathematics that would be of interest to experts and instructive to beginners. In fact, the faultless and ready assimilation of the elementary, though extremely profound principles of mathematical reasoning is essential not just for the professional mathematician. Such a goal is no less important for anyone who must apply mathematical methods in the real world and implement them on a computer. The division between theoretical and effective solutions, between constructive and nonconstructive approaches, and between the abstract object and a representation of the abstract object is often a matter of extremely fine details of mathematical reasoning that nevertheless must be perceived faultlessly. At the same time, the basic foundations of mathematical constructions and reasonings are often set forth in an offhanded manner, scattered about in different courses, or generally assumed to be entirely self-evident.

With the foregoing remarks in mind, we now feel it necessary to touch upon the foundations of mathematical research, at least "in the small." We will present a brief, but highly condensed review of the fundamental concepts insofar as they are used in the book, without, however, begrudging ourselves the time and space for formal digressions wherever they seem pertinent to the basic presentation. We hope that in this way we will be able to expound the essentials of all our concepts to those readers who are learning about them for the first time, and that the approach will not be without interest to the more advanced reader.

2.2. Initial Definitions

Let us once again enumerate the concepts we have introduced in the descriptive analysis of the problem: program schema, statement, argument, result, variable, storage allocation, control flow graph, route, data path, bundle, incompatibility, incompatibility graph. It is now time to give rigorous definitions of each of these concepts. Using these definitions, we will then try to find a solution of our problem.

Definition of Program Schema

The concept of a program schema is clearly a primitive concept here. Now that we have completed the review section, we can state that the notion of a program schema is based on that of a control flow graph whose vertices are statements and whose arcs denote all the possible control transfers from one statement to the next. Each statement has assigned to it a designated number of arguments and results. A storage allocation consists in correlating with each argument and result the name of some variable. The set of all variable names is understood to refer to the storage used to transfer values from results to arguments.

In devising a definition of a program schema, we must first decide whether to define a single, though arbitrarily selected schema, or a set of schemas. This is not an entirely academic question. To specify a set of schemas means describing those "details" or primitive objects that, when combined together in an arbitrary way, create a designated set. This, for example, is how the series of natural numbers is constructed. Here the initial "details" are the zero and the operation of counting that "creates," for some succeeding number, the number that follows it in sequence. The set of all words in some alphabet, the set of designators in ALGOL, and so forth is constructed analogously, though in a more complex way. We must not, however, let these analogies persuade us to attempt at once to give a grammar of all possible program schemas. There is an old saying, "entities should not be multiplied unnecessarily" (William of Occam—trans.), which is of particular importance in mathematics, where the seeming ease with which speculative constructions are created contributes to such a pointless multiplication of entities.*

Returning to our case, let us note that we have not answered our question, nor have we thought through the general outline and problems of our theory. Following Cantor, we must speak of a set of objects if there is a definite need to consider them "all together" or at least "any one of them." Let's try to determine what our situation is now. We are presented with the following problem. Find the optimal admissible storage allocation for a designated program schema. This means that in solving the storage packing problem the schema is fixed, and only the storage allocation changes. We require a set of admissible storage allocations. It is in this set that we must find an allocation that is minimal in terms of the number of variables used. However, we do not have to compare one program schema to any other schema that differs from it any more substantially than in terms of storage allocation, even if it solves the same problem (e.g., Examples 4 and 5 of Chapter 1). Any such comparison

---

* In the folklore of the Moscow Mathematical Society there is the story of the young speaker who briskly began his paper with the words, "Without any serious limitation on generality, let us consider a set with cardinality at most countable." It turned out that he had in mind an alphabet consisting of two letters.

falls outside the scope of our theory. Thus, it is clear that there is no need to construct the set of all program schemas, though we do need a definition of this set if we wish to consider the set of all storage allocations associated with a given program schema and determine which of these allocations are admissible (i.e., preserve the data paths), and finally, find the optimal allocation from among the latter.

Thus, let us proceed to define a program schema. An obvious initial set would be a finite set of statements $F = \{F_1, \ldots, F_n\}$. Now we must determine the arguments and results of these statements. For us these concepts have a double meaning. On the one hand, each of these objects (arguments and results) relates to some statement, while on the other hand, in all the different storage allocations the same variable is correlated to each of these objects. Because of this universality of the concepts of arguments and results we may subsume them under a single common designation. How to think up apt designations and convenient notation is a secret of the creative imagination no book can explain; and so without further ado, we will refer to both the arguments and results as *poles*, by analogy with the inputs and outputs of an electric circuit. Some logical effort is needed to visualize the poles first in the form of an isolated set of objects, and only subsequently as a special mapping that has been "adapted to" a particular statement. Summarizing, we have a set of arguments $A = \{a_1, \ldots, a_p\}$, and a set of results $R = \{r_1, \ldots, r_q\}$, which we have combined into a set of poles $P = A \cup R = \{\pi_1, \pi_2, \ldots, \pi_r\}$, where $r = p + q$. An *allocation of poles* to statements is written out in an obvious way in the form of a mapping V of the set of poles into the set of statements:

$$V: P \to F.$$

We define a *control flow graph* as a directed graph $C = (F, J)$ constructed and defined on a set F of statement vertices and a binary relation J that specifies the immediate successor of any statement in terms of control transfers.

These sets characterize everything there is to know about a program schema, other than the storage allocation. A schema without a storage allocation is no longer a schema, but rather a kind of foundation for a schema, a *skeleton* say, on which different storage allocations may be "superimposed." Thus, a skeleton S is a tuple of sets of statements F, a control flow graph C, a set of arguments A, a set of results R, and an allocation of poles among the statements V:

$$S = (F, C, A, R, V).$$

To turn a skeleton into a schema we require storage, i.e., a set of variables $X = \{x_1, \ldots, x_m\}$ and a storage allocation among the poles, which may be specified most naturally in the form of a mapping of the set of poles onto the set of variables:

$$L: P \to X.$$

(We don't have to consider variables that aren't correlated to any pole.)

Thus, a *program schema* G is a tuple consisting of a skeleton S, storage X, and storage allocation L among the poles:

$$G = (S, X, L).$$

Let us undertake an analysis of this definition of a program schema. The schema G is constructed from given arbitrary finite sets of abstract objects: a set of statements $F = \{F_1, \ldots, F_n\}$, a set of poles $P = \{\pi_1, \ldots, \pi_r\}$, and a set of variables $X = \{x_1, \ldots, x_m\}$ which are part of the construction of the control flow graph C, and two mappings—the allocation of the poles V and the storage allocation L. It is precisely because we have not rigidly defined the composition and properties of the primitive abstract objects that we may claim it is not the set of "all" program schemas we are describing. For designated sets of statements, poles, and variables, however, we may readily imagine the set of "all" control flow graphs C and the set of "all" mappings V and L. Let us ask ourselves whether any tuple whatsoever

$$((F, C, A, R, V), X, L)$$

may be considered a program schema.

This is the sort of question that must be asked every time we introduce rules for the construction of an arbitrary composite object. As in real life, we must be very careful when "poking around in dark corners," i.e., take care to investigate the different degenerate and special cases we did not have in mind in the descriptive analysis, focusing our attention mainly on "typical" cases, though, of course, to investigate these cases we have to encroach upon the sphere of unbounded combinatories of formal definitions.

In fact, the act of verifying the generality of a definition constitutes a permanent part of any mathematical study and is performed only after a careful check of all the stages of this study. The purely aesthetic criteria of simplicity and elegance serve as inducement to mathematicians to maintain a certain level of generality as long as counterexamples are not encountered or as long as a proof cannot be constructed due to the difficulty of the problem. On the other hand, the mathematician must not hesitate to set aside "empty" generalizations, as these make a presentation tiresome and make algorithms cumbersome without adding anything to the store of knowledge. In the present case, our analysis of the generality of the definition of a program schema is also preliminary in nature and relates to the analysis of control flow graphs, storage allocations, and allocations of poles.

Analysis of the Concept of a Control Flow Graph

By definition, a control flow graph is an arbitrary directed graph with vertices $F = \{F_1, \ldots, F_n\}$. Can a program have an arbitrary graph as its control flow graph? Naturally, because of the sequential logic of the programming process, there are any number of interpretations of what constitutes a "typical" program. In a somewhat playful mood, we give a collection of the more unusual graphs in Figure 2.1.

Before delving into the essential variety of these diagrams, let us give several definitions and properties that will help us clarify the discussion and, moreover, make it more useful for what follows. The above examples of graphs may be divided into two categories. In the first category ((a) and (c)) are graphs in the form of "connected" diagrams, while in the second category ((b) and (d)) each graph is clearly divided into parts isolated from each other, but connected "within themselves." But it is difficult to say anything for certain about case (e). Let us try to see why.

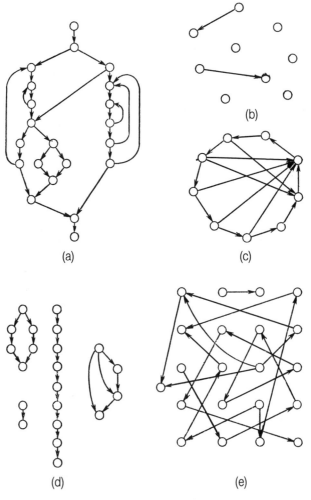

Figure 2.1. Examples of graphs.

The property of connectivity may be understood as asserting that whatever two vertices of the given graph we consider, there exists a path consisting of arcs that connect these vertices. These words may be enough for an intuitive conception, but we need more rigorous definitions.

A. Two vertices in a graph are said to be *neighboring* if one of them is the predecessor of the other (or they are *adjacent* in an undirected graph).
B. Two vertices a and b in a graph are said to be *connected* if there exists a sequence of vertices in the graph $v_1, v_2, \ldots, v_n$ such that $v_1 = a$ and $v_n = b$, and such that any pair (v_i, v_{i+1}) $(i = 1, \ldots, n-1)$ is formed by neighboring vertices.
C. A graph is said to be *connected* if any pair of vertices in it is connected.

Suppose that we are given two graphs $G_1 = (A_1, \Gamma_1)$ and $G_2 = (A_2, \Gamma_2)$. Obviously, the intersection $\Gamma_1 \cap \Gamma_2$ will be a subset of the direct product $(A_1 \cap A_2) \times (A_1 \cap A_2)$. The graph $G' = (A_1 \cap A_2, \Gamma_1 \cap \Gamma_2)$ is called the *intersection* of the graphs G_1 and G_2: $G' = G_1 \cap G_2$. The union of two graphs $G_1 \cup G_2$ is analogously defined. By definition, a graph is said to be *empty* if the set of its vertices is empty. Finally, two graphs are said to be *disjoint* if their intersection is empty.

The meaning of these definitions will become clear once we have formulated the following simple, yet remarkable theorem.

Theorem 2.1. *Any nonempty graph G may be uniquely represented in the form of a union of nonempty pairwise disjoint connected subgraphs* $G_1, \ldots, G_l (l \geq 1)$.

Proof. Let us describe the following uniquely executable procedure. For each vertex a_i $(i = 1, \ldots, n)$ construct the set D_i of all the vertices connected to it, and thus obtain the n sets $D_1, \ldots, D_n$. Let us prove that for any pair D_i and D_j, either $D_i = D_j$ or $D_i \cap D_j = \varnothing$, where $\varnothing$ is the previously introduced symbol for the empty set.

Let us first prove the following lemma.

Lemma. *If each of two vertices a and b in a graph is connected to a third vertex c, they are connected to each other.*

In fact, by the definition of connectivity there exist two chains of neighboring vertices:

$$a = v_1, v_2, \ldots, v_n = c$$

and

$$b = u_1, u_2, \ldots, u_m = c$$

from which a single chain may be created:

$$a = v_1, v_2, \ldots, v_n = c = u_m, \ldots, u_2, u_1 = b,$$

proving that a and b are connected.

Returning now to the sets D_i and D_j, we may at once establish that if a_i and a_j are connected, then, on the one hand, each of them occurs both in D_i and D_j and any vertex connected to one of them is also connected to the other, i.e., in this case $D_i = D_j$. But if a_i and a_j were not connected, D_i and D_j could not have any common vertex, since if such a vertex b were to exist, from the fact that a_i and a_j are both connected to b, it would follow that a_i and a_j are connected, which contradicts the assumption.

As a result we have obtained a unique partitioning of the set $A = \{a_1, \ldots, a_n\}$ into some number of pairwise disjoint sets $B_1, B_2, \ldots, B_l$.

For each of the B_i ($i = 1, \ldots, l$), we construct a subgraph G_i of G having the B_i as its vertices. By the definition of a subgraph, such a construction is also unique, and it is also self-evident that the resulting graphs are pairwise disjoint. It remains for us to prove that

$$G = G_1 \cup G_2 \cup \ldots \cup G_l.$$

We have already proved that

$$A = B_1 \cup B_2 \cup \ldots \cup B_l.$$

Suppose that Γ is the set of arcs of G and let Γ_i be the set of arcs of G_i. We wish to prove that

$$\Gamma = \Gamma_i \cup \Gamma_2 \cup \ldots \cup \Gamma_l.$$

Since the G_i are subgraphs of G,

$$\Gamma_1 \cup \Gamma_2 \cup \ldots \cup \Gamma_l \subseteq \Gamma.$$

Let us prove the converse inclusion. Each arc of Γ either belongs to one of the subgraphs G_i or connects vertices that belong to distinct subgraphs, for example, $a \in G_i$ and $b \in G_j$. This case is, however, impossible, since if a and b were neighboring vertices, by the lemma and the properties of B_i and B_j, any vertex in B_i would have to be connected to each of the vertices of B_j, which, by virtue of the construction of B_i and B_j, is possible only if $B_i = B_j$, which contradicts the fact that they are pairwise disjoint. The theorem is proved.   □

The graphs $G_1, \ldots, G_l$ in the statement of the theorem are called the *connectivity components* of G.

Let us continue with our perusal of the graphs shown in Figure 2.1. We see that in the general case a control flow graph may consist of several connectivity components. Without even waiting for the construction of the general theory, we may at once note that if a program schema is decomposed into isolated parts, i.e., into components of a control flow graph, the storage packing process may be performed in each part separately, since vertices that belong to distinct parts are obviously compatible. From this point of view, it is natural to insist that a control flow graph be connected.

On the other hand, we could imagine an actual situation in which it would be desirable to minimize the storage needed by a group of programs whose structure is not known in advance. Such a group could have been created by means of a compiler, or it may simply be too difficult to determine in advance how many connectivity components there are in the control flow graph (Figure 2.1 (e)). It may then be more convenient to deal with a single storage packing procedure that accomplishes its purpose without letting ourselves be drawn into an analysis of the control flow graph. With these contradictory goals in mind, let us try to establish the potential usefulness of a given partitioning, or—as is usually said—*factorization* of the storage packing process in each of the components of a control flow graph, though we will continue to develop the theory for the general case as long as this seems natural.

By comparing the "typical" control flow graph of Figure 2.1(a) to the other examples, we may discover such features as single-statement components (Figure 2.1(b)), graphs without terminal or without initial statements, and graphs with several initial or several terminal statements. Programming experience suggests that these features must not, in general, be the subject of any *a priori* constraints. The case of several initial or several terminal statements must be permitted if for no other reason than the possibility that several connectivity components might exist. Finally, there are programs that either have no halt instructions or in place of the latter, are supplied with breakpoint instructions that allow the particular program to continue, which is why the graph of Figure 2.1(c) is admissible. In a word, for the time being we are retaining the definition of a control flow graph in all its generality.

Allocation of Poles

Let us consider our analysis of the definition of a program schema supplied with an allocation of poles:

$$V: (A \cup R) \to F.$$

We have already had to deal with statements that have an arbitrary number of arguments and results (including zero arguments or results). The assumption that V may be arbitrarily selected may, however, lead to schemas whose input statement has arguments (which do not have to be loaded) or the output statement may have results (that are never used). In other words, we may encounter "meaningless" program schemas. What should be our attitude in such cases? Usually, such a question can be answered from the standpoint of general considerations no less than through the analysis of particular problems. Everyday experience already suggests that any formal construction always generates objects with "something extra," with respect to which any previously "conceived" objects form a subset. One example of this extra "something" is that created by the grammatical rules of the Russian language, and not only Russian, but any programming language, such as ALGOL, as well. The existence of this extra "something" is no accident. On the one hand, the meaning of an abstract object, i.e., the relation between this object and an event in the real world is, strictly speaking, a category that falls outside the scope of mathematical discourse. We could, of course, give a formal definition of the meaning or, as is usually said, *interpretation* of the particular object and verify that it is satisfied. Such an approach is possible, and in the present book we will repeatedly touch upon questions of interpretation, particularly as regards the theory developed in the present chapter. On the other hand, any explication of a meaning, even if implemented, greatly complicates theory, often without providing any major advantages.

One reason for this complication may be sought in the fact that the meaning of an object is entirely independent of the composition of this object and is not determined by the object itself. To grasp a meaning, it is necessary to take into account a somewhat broader context which it is not always possible to explicate. The present author once heard the sentence, "Last night we had a real cool time at one of the parties," which will no doubt be quite comprehensible to some younger readers. [The original is in the slang of the Russian youth culture.—trans.].

There is a further complication which we now propose to elucidate using our problem as a test case. Suppose it is preferable that exit statements do not have results that are never used. Without giving any thought to the matter, we might write, "An allocation of poles must satisfy a condition which asserts that an exit statement does not have results." And since one thing always leads to another (and any one statement A always leads to some other statement B), we will apparently have to consider, describe, and forbid any other instances of the use of statements with unused results. Suppose we are able to do so. In that case, however, we will have to deal with requirements of quite a different kind. Let us assume (this is a practical example) our computer is provided with an instruction that calculates the integral part of a number, and in addition generates the fractional part of a number, which is also transmitted to memory automatically. In such instances, whether we like it or not, we will have to allow statements with unused results to occur, and the theory will have to take into account this possibility. But if we have truly "let the genie out of the bottle," why do we have to impose any constraints at all on the results of an exit statement if in theory these constraints will never have any effect?

We have allowed ourselves the liberty to digress from the main thread of the reasoning simply because a good understanding of the difference between formal and "interpreted" objects may sometimes be a source of considerable difficulty for specialists concerned with the formulation of applied problems but who lack adequate experience. We may be influenced by the prejudice according to which the more concrete and the more direct a definition, the more correct and the more meaningful the theory. As in the case of excessive generalizations, here the only formal criterion is that of routine logical testing of the theoretical reasonings and constructive algorithms to ensure that any generalization is used exhaustively and, conversely, that any constraint is used essentially.

Thus, we will adopt our definition of an allocation of poles without any constraints.

Storage Allocation

In considering the last mapping

$$L: P \to X$$

the reader may, in keeping with the spirit of the foregoing, wish to retain it in all its generality. Nevertheless, we could just as well try to imagine possible "special" cases of storage allocation. In particular, an arbitrary storage allocation may allow for the possibility of "open" data paths along certain chains of statements, i.e., undefined arguments and unused results. From the example just presented (simultaneous calculation of the integral and fractional parts of a number) and also Example 11 (Chapter 1), we already know that such a situation may be created by the presence of "redundant" results and "unnecessary" arguments, and also whenever there is no way of distinguishing between admissible and inadmissible chains of statements in a program schema. Thus, since we are unable to prevent the existence of open data paths, there is no need to try and limit the storage allocation in this way.

Finally, there is one more aspect of a storage allocation to consider: the same variable may be associated with several arguments or with several results of a single statement. This possibility requires a special analysis. We begin with the results.

If we wish to describe the set of storage allocations that occur in the definition of a program schema, we naturally have to keep in mind not only those allocations that specify the initial schema, but also those that ought to be considered in the search for an optimal storage minimization. From this point of view, we know in advance that a storage allocation that correlates the same variable to distinctly designated (named) results will obviously not be admissible (the simplest examples illustrating our line of reasoning are shown in Figure 2.2). In fact, if a merging together (identification) of names of results is not accompanied by a merging together of names of arguments (Figure 2.2(b)), by the formal attributes a data path will be lost, which is not permitted. But if the merge process is done in a compatible manner, then, without formally violating the principle of preservation of data paths, we will nevertheless be unable to arrive at a reasonable interpretation of the data paths, since for any one argument it will not be possible to determine which result was responsible for transmitting the particular value of the variable used. Obviously, the same kind of uncertainty occurs whenever names are merged together in the initial schema. Of course, we could try and give a

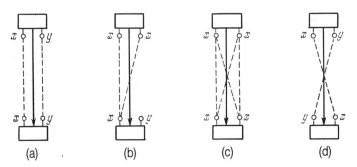

Figure 2.2. The simplest examples of improper renaming.

special interpretation of this kind of merging, and assume that in this case a statement is defined in such a way that the values of the results with which the same variable is associated will always be the same. By this principle, all these results may be considered the same without any fear of contradiction. This stipulation salvages the theory, though as we shall see, it requires a special explanation. Which choice is more convenient—that's for us to decide. We are supposing that the reader is in agreement with our preference to impose the following constraint on the storage allocation: If $r_i \neq r_j$ and $V(r_i) = V(r_j)$, then $L(r_i) \neq L(r_j)$.

Now let us consider the case when it is the names of arguments which are to be identified. Unlike the case of results, no special interpretation is needed if some statement has two arguments with the same variable. Of course, we know that in any storage allocation the theory enjoins us to always label these two arguments with the same variable; therefore, it would seem that in passing from a program to a schema we could treat these two arguments as one without detriment to our discussion, supposing here that distinct arguments also have distinct variables assigned to them. Before formulating the corresponding constraint, however, we must verify that a merging of argument names yields an admissible allocation. Thinking a bit about this problem leads us to the conception of the schema depicted in Figure 2.3(a), in which the data paths are consistent according to all the formal attributes, so that it is entirely proper to associate the same variable with both arguments of statement F_4 (Figure 2.3(b)). Of course, not all readers will find this example entirely convincing, as it permits open data paths, e.g., argument y is undefined if F_4 is reached via $F_1 F_2$. In that case, we may allude to our previous discussion about the admissibility of open data paths even along chains of statements admissible in the structure of the schema. There is an interpretation (again taken from real life) for this special case: F_4 "knows" along which chain control is transferred to it and functions precisely with a labeled argument without resorting to any other still undefined argument. Thus, we do not impose any sort of constraints on the allocation of variables to arguments.

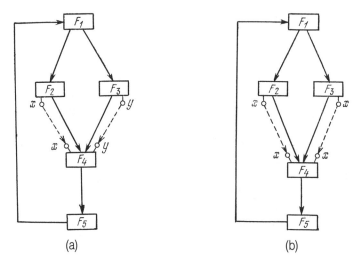

Figure 2.3. Merging the names of arguments.

Now that we have analyzed the definition of a program schema, it is time to give a rigorous definition of the set of data paths, understood as an invariant of the schema that must be preserved in accordance with the demands of an admissible storage allocation.

To describe this invariant, we will have to make use of statements and chains of statements in a control flow graph and the arguments, results, and variables associated with them. For this purpose, we must introduce additional notation and terms that may serve as exact and rigorous concepts compatible with the notation used in the definition of a program schema. At this point, it is pertinent to again digress and talk about certain principles of mathematical terminology and symbolism in general.

Digression on Terms

The demand for rigorous definitions and exact notation is the first thing the beginning mathematician must get accustomed to. The art of combining rigor and exactitude with simplicity and clarity in the writing of a mathematical text is a far more difficult task, which is only aggravated by the fact that today the principal form of publication of original mathematical studies is the journal article, a form in which space limitations are generally the chief factor governing the style of presentation. Later on we will again discuss ways of handling this problem, but for now wish to make just two digressions, one on the use of meaningful terminology, and the other on what may be called "indexomania."

A term is either a primitive word of the language in which the particular mathematical article is written or is introduced into the language by the author and used to denote an abstract object or certain properties of an abstract object. For example, "set" and "separable" are terms of the first and second type, respectively. Note that in mathematics there is no real difference between a term and its symbolic notation. We may state, "Suppose that F is a continuous function," and then use the symbol F alone without having to say the word "function." On the other hand, any symbol used in a text that has been written properly in accordance with the grammatical rules becomes an entirely definite member (word) of a sentence. It is no accident that a thoughtfully written textbook will always give rules for "reading" symbolic expressions in which the grammatical role played by the notation is stated. From this point of view, the mathematical term is distinguished by the fact that it is used exclusively in the sense imputed to it in a definition, i.e., in its defining sentence. When we speak of a "prime number," we must always recall that the only meanings we have "conferred" on this term are the fact that such a number is different from 1 and that it has as its divisors only 1 and itself. At the same time, the overwhelming majority of the words of one's native language that have been fully assimilated always bear all sorts of "other" meanings implanted in these words by the very life of the language. We speak of the set of integers and the set of people, Weierstrass' function and managerial functions, the group of motions (movements) in the Euclidean plane and members of the trade union movement. Even someone with a highly developed propensity for logic is unable to part with these "other" meanings, which find their way into one's subconscious and form one's conception of this or that term involuntarily.* This circumstance has given rise to the tradition of employing rarely used words as mathematical terms, chiefly foreign words that are meaningless to a native speaker (of the language of the mathematics text); a meaning established by the author can then be conferred on these words.

Moreover, tradition is supported by many centuries of the use of Latin as the language of scientific discourse. This is why in the mathematical literature there are so many instances of such words as "epicycloid," "factorial," "trisector," "quaternion," "asymptote," and other high-flown words responsible for the outward appearance of the professional literature. Unfortunately,

---

* In his defense of his Master's thesis, a student at Novosibirsk University, in speaking of a partitioning of some finite set M into subsets, insisted on referring to the latter as "groups of elements of M." This seemingly inoffensive usage turned out to be quite unacceptable to one member of the committee, a leading specialist in group theory. Because of his natural desire to see identity elements, inverse elements, and all the other accoutrements of the broad concept of a group, he had difficulty understanding the paper. At the same time, the student could not reformulate the thesis, and the minimal amount of mutual understanding needed for a successful defense could not be established.

this external form sometimes creates the wrong impression as to what constitutes the essence of literary style in science.*

This does not mean that figurative terms (i.e., those with a supplementary descriptive meaning) are contraindicated in mathematics. There are terms that restore to mathematics the nature of the real object standing for (representing) the formal object defined by this term. This category includes such terms as "wave function," "game" (in game theory), "potential," "proposition" (in mathematical logic), "expectation" (in probability theory), and so forth. Another category (the most numerous) consists of figurative terms that create essentially an image, mainly visual, of the defined object or word simply by virtue of the selected word, thus: "curve," "continuous," "lune," "edge" (in a graph), "tree," "route" (in the present book), and many others. Finally, the next category of figurative terms consists of terms used in language proper as abstract concepts whose sense is in consonance with their adopted use in mathematical discourse, for example, "set," "probability," "measure," "union," "complement," "connectivity," "distance," "weight," and so on. The figurative aspect of terminology is thereby a powerful tool for making a presentation more effective in the sense of helping the reader not only comprehend and assimilate the logical structure of a text, i.e., become convinced of the correctness of the proofs, but also—and this is far more important—enriches the reader's intuition and establishes a relation between the mathematical text and the reader's own experience and previously acquired knowledge.

In concluding this digression on terminology, we would like to encourage the use of figurative terminology so long as the following conditions are observed:

a term must be defined precisely in a mathematical sense;

the figurative "weight" of a term must not be a matter of chance, but rather should be carefully chosen in light of the previously adopted definition of figurativeness;

informal reasonings that employ words in their everyday sense that have already been introduced as terms, however, must be avoided in an article;

the current "usage" of a term in the literature the intended reader may be assumed to know must be respected;

the creation of terms must be considered just as valuable a contribution to science as the proof of theorems, and thereby must be the subject of

---

*Continuing our series of interlinear vignettes, we should not forget the ironical remark made by one of the best lecturers of our time, Academician S.L. Sobolev, at a seminar held at the Computer Center of Moscow University regarding a speaker's use of the Russian word, *Vyzyrator* (caller). The term was used by the speaker to denote a subroutine that calls the modules of a large software package. The meaning of the remark was obvious: Do not mangle language for the sake of a false scientologism by appending a Latin suffix to a true Russian word (contrary to the rule for creating compounds in Russian—trans.).

recognition in terms of priority, citation, and all the other requirements of professional ethics.

Digression on Indices and Symbols

Let us now consider what are the features of "indexomania," a widespread childish habit peculiar to the beginning author. There are two objective grounds for the use of indices:

a numbering of elements of the same kind of a finite set is a convenient means of distinguishing them, and at the same time retains the uniformity of the notation and emphasizes this uniformity;

the application of arithmetic operations to the natural numbers so as to enumerate the elements of a set or components of an ordered sequence makes it possible to describe complicated manipulations with numbered objects in a concise manner.

There is one difficulty, however. Usually, a numbering of the elements of some set is assumed to be fixed once and for all within a mathematical work (article, chapter, etc.). Therefore, if the set $M = \{m_1, m_2, \ldots, m_k\}$ is defined somewhere, then m_2 or m_k will naturally always be understood as precisely the second and final element of this set. The following example shows what this leads to.

We suggest that the reader look over the page he is reading right now. It consists of letters from some alphabet $\{a_1, \ldots, a_n\}$. Let's try to see what is involved in automatic text processing on a computer. For this purpose, each letter of the text is replaced by the number of the compartment in a type set from which this letter may be selected by the computer. Let us suppose, further, that as in the case of poetry, the text is formed in such a way that there is an exact correspondence between the handwritten lines and the printed lines. Thereby, the position of each letter in the text may be specified by means of the number of the row i in which the letter is found and the number of the letter in its row j, so that at position (i,j) is found the number n_{ij} of the corresponding letter, and the letter itself will consequently have the form $a_{n_{ij}}$. The number of letters in the ith row is naturally denoted k_i. Suppose, further, that there are m paragraphs in the page, and that the rows at which these paragraphs begin are numbered $i_1, i_2, \ldots, i_m$. Finally, suppose that the text processing rules are chosen in such a way that a line can begin a paragraph only if the last character of the preceding line is some special control character, say $\#$. Then, if rules for the proper layout of paragraphs in the page must be formulated rigorously, they will have the form of a multi-level construction:

$$(\text{for} \quad r = 1, \ldots, m) \qquad a_{n_{i_r}-1, k_{i_r}-1} = \#.$$

"Indexomania" does not consist in simply "glorifying" such expressions, and combatting it does not mean eliminating indices entirely. It may be entirely legitimate to use the above ladder of indices in some program for automatic text processing. It is unfortunate that authors sometimes do not know when an index is really necessary and when indices may be omitted, and even whether they may by omitted in general. One reason for this difficulty is the result of the confusion we have already alluded to, that is, whether a set has been numbered for the purpose of ordering it, for the purpose of denotation, or for the purpose of counting the number of elements in the set. The use of an index is unavoidable only when it is necessary to speak of all the elements of a set or subset that cannot be denoted simply in a unique way without introducing an index for counting them. Whenever we take an arbitrary sample and assert, "Suppose that m_i is some element of a set M," we could use any related notation for the element instead of m_i but without an index. Among such related notation there is the symbol itself but without an index (m), the same symbol with primes $(m', m'',$ etc.), and finally, letters close to it in alphabetical order (each notation symbolized by combinations to which the eye has become accustomed, e.g., (a, b, c), (f, g, h), (i, j, k), (m, n), (p, q, r), (u, v), (x, y, z), and so on).

The introduction of such variety into symbolism requires, on the part of the writer, however, a serious and exacting attitude towards the alphabet and the observance of certain standards that are, on the one hand, aesthetic and stylistic and, on the other hand, that are of logical necessity.

The notation used in mathematical texts, like names in programs written in algorithmic languages, obeys rigorous rules of localization established by means of defining sentences. As a rule, most of the notation is localized within extremely small segments of texts, such as the statement of a theorem, a paragraph, or a logical stage of a proof. At the same time, the explicit use of defining sentences economizes on notation and, conversely, accustoms the reader to the use of global notation and objects whose definitions remain in force throughout significantly lengthy portions of text.

In selecting notation, it is necessary to take into account the formally inessential, though actually existing, hierarchy of alphabets and letters that reflects the structural hierarchy of objects, thus lowercase letters for initial abstract objects, uppercase letters for "simple" compound objects and sets, boldface capital letters for denumerable sequences and sets, script letters for the most all-inclusive objects, classes of sets, and so on. Of course, many of the more restricted branches of mathematics have their own typographical conventions.

As in the case of terms, it is necessary to avoid the use of previously "employed" notation and likewise try to avoid denoting by, say, the letter N (which is usually associated with the natural number) a set of functions or set of real numbers. But if such "overused" letters as x, F, n, etc., must be resorted to, there is no need to worry about seeming unoriginal; x could be made an unknown, F a function, and n an integer, or these letters could be employed in precisely defined, though transitory application so that the "sound" of the defining sentence just expressed would vouchsafe the ordinary perception of the symbol for a short time.

All other conditions being equal, the alphabet of employed symbols should not be increased unnecessarily. Preparing a mathematical text for the printer has now taken on the appearance of a mass production process, and not just at special printing houses, but also at institutes and commercial publishers (and in vast quantities there) that lack full sets of type, where the text may be set on a computer, or where there are other restricting factors that nevertheless make possible rapid production. Latin type of a single font is the routine minimum; the addition of the Greek alphabet, semi-boldface, and italic fonts can make the process extremely difficult.

Rigorous Definition of Incompatibility

Now that we are armed with these remarks on style, let us proceed to develop the terminology and symbolism needed for our study. A substantially greater degree of consistency may be achieved if all the symbolism is developed simultaneously and early on; this we can do, as we have already drawn the outlines of the theory in the descriptive analysis of the problem.

The incompatibility graph [also translated as "inconsistency graph"—trans.] is the final construction of the theory of storage packing. Let us introduce a symbol for this graph, say the letter I. The choice of notation depends upon a combination of chance, tradition, and sometimes a concealed intention of the author the reader may not know anything about. In working with the Latin alphabet, we will sometimes consider capital letters of the different English words relevant to the subject at hand. We have already used the words argument, result, and pole this way in arriving at the symbols A, R, and P, and will use the word incompatibility [uncompatibility] similarly. The vertices of graph U are "bundles" of data paths. A bundle, an object we have yet to define rigorously, is a subset consisting of related data paths in some program schema. A *data path* is a pair of poles (r, a) with which we associate the same variable and for which there exists at least one route by means of which it may be implemented. A route is some sequence of vertices in a control flow graph that may be "traversed" along the arcs of this graph. To define a route, we require the definition of a "path" in a directed graph and notation for its initial, terminal, and internal vertices. Moreover, we need notation for the arguments and results of the statements in the route. To determine an admissible storage allocation, we must consider the set of all the routes of all the data paths. It deserves its own name, and for obvious reasons we call it a [support] *carrier* (of data paths), denoted CR. To construct the graph U, we must specify a binary relation of incompatibility on the bundles. This relation, recall, depends on the relative position of routes that implement the data paths in the bundles (the initial vertex of one route may turn out to be an internal vertex or even the initial vertex of another route).

These constructions are all quite simple, and most of them have been defined only in passing, though on the basis of just the foregoing discussion we may demonstrate a different approach to the definition of concepts.

Let us begin with the definition of a path in a graph. Suppose we are given a graph $G = (A, \Gamma)$, where $A = \{a_1, \ldots, a_n\}$ is the set of vertices and Γ the set of arcs. By a *path* in G, we understand the sequence of vertices

$$a_{i_1} a_{i_2} \ldots a_{i_n} \qquad (n \geq 2),$$

such that $(a_{i_j}, a_{i_{j+1}}) \in \Gamma$ for all $j = 1, \ldots, n-1$.

This may be stated differently. A *path* in a graph G is any finite sequence W of vertices in the graph of length at least two such that any vertex in W (other than the final vertex) is the successor in G of a preceding vertex in W.

These definitions are equally rigorous, and each has its own advantages and drawbacks. The first definition requires the introduction of notation for the vertices and indices; the second definition does not make use of any indices or symbolism, but relies on the properties of a sequence (existence of succeeding element, the concept of the length of a sequence) and the definition of a successor. The choice of one approach to the definition of a path versus another also determines the style of the presentation. Though each approach is "legitimate," as this example shows symbolism does not always make a presentation more concise nor does it always make it easier to understand.

Let us now define the concept of a route. Continuing the style of the symbolic presentation, we will say that a *route* of a data path (r, a) is to be understood as referring to any path

$$F_{i_1} \ldots F_{i_k}$$

in a control flow graph such that $L(r) = L(a) = x$, $V(r) = F_{i_1}$, $V(a) = F_{i_k}$, and for any r' such that $V(r') = F_{i_j}$ $(j = 2, \ldots, k-1)$, $L(r') \neq x$.

For the sake of comparison, let us give another, "verbal" definition of a route, but before doing so we give two more definitions that will be useful in what follows.

Any vertex occurring at any but the initial or terminal position in some path in a graph is called an *internal vertex*.

A statement *reads in* (*generates*) a variable x if it has an argument (result) to which the storage allocation correlates x.

A *route* of a data path (r, a) is understood to refer to any path in a control flow graph whose initial statement generates the value of x correlated with r and whose terminal statement reads in a value of x correlated with a, such that no internal statement generates x.

Let us analyze this definition. First, the concept of a route includes not only a path in a control flow graph, i.e., some sequence of statements, but also the data path this route implements. Thus, there are two routes in the program schema of Figure 2.4(a). This means that a route must be represented as a tuple of two components: a pair of poles (output, argument) that form the data path and a path in the control flow graph that implement the data path. For

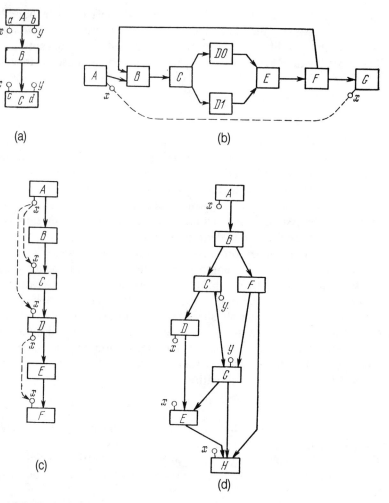

Figure 2.4. Examples of routes of data paths: (a) control flow graph with two routes; (b) graph with infinite number of aperiodic routes that realize a data path; (c) control flow graph with two liveness domains of definition of the variable x; (d) control flow graph in which the data path is preserved when x and y are identified, but in which a route disappears.

the schema of Figure 2.4(a), this will be given as

$$(a, c), ABC \quad \text{and} \quad (b, d), ABC$$

Second, it must be borne in mind that though there cannot be more than $p \times q$ data paths in a program schema, where p is the number of arguments in the schema and q is the number of results, there may be an infinite number of routes that implement any one path. Figure 2.4(b) convincingly demonstrates why this is so: the existence of loops in the graph, for example, *B C D0 E F B*. If a graph has loops, we may naturally think of its paths being periodic, even though the example of Figure 2.4(b) suffices to demonstrate that it can also happen that a set of paths does not satisfy any sort of periodicity condition. Let us take an arbitrary binary number, and for each of its digits *d*, repeat the loop

$$BC \begin{array}{c} D0 \\ \\ D1 \end{array} EF$$

once; here if $d = 1$, we proceed along the branch with $D1$, and if $d = 0$, along $D0$.

Figure 2.4(c) shows why we don't have to insist that the exit statement of a route not generate a value through which the data path could be realized. This is in accord with the meaningful interpretation of the concept of a statement according to which a statement first reads in the value of an argument, and then generates a result. The creation of the new value *x* by statement *D* therefore still allows us to implement a path from *A* to *D*. That the value of the argument has been read in does not nullify this value, and therefore *C*, which is the exit statement of the route from *A* to *C*, turns out to be an internal statement in the route from *A* to *D*.

The example of Figure 2.4(d) demonstrates another reason why more than one route may implement one and the same path: the existence of branchings in the control flow graph. Each path creates its own route, except for *A B C D E H*, in which *D* interrupts the possible paths from *A* to *E* and from *A* to *H*, creating its "own" routes *D E* and *D E H*.

Now that we have a rigorous definition of a route (a route is a construction that "implements" the concept of a data connection), we may at once proceed to the concept of a carrier CR, understood as the set of all the routes of a program schema. Note that though routes are constructed for a designated program schema, i.e., skeleton + storage + storage allocation, the carrier itself consists of constructions created exclusively from elements of the skeleton (statements and poles). Because of this important property of a carrier, we may compare carriers of schemas with the same skeleton but different *X* and *L*. Now suppose that a carrier CR has been constructed for some schema *G*. To underscore this relation, we let CR(*G*) denote the carrier CR(*G*). We now give the following definition.

Definition. Suppose we are given two program schemas $G = (S, X, L)$ and $G' = (S, X', L')$. We will say that *G' computes G* ($G' \succ G$) if CR(*G'*) $\succ$ CR(*G*).

Now we may assert that the storage packing problem for a given schema *G* $= (S, X, L)$ consists in finding in the set of schemas $G' = (S, X', L')$ the schema that computes *G* whose *X'* is of least cardinality.

Our descriptive analysis of the problem suggests that it may be solved in two stages: construction of the incompatibility graph, and then the coloring of the graph. In the next section, we will attempt to evaluate this strategy.

2.3. General Theory

Data Flow Graph

Let us begin our investigation with a description of the graph *I*. Its vertices are "bundles," i.e., certain types of collections of data paths (*r*, *a*) which are in turn specified by a binary relation *M* that asserts the existence of a route that implements a "data transfer" from *r* to *a*.

With the foregoing in mind, we are justified in considering a directed graph whose vertices are poles *P* and whose set of arcs is specified by a binary relation *M*. This graph, which we have already drawn in all our examples by means of broken arrows without calling it by any special name, may now be

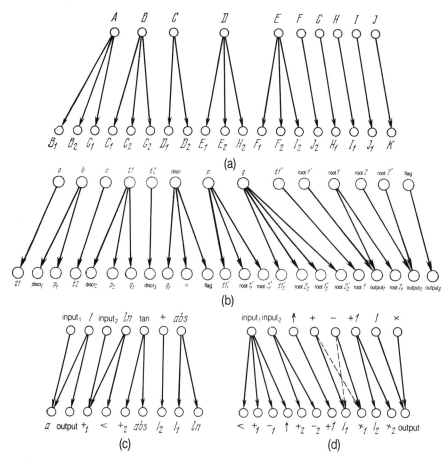

Figure 2.5. Data flow graphs: (a) Examples 5, 6, 7, and 8; (b) Example 9; (c) Example 10; (d) Example 11.

referred to in a natural way as a *data flow graph* $I = (P, M)$. Having thus arrived in this offhanded way at a definition of a data flow graph, we will, as usual, undertake its analysis. We begin by redrawing the data flow graphs from all the examples constructed in Chapter 1 and collect them together in Figure 2.5. For the sake of greater visualization and to achieve a more clear-cut relation to the initial schemas, we have placed the results in the upper row and the arguments in the lower row, labeling the poles by the symbols of the statements these poles refer to. Simple examination of the resulting graphs leads to the following observations.

First Observation. The arcs in a data flow graph are of a special type. A result in these arcs can only be a predecessor, and an argument only a successor. Basically, the binary relation M is defined not on the direct product $P \times P$, but rather on the direct product $R \times A$, where $R \subseteq P$, $A \subseteq P$, and $R \cap A = \varnothing$. This type of graph is called a *bipartite graph*.

Second Observation. Theorem 2.1 of the preceeding section demonstrates quite convincingly that the "bundles" of data paths used in Chapter 1 are basically nothing other than the connectivity components of a data flow graph.

In the present context, this observation is almost trivial, and is little more than a "dry well." It completely formalizes the concept of a bundle and at the same time demonstrates how important a construction is the data graph.

Third Observation. In a number of cases, a data flow graph is a more profound invariant than is a carrier. For example, in the program schemas of Examples 5 and 6, 7 and 8, it is clear that in each pair of examples the carriers are distinct, whereas the data flow graphs are the same. The curious reader may at once wonder about the data flow graph's special role as an invariant in the storage packing problem. In attempting to arrive at an answer, the reader should have no trouble proving the following assertion.

Theorem 2.2 *Suppose that $I(G)$ is the data flow graph of a program schema G. Then if $G' \succ G$, $I(G)$ is a subgraph of $I(G')$.*

Unfortunately, Figure 2.4(d) demonstrates just as convincingly that the converse assertion is not true. If x and y are identified, none of the arcs gets ejected from the data flow graph, though the pattern of data paths is entirely distorted.

The truly curious reader will nevertheless remain unsatisfied with such an all-embracing negative conclusion and will try to find out when a data flow graph can still be preserved as an invariant. Such a reader may incidentally discover rather quickly that the data flow graph of a linear program schema is a universal invariant not only of a storage allocation, but also of a broader class of transformations of schemas related to permutations of statements. For the more general case, the reader may draw upon a class of schemas in which distinct storage allocations rigorously preserve the set of data paths without augmenting this set. We will not, however, digress from the basic line of our general theory just now.

Refining the Concept of Incompatibility

Based on the minor discovery just made, our hypothesis may be re-formulated so that the connectivity components of the data flow graph of a program schema become the vertices of an incompatibility graph. As such, they deserve a special name. Historically, a connectivity component has been referred to as the *liveness domain* (of some variable). Since the descriptive analysis is now behind us, the meaning of the term is clear: in any liveness domain, the same variable is associated with all the poles, since it preserves a generated (live) value of the variable.

To arrive at a complete description of U, we must describe the binary relation of incompatibility between different liveness domains. Let us first give a strictly verbal formulation of the relation of incompatibility.

Definition. Two liveness domain are *incompatible* if there is a data path in each of them such that the initial statement of a route of one of the paths is the initial or an internal statement of a route of the other path.

Though it takes a deep breath to enunciate the definition without faltering, it is nevertheless entirely rigorous and strictly in accord with the conjectures made in the first chapter. There is, however, still something we are not sure of, something that was not entirely clear to us in our discussion of the illustrative examples and which until now would not have been a simple matter to guess at, provided we didn't glance once again at Figure 2.1 with all its examples of connectivity components in directed graphs. One of the examples depicts connectivity components consisting of isolated vertices. We might then ask whether a data flow graph can have isolated vertex poles. The definition of a program schema clearly suggests this is entirely possible. An isolated result is a result which is used nowhere, and an isolated argument an argument into which no results "feed." But then we might ask how is it possible to define an incompatibility relation on isolated poles, since we cannot speak of routes if there are no arcs (data paths) in a data flow graph, as there are then no routes either.

Here we face a traditional dilemma. Should we expunge the isolated vertices from any data flow graph so as to shrink the scope of the definition of incompatibility, or should we generalize the definition of incompatibility to the case of arbitrary data flow graphs. In the latter case, we must also decide how to formulate this generalization so as not to contravene the assumption that all associations between the same variables and connectivity components are consistent.

Let us first consider the case of an isolated result r. We turn to the descriptive interpretation of a statement. When a statement generates a result, it "does not know" when this result will, in general, be used. An incompatibility relation arises from the assignment of the value of a result to an improperly selected variable. This result then "nullifies" (in the American literature, it is even said it "kills") the desired value (formally speaking, this makes it impossible to determine the same route in a schema with reallocated storage). It will be impossible to determine "this same" route if a competing result is the result of one of its internal statements or is its initial statement. Thus, as compared with a data flow path, statement $V(r)$ behaves like the initial statement of a route which is in competition in the sense of the definition made above.

Let us now compare two isolated results r and r'. It is evident that there is nothing wrong in nullifying an unused result, and therefore incompatibility can arise only if the isolated results are the results of the same statement $V(r) = V(r')$. If they were inconsistent, this would go counter to the rules for constructing a program schema.

Now consider an isolated argument a. In the descriptive interpretation of an isolated argument, it is asserted that the value of such an argument will not affect how statement $V(a)$ is executed; $V(a)$ will be executed the same way whatever variable is associated with a. Thus, we may assume that an isolated argument is compatible with any liveness domain in a data flow graph.

We have now considered all the possible ways of combining connectivity components and know how the definition of incompatibility has to be modified.

Definition. Two liveness domains are *incompatible* if and only if two results r and r', respectively, may be found in each of them such that either $V(r) = V(r')$ or $V(r)$ is an internal statement of some route of data flow path (r', a') or $V(r')$ is an internal statement of some route of data flow path (r, a), where a and a' are designated arguments.

Now the incompatibility relation has been defined for all liveness domains $\{a_i, \ldots, a_1\}$ of data flow graph $I = (P, M)$. Suppose that $A = \{a_1, \ldots, a_1\}$. Then the incompatibility graph U is completely defined as $U = (D, H)$.

Incompatibility Criterion

By virtue of these definitions and our analysis, we may now undertake a rigorous proof of the basic hypothesis made in the illustrative discussion of the storage packing problem, i.e., the admissible storage allocations are those in which the same variable may be associated with all the poles of any pair of compatible liveness domains. Let us give a rigorous formulation, preceding it by one more symbolic notation. If in some storage allocation L, the same variable is associated with all the poles of some liveness domain d, we denote this variable $L(d)$.

Theorem 2.3 *Suppose we are given two program schemas $G = (S, X, L)$ and $G' = (S, X', L')$ and let $d_1, \ldots, d_1$ be the liveness domains of graph $I(G)$. Under these conditions, $G' \nmid G$ if and only if:*

(a) *for any d_i $(i = 1, \ldots, l)$, $L'(p)$ is the same for any pole p from among the d_i;*

(b) *$L'(d_i) \neq L'(d_j)$ for any pair d_i and d_j satisfying the incompatibility criterion in $I(G)$.*

Let us now prove the theorem. It contains a necessary and sufficient condition, and therefore we must conduct our reasoning in both directions: from the computability of schema G by schema G' to the premise, and conversely.

Necessity. Suppose that $G' \nmid G$. Let us verify that the premises are satisfied. Condition (a) holds trivially for liveness domains formed by isolated poles. Let us assume that there are two poles p and p' in some domain d containing the arcs such that $L(p) \neq L(p')$. Then there must be an arc (r, a) in d such that $L(r) \neq L(a)$ also. (A detailed proof of this mini-lemma requires some discussion that would essentially make use of the property that d is a connected domain.) But in this case, the pair (r, a) cannot form a data flow path in G' that would implement an arbitrary route. This contradicts the condition $G' \nmid G$.

Let us now assume that we have found two incompatible liveness domains d_i and d_j in $U(G)$ for which it is nevertheless true that $L'(d_i) = L'(D_j) = x$. By the definition of incompatible, in this case we find either that there is a statement with two results in G' with which the same variable may be associated (this contradicts the rule for specifying G') or two results r and r', an argument a, and a path

$$V(r) \ldots V(r') \ldots V(a)$$

(the other statements are not shown) may be found which form a route m of the data flow path r, a and G:

$$m = ((r, a), V(r) \ldots V(r') \ldots V(a)),$$

whereas in G', we nevertheless have $L'(r) = L'(r') = L(a) = x_1$. This means that m is not a route in G', which again contradicts the condition $G' \nmid G$. Necessity is proved.

Sufficiency. Now suppose that the premises of the theorem hold. Let us assume that G contains a route m not in G'. Let $m = ((r, a), V(r) \ldots F_i \ldots V(a))$, where F_i is an arbitrary internal statement of m, possibly absent. Let us consider under what conditions this sequence might not be a route in G'.

One way this might happen is if $L'(r) \neq L'(a)$. This, however, cannot be, since both r and a belong to the same liveness domain d in G and also since $L'(r) = L'(a)$. Thus, if m does not contain any internal statements, it is a route of the path (r, a) in G'.

It could also happen if there is a result r' such that $V(r') = F_i$ and $L'(r') = L'(r)$. Since F_i is an internal statement of m in G, r' must belong to some d' in

G which is different from the liveness domain d containing (r, a). (This is another mini-lemma requiring a critical analysis of the definitions of a route and connectivity component.) By definition, in this case the two liveness domains d and d' are incompatible. But by condition (b), we must then have $L'(r') \neq L'(r)$. Thus, if the conditions of the theorem hold, there is nothing preventing any m from also being a route in G'. $\qquad\square$

The theorem just proved is fundamental to our general theory and underlies our entire approach to the storage packing problem.

Description of Incompatibility Graph

Now we wish to focus our attention on the different methods of specifying an incompatibility graph. We have already analyzed its vertices, i.e., the connectivity components of the data flow graph, and we have also given a rigorous definition of incompatibility. In the general case, the latter concept makes use of routes that are in a designated relative position (the initial statement of one route being the initial statement or an internal statement of the other route). We already know that the approach we are following in developing the theory presumes that the initial definition of what it means to say that one schema is "computable" by another is a constructive definition. We are not able to decide whether some storage allocation is admissible simply by studying the carrier directly, as the latter is a set of routes that is, in general, infinite. By means of Theorem 2.3, we have already reduced the problem of deciding whether a particular storage allocation is admissible to the analysis of the incompatibility graph. Now we must take one more step and expunge the routes from the very definition of incompatibility and no longer think of them as "working hypotheses." Incidentally, an analysis of the isolated poles in a data flow graph would be of assistance here. We hope that the generalized formulation of the incompatibility criterion will help the reader see how natural is the next theorem which, however, we precede with the definitions of two new symbols.

Suppose that d is some liveness domain in the data flow graph of a schema G. Then we let $R(d)$ denote the set of all statements whose results are poles in d, and $T(d)$ the set of all statements each of which is an internal statement of at least one of the routes of the data flow paths in d.

Theorem 2.4 *Two liveness domains d and d' of the data flow graph of a schema G are incompatible if and only if the set*

$$R(d) \cap R(d') \cup R(d) \cap T(d') \cup R(d') \cap T(d)$$

is nonempty.

Proof. The proof of this theorem is extremely simple as it is little more than a rephrasing of the definition of incompatibility. If the above set is not empty, this means that there exists a statement that generates results for both liveness domains d and d' or, if it generates a result for only one domain, this statement is an internal statement in the route of some path in the other domain. Conversely, if the incompatibility condition holds, this means that the set is nonempty.   □

With this, the construction of the general theory is complete. We have derived a rigorous formulation of the problem, and described both given and unknown objects that, once found, will help in solving the storage packing problem, by virtue of the theorems proved above. The objects in question are the connectivity components of a data flow graph and also the sets $R(d)$ and $T(d)$, by means of which an appropriate coloring of an incompatibility graph may be constructed.

CHAPTER 3

Algorithmization

The present chapter may be thought of as an effort to investigate the general theory at a deeper level along one particular line of inquiry. In the preceding chapter, we focused our attention on the description of objects whose existence was vouchsafed by the theorems proved there and by means of which the storage packing problem could be solved. If a data flow graph could then be constructed for a given program schema, its connectivity components would have to be made the vertices of an incompatibility graph. If for each connectivity component d we know the set R of statements whose results occur in d and the set T of internal statements of routes that implement the data flow paths in d, the incompatibility criterion could then be determined completely. Finally, distinct colorings of the vertices of an incompatibility graph yield distinct methods of storage allocation; a coloring consisting of a minimal number of colors yields the most economical storage allocation.

In this chapter we will continue at the level of abstract objects and try to understand how all these objects may be constructed, e.g., how to find the connectivity components of a data flow graph, how to determine the set R (which is a simple matter) and how to determine the set T (which is a far more difficult problem), and, finally, how to find an optimal coloring of an incompatibility graph. In all these constructions, we have to find systematic procedures that may serve as a basis for the practical solution of the storage packing problem, for example, on a computer using ALGOL programs.

Recall that the descriptive analysis of the problem, though based on special examples, provided some hints as to what might be the nature of these computational procedures.

3.1. Data Flow Graph

The data flow graph I of a schema G is given as $I = (P, M)$, where P is a set of poles and M is a binary relation between the pairs (r, a) which asserts that "there exists a data path from result r to argument a." To find the set $D = \{d_1, \ldots, d_l\}$ of connectivity components, we only have to know which poles are correlated with which components. Of all these objects, the initial schema gives us only P. Without delving too deeply into the problem just yet, we can still hope that the procedure for computing I will show us a way of finding the connectivity components, if at all possible, "on their own," in the process of finding the data paths. Yet another hint guiding our approach to the partitioning of vertices into groups in the same component yields a proof of Theorem 2.1: Every vertex a_i in a group "searches" for its neighbors, beginning with itself (which it assumes is an isolated vertex). Then in the course of constructing the set D_i (from Theorem 2.1), all the connected vertices are placed in the same set, and the isolated vertices remain isolated.

Transitive Closure

Practice in the construction of data paths in the examples of Chapter 1 gave us an important key to the procedure for constructing data flow graphs. Starting with an assignment to the variable x, we travel along some path (in linear schemas, there is only one such path) until an occurrence of x as an argument is found (which thereby establishes the data path), or until a new assignment to x is encountered that at once puts an end to any attempt at continuing the route of the variable begun by the preceding assignment.

This rather graphic reminder must, however, be formulated using more rigorous terms than "travel along" and "encounter." Here it will be pertinent to learn one more definition.

Definition. Suppose that B is a binary relation on the elements of a set A. A *transitive closure* $\mathrm{Tr}(B)$ is understood to refer to a binary relation B' on these elements that holds for a pair (a, a') if and only if there exists a finite sequence $a a_1 a_2 \ldots a_n a'$ $(n \geq 0)$ of elements of A such that any pair of neighborhing elements in this sequence satisfies B.

With regard to graphs, two vertices (a, b) satisfy the transitive closure of the neighbor relationship if there is a path in the graph from a to b.

The notion of step-by-step movement along paths connecting vertices in a graph leads to an obvious algorithm for finding the transitive closure. We can be certain that the transitive closure $\mathrm{Tr}(\Gamma)$ of a directed graph (A, Γ) has been found if for every vertex $a \in A$ we can specify the set $\mathrm{Tr}(a) = \{x\}$ of all x such that the pair (a, x) satisfies the relation $\mathrm{Tr}(\Gamma)$. We call $\mathrm{Tr}(a)$ the *transitive image* of the vertex a. For this purpose, we introduce for each vertex a its *start set* S and *augmented set* T. At the initial point, we set $S^{(0)} = \{a\}$ and $T^{(0)} = \varnothing$. Then we define a recursive process determined by the relation

$$T^{(n+1)} = T^{(n)} \bigcup \Gamma(S^{(n)}), \qquad S^{(n+1)} = T^{(n+1)} \setminus T^{(n)}.$$

The symbol $\Gamma(S)$ denotes the set of successors of vertices of S. The relation is applied repeatedly until the least $n = N$ is found such that $S^{(n+1)} = \varnothing$. In this case $T = T^{(N)}$. Since $T^{(n)}$ cannot be expanded without limit, it is self-evident that such a point will be reached. It remains for us to prove the following assertion.

Lemma. $T = \mathrm{Tr}(a)$.

Proof. Let us show that $\mathrm{Tr}(a) \subseteq T$. In fact, if the vertex $a' \in \mathrm{Tr}(a)$, there will exist a path $aa_1 \ldots a_n a'$ in the graph. This fact may also be expressed by the relations

$$a_1 \in \Gamma(a),$$

$$\cdots\cdots$$

$$a_n \in \Gamma(a_{n-1}),$$

$$a' \in \Gamma(a_n).$$

This path may always be selected in such a way that the $a, a_1, \ldots, a_n$ are all distinct. From the relation for $S^{(n)}$ it is clear that

$$a \in S^{(0)},$$

$$a_1 \in \Gamma(S^{(0)}), \qquad a_1 \in S^{(1)},$$

$$\cdots\cdots$$

$$a_n \in \Gamma(S^{(n-1)}), \qquad a_n \in S^{(n)},$$

$$a' \in \Gamma(S^{(n)}),$$

whence it follows that $a' \in T^{(n+1)}$ and, consequently, $a' \in T$.

Let us show that $T \subseteq \mathrm{Tr}(a)$. Suppose that $a' \in T$. This means that for some $n > 0$, $a' \in \Gamma(S^{(n)})$. Let us prove by induction that the inclusion $b \in \mathrm{Tr}(a)$ holds for any vertex b in $S^{(n)}$. For $n = 1$, this is self-evident: $S^{(1)} = \Gamma(a) \backslash \{a\}$. If the inductive hypothesis $S^{(n-1)} \subseteq \mathrm{Tr}(a)$ holds, any successor of any vertex in $S^{(n-1)}$ will consequently also belong to $\mathrm{Tr}(a)$. $\qquad\square$

We have taken the time to discuss this very simple proof in some detail even though the proof seems so simple as to make any formalization appear clumsy. Nevertheless, because the recursive method of finding transitive closures is so important in a number of algorithms based on the use of graphs, the reader should gain a ready fluency in the process of deriving rigorous proofs of these and analogous assertions.

In certain cases, besides the "free" transitive closures, we may also consider so-called *restricted* transitive closures in which we encounter "impassable" vertices as we move along the paths; these vertices do not belong to paths that connect vertices associated with this type of transitive closure. If X is a set of such impassable vertices, the construction of what we are calling a *restricted transitive closure* $\mathrm{Tr}(a|X)$ has the form

$$S^{(0)} = \Gamma; \qquad T^{(0)} = \varnothing;$$

$$T^{(n+1)} = T^{(n)} \cup \Gamma(S^{(n)}), \qquad S^{(n+1)} = T^{(n+1)} \backslash T^{(n)} \backslash X.$$

Connectivity Components

At the start of the section we expressed a number of conjectures regarding the construction of a data flow graph and its connectivity components. In light of the above definitions and the recursive procedures, we may now combine these conjectures as follows.

We introduce the concept of a "current" connectivity component. The word "current" will be taken to mean "at some point in the construction of the data flow graph." Suppose we are given a schema $G = (S, X, L)$. At the initial moment, we have as many current components as there are poles, so that each pole belongs to its "own" component. Suppose r is some result and let $d(r)$ be its current component, the statement $F = V(r)$, the variable $x = L(r)$, and $R(x)$ is the set of statements of the schema that generates x. We will construct the restricted transitive closure $\mathrm{Tr}(F \mid R(x))$ for F, which we denote briefly by $E(r)$. Suppose that $a_{i_1}, \ldots, a_{i_k}$ are arguments of statements in $E(r)$ such that $L(a_{i_1})$ $= \ldots = L(a_{i_k}) = x$, and let $d(a_{i_1}), \ldots, d(a_{i_k})$ be their current components. Then the data flow graph has now been augmented with the addition of the data paths $(r, a_{i_1}), \ldots, (r, a_{i_k})$, and a new general current component $d' = d(r)$ $\cup \, d(a_{i_1}) \cup \ldots \cup d(a_{i_k})$ is associated with all the poles $r, a_{i_1}, \ldots, a_{i_k}$. This construction is carried out for each result of the schema. We finally obtain a set M of data paths and a set of subsets of poles: $D = \{d_1, \ldots, d_l\}$. We say that the graph (P, M) is the data flow graph I of the schema G and that D is the desired partitioning of its poles among the connectivity components of I.

The following proof of the assertion just made may be omitted by the reader, but only if he is able to carry out an appropriate line of reasoning on his own. We are presenting the proof if for no other reason than to help the less experienced reader test himself. We first describe the construction procedure more rigorously so that the description in fact resembles an algorithm. The standard notation for a program schema introduced in the preceding chapter will be used here.

At the start, we set $d_1 = \{\pi_1\}, \ldots, d_r = \{\pi_r\}, M' = \varnothing$.

We consider result r_i for each $i = 1, \ldots, q$. Let us find the succeeding objects and sets in some designated schema; $x = L(r_i); F = V(r_i);$ and $R(x)$ is the set of statements that generate x.

We construct the following sets by induction:

$$S^{(0)} = \{F\}, \qquad T^{(0)} = \varnothing$$
$$T^{(n+1)} = T^{(n)} \bigcup \Gamma(S^{(n)}); \qquad S^{(n+1)} = T^{(n+1)} \setminus T^{(n)} \setminus R(x).$$

In the course of the construction, we form $d' = d_i \bigcup d_j$ for each a_j such that $L(a_j) = x$ and $V(a_j) \in \Gamma(S(n))$, and substitute them for both the d_i and the d_j, inserting the pair (r_i, a_j) into M'. Once a value of n is attained such that $S_{(n+1)} = 0$, this will mean that no further processing using r_i is necessary.

Suppose that M' is the resulting set of pairs and $d'_1, \ldots, d'_l$ the resulting distinct sets among the current components $d_1, \ldots, d_r$. Let $I = (P, M)$ be a data flow graph and $D_i = (P_i, M_i)$ its connectivity components $(i = 1, \ldots, l)$. Let us show that $M = M'$, $l = l'$, and that $\{d_1', \ldots, d_{l'}'\} = \{P_1, \ldots, P_l\}$. The proof may be divided into several lemmas.

(a) $M \subseteq M'$. By the definition of a data pair (r_i, a_j), there exists a route

$$(r_i, a_j)F_{i_1} \ldots . F_{i_k}$$

in which $L(r_i) = L(a_j) = x$; $F_{i_1} = V(r_i)$ and $F_{i_k} = V(a_j)$, and such that none of the $F_{i_2}, \ldots, F_{i_{k-1}}$ generates x. Then by the definition of the transitive image $\mathrm{Tr}(V(r_i) | R(x))$, it follows that the statement $F_{i_k} \in E(r_i)$, consequently there exists a value of n such that $F_{i_k} \in \Gamma(S^n)$. By the construction of the pair, (r_i, a_j) in this case is embedded in the set of pairs.   □

(b) $M' \subseteq M$. Let us consider a pair (r_i, a_j) embedded in M'. By the construction, this could have happened in the course of determining the sets $T^{(n+1)}$ and $\Gamma(S^{(n)})$ for some value of n. In other words, $V(a_j) = \Gamma(S^{(n)})$, and thus $L(a_j) = L(r_i) = x$. By the construction of $S^{(n)}$, there exists a chain of statements $F_{i_0}, \ldots, F_{i_n}$ such that $F_{i_0} = V(r_j)$ and $F_{i_m} \in \Gamma(F_{i_{m-1}})$ $(1 \leq m \leq n)$; here none of the F_i generates x. But in this case, the construction

$$(r_i, a_j)F_{i_0} \ldots F_{i_n} V(a_j)$$

satisfies the definition of a route, whence it follows that $(r_i, a_j) \in M$.   □

(c) For every d_i, if the results $r_1, \ldots, r_q$ are considered in some fixed order, the construction specifies a unique sequence of unions of elements of the sequence in the set of results. Let us prove the property of the d_i' we are interested in by induction on the ordinal number of this sequence. At the initial point, clearly, all unequal current components are either:

(a) pairwise nonintersecting;
(b) sum to all the sets of poles; or
(c) each set occurs completely in one of the P_k $(k = 1, \ldots, l)$.

Let us now consider an arbitrary step in the process of combining a pair of current components d_i and d_j into $(d' = d_i \cup d_j)$. The other sets remain unchanged in this process. Clearly, as before d' in combination with the other sets will satisfy properties (a) and (b). Suppose that $d_i \subseteq P_u$ and $d_j \subseteq P_v$ $(1 \leq u, v \leq l)$. By the construction, there exist $r_i \in d_i$ and $a_j \in d_j$ which together form a data pair in the schema. By the transitivity of the relation of connectivity (lemma preceding Theorem 2.1, Section 2.2), we at once find that both d_i and d_j, and consequently their union d' as well, belong to one and the same set of vertices P_u of the connectivity components D_u.   □

(d) It remains for us to prove that $l = l'$ at the conclusion of the construction of $E(r_j)$ for all the results of the schema. We leave it for the reader to figure out why l' cannot be less than l, and thus suppose that $l < l'$. This means that there exist at least two distinct current components d_i' and d_j' each of which is in some P_u. From this fact, and also property (a), it follows that d_i' *and* d_j' each have one pole such that the two poles together form a pair (r, a) which is an arc in the connectivity component P_u of the data flow graph of the schema. By Lemma (a), $(r, a) \in M'$, and this means that by the construction of M' there exists some n such that $V(a)$ belongs to $\Gamma(S^{(n)})$, the pair (r, a) is embedded in M', and $d(r)$ and $d(a)$ are combined into a new current component common to both r and a, which contradicts the assumption that d_i' and d_j' are distinct.   □

By the last two lemmas, we may conclude that

$$\{d_1', \ldots, d_l'\} = \{P_1, \ldots, P_l\}. \qquad\qquad\qquad □$$

(Here is a question for the reader: Why is it that the last conclusion cannot be written in the form $d_i' = P_i$ $(i = 1, \ldots, l)$?)

To get a better understanding of the algorithm and to learn how to identify its connectivity components, we suggest the reader apply it at least to the examples of Chapter 1. We reproduce the results from the application of the algorithm to Example 11 (ALGOL program with procedures) to provide some direction and suggestions for arranging the information on a sheet of

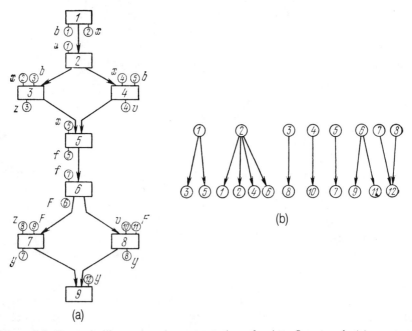

(a)

(b)

Figure 3.1. Example illustrating the construction of a data flow graph: (a) program schema; (b) data flow graph.

paper. In Figure 3.1, the program schema has been redrawn; here the statements and poles are denoted by their ordinal numbers.

Since it is clear in both the diagram and at each position in the table which number occurs in the position for which ordinal number, we will not use literal notation for the elements of the schema, except for variable names from memory. This policy will help the reader test the operation of the algorithm more formally, and also prepare the way for an "arithmetization" of the algorithm, which we will carry out in the chapter devoted to realization.

The construction of the transitive images is shown in Table A. The tabular column corresponds to the construction of $\text{Tr}(V(r)|R(L(r)))$ for some result r. Statements that accept $L(r)$ are underscored, and the data paths thus created are indicated in the upper portion of the corresponding position. The formation of the current components is shown in the neighboring columns. Results that have been combined together are shown in the numerator, while arguments that have been combined together are given in the denominator. The resulting data flow graph is shown in Figure 3.1(b).

There exists a storage allocation that may be implemented without having to construct any incompatibility graph. This is the allocation in which we associate with each connectivity component its own variable. This, the least "economical" storage allocation is referred to as the "canonical" allocation, as all possible storage allocations may be obtained from it by means of a procedure that resembles a substitution of variables, i.e., all occurrences of the same variable in the schema are replaced by the symbol of another variable. Naturally, an acceptable level of economy occurs whenever a new variable replaces several variables associated (in the canonical allocation) with pairwise compatible liveness domains.

3.2. Incompatibility Graph

Let us recall the statement of Theorem 2.3: Two domains d and d' are incompatible if and only if

$$R(d) \bigcap R(d') \bigcup R(d) \bigcap T(d') \bigcup R(d') \bigcap T(d) \neq \varnothing,$$

where $R(d)$ is a set of statements that contains a result that belongs to d, while $T(d)$ is a set of statements each of which is an internal statement of at least one route that realizes a data path belonging to d.

The set $R(d)$ is constructed step by step. If we are given a partitioning of poles with respect to connectivity components, we select from d all the results $r_{i_1}, \ldots, r_{i_t}$ occurring in it such that

$$R(d) = \{ V(r_{i_1}), \ldots, V(r_{i_t}) \}.$$

Direct Closure

To construct $T(d)$ we must "traverse" routes of data paths in d and label the statements we have "passed by." With the preceding section in mind, the

Table A. Construction of data flow graph.

Initial sets:

Results   r: 1 2 3 4 5 6 7 8
Statements V(r): 1 1 3 4 5 6 7 8

Step		1	2	3	4	5	6	7	8
						Results			
0		1	1	3	4	5	6	7	8
1		2	(2,1) 2	5	5	(5,7) <u>6</u>	(6,9) (6,11) <u>7,8</u>	(7,12) <u>9</u>	(8,12) <u>9</u>
2		(1,3) (1,5) <u>(3,4)</u> 5	(2,2) (2,4) <u>(3,4)</u> (2,6)						
3			<u>5</u> 6	(3,8) <u>7,8</u> 9	0 (4,10) <u>7,8</u> 9	7,8 9	9	∅	∅
4		6	6	∅	∅	∅	∅		
5		7,8	7,8			∅			
6		9	9						
7		∅	∅						
E(r)		2–9	2–9	5–9	5–9	6–9	7–9	9	9

Initial Sets:

Variables $L(r)$: $b \; x \; z \; v \; f \; F \; y \; y$

Statements

That compute $L(r)$: 1 1 3 4 5 6 7 8

Current components

r:	1	2	3	4	5	6	7	8	a:1	2	3	4	5	6	7	8	9	10	11	12
	$\bar{1}$	$\bar{2}$	$\bar{3}$	$\bar{4}$	$\bar{5}$	$\bar{6}$	$\bar{7}$	$\bar{8}$	$\bar{1}$	$\bar{2}$	$\bar{3}$	$\bar{4}$	$\bar{5}$	$\bar{6}$	$\bar{7}$	$\bar{8}$	$\bar{9}$	$\bar{10}$	$\bar{11}$	$\bar{12}$
							$\dfrac{7}{7}$	$\dfrac{8}{}$	$\dfrac{2}{1}$	$\dfrac{2}{}$	$\dfrac{3}{3,5}$	$\dfrac{2}{}$	$\dfrac{1}{3,5}$	$\dfrac{2}{}$	$\dfrac{5}{7}$					
	$\dfrac{2}{1}$			$\dfrac{4}{}$	$\dfrac{5}{7}$	$\dfrac{6}{9,11}$		$\dfrac{7,8}{12}$	$\dfrac{1,2,4}{2}$	$\dfrac{1,2,4}{2}$		$\dfrac{1,2,4}{2}$	$\dfrac{1}{3,5}$	$\dfrac{2}{}$		$\dfrac{8}{}$	$\dfrac{6}{9,11}$	$\dfrac{10}{}$	$\dfrac{6}{9,11}$	$\dfrac{7,8}{12}$
	$\dfrac{1}{3,5}$		$\dfrac{3}{8}$	$\dfrac{4}{10}$					$\dfrac{1,2}{}$	$\dfrac{1,2}{}$		$\dfrac{1,2}{}$		$\dfrac{1,2}{}$						
	$\dfrac{1,2,4}{2}$	$\dfrac{3}{8}$				$\dfrac{2}{1,2}$	$\dfrac{5}{7}$	$\dfrac{7,8}{12}$	$4,6$	$4,6$		$4,6$		$4,6$						
	$1,2,4,6$																			

$$d_1 = \frac{1}{3,5}; \quad d_2 = \frac{2}{1,2,4,6}; \quad d_3 = \frac{3}{8}; \quad d_4 = \frac{4}{10}; \quad d_5 = \frac{5}{7}; \quad d_6 = \frac{6}{9,11}; \quad d_7 = \frac{7,8}{12}$$

word, "traverse," recalls the definition of a transitive closure and encourages us to try and apply it in our case. In fact, if we were to construct the transitive closure of some statement $V(r)$, *a fortiori* we will have included in it all the internal statements of routes that begin with $V(r)$. However, we are interested in all the results of d, and so we find the natural definition

$$\text{Tr}(d) = \bigcup_{k=1}^{t} \text{Tr}(V(r_{i_k})),$$

from which we derive the fact that $\text{T}(d) \subseteq \text{Tr}(d)$. This, however, is a very weak inclusion, since a transitive image contains all the statements reachable from $R(d)$. Recalling the definition of a route, we may at once see that $\text{T}(d)$ may be given an improved upper bound if we take the restricted transitive image $\text{E}(r_{i_k})$. Setting

$$E(d) = \text{Tr}(R(d)\,|\,R(d)) = \bigcup_{k=1}^{t} \text{Tr}(V(r_{i_k})\,|\,R(d)) = \bigcup_{k=1}^{t} E(r_{i_k}), \qquad (1)$$

we obtain $T(d) \subseteq E(d)$.

Let us step aside for a moment from the main theme of our discussion. In our last paragraph we have yet another example of the conciseness of mathematical language, a language that requires on the reader's part the ability to distinguish between denotational and applicative occurrences of notation for particular objects. In Eq. (1), the different terms of this compound equality have different senses. There is the set $E(r_{i_k})$ which by definition is equal to $\text{Tr}(V(r_{i_k})\,|\,R(d))$. The equality $E(d) = \bigcup_{k=1}^{t} E(r_{i_k})$ is the definition of the new set $E(d)$. The equality

$$\text{Tr}(R(d)\,|\,R(d)) = \bigcup_{k=1}^{t} \text{Tr}(V(r_{i_k})\,|\,R(d))$$

is the definition of the restricted transitive image of some set (in this case $R(d)$) analogous to the ordinary transitive image of the set of vertices we have just defined. The equality $E(d) = \text{Tr}(R(d)\,|\,R(d))$ is a corollary of the above definitions, a kind of mini-theorem. Note that this is not the only interpretation possible. We could also define $\text{Tr}(R(d)\,|\,R(d))$, and then define $E(d)$ in terms of the latter, finally deriving the conclusion $E(d) = \bigcup_{k=1}^{t} E(r_{i_k})$.

We require one additional logical step. We have introduced the concept of the transitive image of a vertex to formalize such properties as reachability of one vertex from another. We obtained a definition of the transitive image of a set purely formally as the union of the transitive closures of its elements. The question then arises as to whether the concept of the transitive image of a set formalizes the concept of reachability. Rereading the beginning of this section once again leads us to the formulation of the following lemma (for the case of a free transitive closure):

Lemma. *Suppose that* $M = \{m_1, \ldots, m_r\}$ *is a set of vertices of some graph G,*
$\text{Tr}(M). = \bigcup_{k=1}^{r} \text{Tr}(m_k)$, *and let* $S(M) = \{s\}$ *be a set of vertices such that for any s there exists a vertex* $m \in M$ *for which there is a path in G from m to s. Then* $S(M) = \text{Tr}(M)$.

Proof. (a) $S(M) \subseteq \text{Tr}(M)$. Let us assume the contrary, i.e., that there exists a vertex $s \in S(M)$ and another vertex m_i such that there exists a path from m_i to s, though s does not belong to $\text{Tr}(M)$. But in this case s does not belong to $\text{Tr}(m_i)$ either, which contradicts the property $\text{Tr}(m_i)$.

(b) $\text{Tr}(M) \subseteq S(M)$. Consider an arbitrary element $t \in \text{Tr}(M)$. As it belongs to the sum, it thereby belongs to one of the terms $\text{Tr}(m_i)$. From this it follows that there exists a path from m_i to t in the graph, which proves that it belongs to $S(M)$. □

The proof of the analogous property for a restricted transitive closure is left as an exercise for the reader.

Inverse Closure

Now we must consider very carefully what might be redundant in $E(d)$. As we move along the arcs of the control flow graph, we may end up either in a loop from which there is an exit or in an infinite loop, or we might encounter a statement that processes a variable that has already been processed, or we might halt at the terminal statement.

Let us try to sketch out an arbitrary program schema in simplified form (single domain), provided that all the logical possibilities for traversing the arcs of the control flow graph just enumerated are implemented (Figure 3.2(a)). In this figure, we have labeled statements in both $E(d)$ and in $T(d)$. By traversing arcs emanating from the assignment statements and for the time being placing statements already traversed into $E(d)$, we capture the redundant statements, and therefore cannot know in advance whether we can reach the read statements along this path.

Unlike the statements listed above, the transitive statements are accessible not only from assignment statements, but also from read statements (if we move towards the arrows). Now that we have let slip a rather obvious observation, let us take a breather from the construction of our logical edifice and think about what we have just said. We have associated motion along the arcs of a graph with the construction of a transitive closure. Since motion in the direction counter to the orientation of the arcs is possible, we are led to introduce the concept of an *inverse transitive closure* and to define the *transitive pre-image* of a vertex a as the set $\text{Tr}^{-1}(a)$ of vertices x ($\text{Tr}^{-1}(a) = \{x\}$) such that the pair (x, a) satisfies the relation $\text{Tr}(\Gamma)$, where Γ is, as usual, the set of arcs of the particular graph. Since each path in a graph may be traversed in the direction of the arcs or in the opposite direction, by

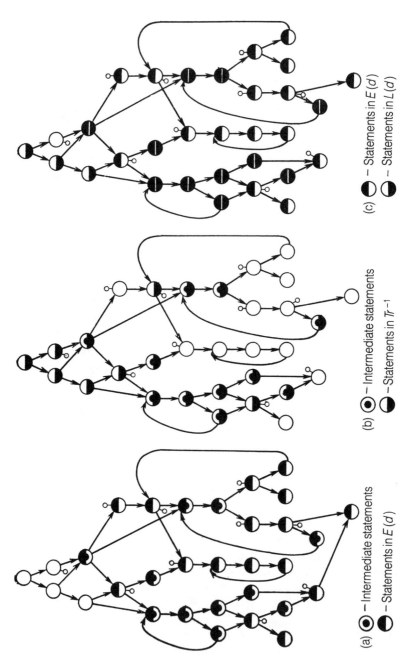

(a) ⦿ – Intermediate statements

◑ – Statements in $E(d)$

(b) ⦿ – Intermediate statements

◐ – Statements in Tr^{-1}

(c) ◑ – Statements in $E(d)$

◐ – Statements in $L(d)$

Figure 3.2 Finding the internal statements.

introducing the notation $\Gamma^{-1}(a)$ for the set of predecessors of a, we at once obtain a procedure for finding the transitive pre-image analogous to the procedure given in the preceding section:

$$S^{(0)} = \{a\}, \qquad T^{(0)} = \varnothing,$$

$$T^{(n+1)} = T^{(n)} \bigcup \Gamma^{-1}(S^{(n)}), \qquad S^{(n+1)} = T^{(n+1)} \setminus T^{(n)}.$$

Analogously, we may define the *restricted* (with respect to the set of vertices X) *transitive pre-image* $\mathrm{Tr}^{-1}(a \mid X)$:

$$S^{(0)} = \{a\}, \qquad T^{(0)} = \varnothing,$$

$$T^{(n+1)} = T^{(n)} \bigcup \Gamma^{-1}(S^{(n)}),$$

$$S^{(n+1)} = T^{(n+1)} \setminus T^{(n)} \setminus X.$$

In both cases, Tr^{-1} is understood as the first $T^{(n)}$ equal to $T^{(n-1)}$.

Suppose that the arguments $a_{j_1}, \ldots, a_{j_s}$ occur in the domain d. Reasoning again by analogy and recalling that $E(d) = \mathrm{Tr}(R(d) \mid R(d))$, we arrive at the conclusion that $T(d) \subseteq \mathrm{Tr}^{-1}(A(d) \mid R(d))$, where $A(d) = \{V(a_{j_1}), \ldots, V(a_{j_s})\}$ is the set of statements that read in the variable that correlates the liveness domains d (Figure 3.2(b)), while

$$\mathrm{Tr}^{-1}(A(d) \mid R(d)) = \bigcup_{t=1}^{s} \mathrm{Tr}^{-1}(V(a_{j_t}) \mid R(d)).$$

Now bearing in mind once again the conjecture we made in passing, that the "internal statements are reachable not only from the assignment statements, but also from the read statements," we may at once improve this hypothesis, turning it into the following rigorous assertion:

$$T(d) \subseteq E(d) \bigcap \mathrm{Tr}^{-1}(A(d) \mid R(d)).$$

The reader who can barely restrain himself from beginning the search for a solution to the problem may very well wonder with some impatience why we have even written an inclusion here, and not an equality. Note that though it is precisely this assumption which turns out to be incorrect (look at the intersection of the set $E(d)$ in Figure 3.2(a) and the set $\mathrm{Tr}^{-1}(A(d) \mid R(d))$ in Figure 3.2(b), and you will at once see four redundant statements), nevertheless the sense of the question is quite promising, and so we will try to find out how to correct the definition of a covering set constructed by means of an inverse transitive closure (giving right now another, as yet inessential, notation—$L(d)$) that preserves our approach to the process of finding the internal statements:

$$T(d) = E(d) \bigcap L(d).$$

From an analysis of the example in Figure 3.2, it is clear that a restricted inverse transitive closure may contain assignment statements that are reachable even if they are "impassable." Analogously, in $E(d)$ the assignment statements may also turn out to be reachable. For this reason, an assignment statement may also occur in an intersection. Similarly, terminal assignment statements (i.e., statements that belong to one of the end-points of a route) are the only "garbage" that reaches the desired set of internal statements. The method of constructing $L(d)$ must therefore be corrected so that the assignment statements are not merely impassable on the next step, but also unreachable, constituting a boundary to further movement towards the arcs. Of course, we will achieve our goal if we eliminate the assignment statements $R(d)$, but not from the start set for the next step, but rather a half-step earlier without letting them end up in the complement to the accumulation set $T^{(n+1)}$. Thus, for every argument a_{j_l} in d,

$$S^{(0)} = \{ V(a_{j_l}) \}, \qquad T^{(0)} = \emptyset,$$

$$T^{(n+1)} = T^{(n)} \bigcup \Gamma^{-1}(S^{(n)}) \setminus R(d), \qquad S^{(n+1)} = T^{(n+1)} \setminus T^{(n)} \qquad L(a_{i_l}) = T^{(N)},$$

where N is the least n such that $S^{(n+1)} = \emptyset$. For the entire domain, however,

$$L(d) = \bigcup_{l=1}^{s} L(a_{j_l}).$$

Figure 3.2(a) demonstrates graphically how the two sets E and L serve to segregate out the set of internal statements in their intersection.

To relate the construction of $L(d)$ more closely to the concept of a transitive closure, we could have referred to it as a *restricted transitive pre-image*, bearing in mind that statements from a restrictive set (in this case, $R(d)$) are not just impassable, but also unreachable. This additional property of a transitive closure (which is meaningful for both direct and inverse closures) may be denoted by a double line so as to distinguish it from a restricting set. The theorem that shows how to find the internal statements of some domain then has the following formulation.

Theorem 3.1. *Suppose that d is the liveness domain of a data graph, and let $T(d)$, $A(d)$, and $R(d)$ be sets of internal (intermediate), read, and assignment statements, respectively. Then*

$$T(d) = \mathrm{Tr}(R(d) \mid R(d)) \bigcap \mathrm{Tr}^{-1}(A(d) \mid R(d)).$$

The proof is left as an exercise for the reader, and we give only an outline here. For the sake of brevity, let EL denote the set on the right side.

Let us first prove that $EL \subseteq T(d)$. We take any $F \in EL$, and, putting to good use, so to speak, its membership both in the direct and the inverse closure, show that it does not evaluate variables correlated with the domain d. We proceed along both arc s_1, starting from some generating statement, and along an oppositely directed arc s_2^{-1} from some read statement (-1 denotes motion towards the arcs). We then prove that the path $s_1 s_2$ satisfies the definition of a route. To prove that $T(d) \subseteq EL$, we restate the definition of intermediacy in terms of reachability both from $R(d)$ and (moving towards the arcs) from $A(d)$. ☐

Frontal Construction of Closures

Let us make one further remark before finishing up with our procedure for constructing the incompatibility graph. Our remark merely extends a thought that may very well have flashed by the minds of readers not fully convinced by Figure 3.2, and who therefore constructed the two sets $E(d)$ and $L(d)$ on their own. Now then, note that $E(d)$ is obtained as a by-product in the course of constructing the data flow graph. Once we have constructed $E(r_i)$ for each result r_i, we integrate into $E(d)$ those $E(r_i)$ whose r_i are in the same d. We then begin to construct $L(d)$, but only when the two sets $R(d)$ and $A(d)$ have already been found (as is shown in the example of Figure 3.2). In this case, it is entirely natural to attempt to construct both $E(d)$ and $L(d)$ "frontally," by moving either along or towards the arcs simultaneously from all the assignment or application statements. Let us make two copies of the control flow graph in Figure 3.2 (Figure 3.3). In the first copy (Figure 3.3(a)), we depict $T(d)$, and in the second (Figure 3.3(b)), $R(d)$ and $A(d)$ along with "layers" of statements included in $E(d)$ and $L(d)$ at the stages of the direct construction. The layers are numbered by arabic numerals in the case of $E(d)$, and by roman

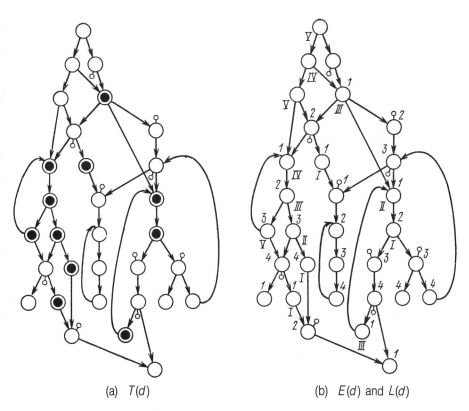

(a) $T(d)$ (b) $E(d)$ and $L(d)$

Figure 3.3. Frontal construction of transitive closure.

numerals in the case of $L(d)$. Note that if the closures are constructed separately, the number of stages in the direct construction will be less than the maximal number of stages. Our construction demonstrates that we obtain the same $E(d)$ and $L(d)$ and, consequently, $T(d)$.

However, we must prove rigorously that the direct method of finding transitive closures yields the same result as finding them separately from some subsequent union. Let us start by refining what we mean by the term, "frontal method." In the frontal method, once we have constructed, for example, the transitive image of a set of vertices A relative to a restricting set B, our initial start set will at once be all of A, after which all the recursive steps and termination criteria are applied in the same way as for a single-element start set. In one proof the line of reasoning would show that a set constructed by the frontal method satisfies the properties of a transitive image as a set of reachable vertices.

Lemma. *Suppose that* $\mathrm{Tr}(A|B)$ *is a set of vertices constructed by the frontal method. Let* $S(A|B)$ *be a set of vertices such that for every vertex* $s \in S(A|B)$ *there exists a vertex* $a \in A$ *for which there is a path from* a *to* s *whose internal vertices do not belong to* B. *Then* $\mathrm{Tr}(A|B) = S(A|B)$.

Proof. $S(A|B) \subseteq \mathrm{Tr}(A|B)$. Consider the vertex $s \in S(A|B)$. A path from some $a \in A$ to s, i.e., $av_1 \ldots v_k s$ $(k \geq 0)$, may be selected in such a way that all the v_i are distinct and none belong to A. By considering the first $k+1$ stages in the construction of $\mathrm{Tr}(A|B)$, it may be verified by induction that s is in the kth augmented set $T^{(k)}$.

$\mathrm{Tr}(a|B) \subseteq S(A|B)$. Consider the vertex $t \in \mathrm{Tr}(A|B)$. The ordinal number of the stage k at which t first occurs in the augmented set $T^{(k)}$ may be found. For $t = t^{(k)}$, a vertex $t^{(k-1)} \in S^{(k-1)}$ may be found such that $t^{(k)} \in \Gamma(t^{(k-1)})$. Moving in the same way with respect to decreasing k, we ultimately arrive at the start set $S^{(0)} = A$. The resulting chain of vertices from $t^{(k)}$ to $t^{(0)} A$ gives us a path which proves that t belongs to $S(A|B)$.   □

Returning to Figure 3.1, we construct $E(d)$ for the seven domains found, combining together the already created $E(r_i)$ for each of the results r_i. The sets $L(d)$ are constructed directly, though the example does not give us much helpful information for this purpose. The process and results of the construction are shown in Table B. For the sake of maximal clarity, an outline of the program schema is redrawn in Figure 3.4(a). Once again, note that in our construction of $L(d)$ the initial start set $S^{(0)}$ is not a subset of the complementary set. Some of its vertices may, however, occur in $L(d)$ at later stages (cf. the second column in the construction of $L(d)$). This is not surprising. We have already seen that the terminal statement of one route may be an internal statement of another route from the same domain.

We have previously remarked that the set of internal statements may be found at once from the already constructed domains $d_1, \ldots, d_l$ and sets $E(d_i)$

Table B

Liveness domain

$d_1 = 1/3, 5$; $d_2 = 2/1, 2, 4, 6$; $d_3 = 3/8$; $d_4 = 4/10$; $d_5 = 5/7$; $d_6 = 6/9, 11$; $d_7 = 7, 8/12$

$E(d_1) = 2\text{–}9$; $E(d_2) = 2\text{–}9$; $E(d_3) = 2\text{–}9$; $E(d_4) = 5\text{–}9$; $E(d_5) = 6\text{–}9$; $E(d_6) = 7\text{–}9$; $E(d_7) = 9$

	Domains d:1	2	3	4	5	6	7
0	3,4	2,3,4,5	7	8	6	7,8	9
1	2	2,3,4	6	6	∅	∅	∅
2	∅	∅	5	5			
3			4	3			
4			2	2			
5			1	1			
6							
$L(d)$:	2	2–4	1,2 / 4–6	1–3 / 5,6	∅	∅	∅

(Step)

(a) Construction of $L(d)$

	Domains d:1	2	3	4	5	6	7
$k(d)$	2	1	3	4	5	6	7
$T(d)$	2	2,3,4	5,6	5,0	5	6	7,8
1	·						
2	1	·					
3	∅	3	·				
4	∅	4	∅	·			
5	∅	∅	5	5	·		
6	∅	∅	6	6	∅	·	
7	∅	∅	∅	∅	∅	∅	·

(Start set)

(b) Construction of incompatibility relations

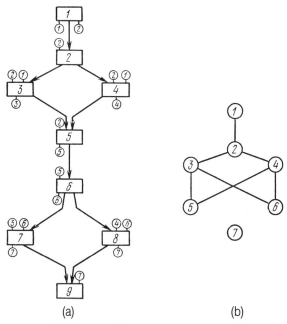

Figure 3.4. Constructing an incompatibility graph: (a) skeleton of program schema (poles are labeled by the ordinal numbers of the domains); (b) incompatibility graph.

and $L(d_i)$, thus: $T(d_i) = E(d_i) \bigcap L(d_i)$ $(i = 1, \ldots, l)$, and that the set of initial statements $R(d_i)$ may be extracted directly from the skeleton of the program schema. Once this is done, it is a simple matter to find the incompatibility relation between the different domains. Once the two sets R and T have been arranged in "parallel," we may then compare for each $i = 1, \ldots, l$,

$$R(d_1) \ldots R(d_l) \to R(d_j) \ldots R(d_l),$$
$$T(d_1) \ldots T(d_l) \nearrow\!\!\!\!\!\!\!\times\, T(d_j) \ldots T(d_l),$$

the three pairs of sets (as shown in the diagram) $R(d_i)$ and $R(d_j)$, $R(d_i)$ and $T(d_j)$, and $T(d_i)$ and $R(d_j)$ in turn, for all $j > i$, to find out whether any pair shares common elements. The result of the comparison (empty—not empty) is entered into an $l \times l$ matrix. This procedure causes the upper triangle of the matrix (the part above the principal diagonal) to be filled. Since the incompatibility relation is symmetric, the lower triangle is filled symmetric to the upper triangle (relative to the principal diagonal). Elements of the nonempty set $R(d_i) \bigcap R(d_j) \bigcup R(d_i) \bigcap T(d_j) \bigcup T(d_i) \bigcap R(d_j)$ are used in the table as the symbol for "not empty" as a control. Once the elements of the now constructed matrix H_{ij} have been identified, we find that this matrix specifies precisely the incompatibility relation for the incompatibility graph $U = (D, H)$, where (recall) $D = \{d_i, \ldots, d_l\}$; d_i and d_j are incompatible, i.e., are adjacent in U if and only if H_{ij} is not empty. The resulting incompatibility graph is depicted in Figure 3.4(b). Naturally, it coincides (to within notation) with the graph drawn in Figure 1.11.

Having made passing reference to topics covered in the first chapter, let's now take a breather from the rather serious tone of the present chapter and try to evaluate our progress. However modest it may seem, our storage packing problem nevertheless reflects commonplace elements of many mathematical investigations. In particular, with the subject matter of the first three chapters in mind, the reader might wish to consider the difference between the cognitive and applied, more precisely, constructive aspects of our study. A cognitive process dominated in the first two chapters. We identified the essential elements in the storage packing problem and found the most appropriate mathematical abstractions for these elements. The present chapter is quite a different matter. To some degree the discussion in this chapter has lost some of its pertinence. We have been speaking less and less about storage packing, even though we have continued to discuss statements, variables, arguments, and results. We have spoken of transitive closures and will soon begin to speak of the process of coloring the vertices of a graph. The problem has lost its original unity, and has been broken up into "chunks" of processes, each of which may be best explained in some other general terms. It may be that some readers may find this technical material tedious, and may thus lose interest in the discussion. But at this point it is worth noting that it is this intermediate step which is the most enticing element of the work of the professional mathematician. In any concrete problem, the theoretician is always in search of a core of abstract constructions and general theories that would be far more interesting than the original problem. The constructive mathematician and the mathematician concerned with applications always place their faith in the "algebra of harmony," and as they do not have to keep to a universal standpoint, are in the habit of breaking up any given problem into a sequence of simple procedures that are elegant in their degree of clarity and transparency. Such, undoubtedly, are the effective and quite regular procedures for the construction of transitive closures to which we have reduced our two subproblems (finding the connectivity components of a data flow graph and constructing the incompatibility relation). But if we were to continue thinking of ourselves as mere advocates of the value of our problem, we would be justified in noting with some satisfaction that, though we have not added much to the knowledge gained in the earlier chapters, we have enriched this knowledge with the universality of the procedures we have developed. And these procedures are bringing us closer to our ultimate goal: Transmit our knowledge to the computer in an effective form, i.e., in a form that can be applied under normal circumstances.

3.3 Coloring the Vertices of a Graph. General Remarks

Let us give a formal description of the problem of finding a minimal coloring. By a *coloring of the vertices* of an undirected graph $G = (X, R)$, we understand an arbitrary mapping

$$C: X \to K$$

of the set of vertices $X = \{x_1, \ldots, x_n\}$ onto an arbitrary finite set $K = \{k_1, \ldots, k_m\}$ $(m \leq n)$. The elements of K are called *colors*. A coloring is said to be regular if for any i and j, $(x_i, x_j) \in R \Rightarrow k(x_1) \neq k(x_j)$. (The expression $A \Rightarrow B$ is an abbreviation of the ordinary assertion that from the fact that A holds, it follows that B holds.) A *minimal coloring* of some graph is a regular coloring in which the number of colors is less than or equal to the number of colors in any other regular coloring of this graph. Clearly, the number of colors used in any minimal coloring is always the same, and in fact is a characteristic of the graph itself. It is denoted $\chi(G)$ or simply χ whenever it is clear which graph we are speaking of, and is referred to as the *chromatic number* of the graph G. If it is necessary to refer to the number of colors used in any other coloring C of G, it is denoted $h(G, C)$.

Analysis of the Trivial Solution

From the definition it follows at once that if we wish to prove that some coloring is minimal, we must be able to prove that there does not exist a regular coloring that uses a lesser number of colors than $h(G, C)$. It is no less obvious that, inasmuch as the number of distinct colorings of a graph is finite, the problem of finding the minimal coloring and the chromatic number is in some sense trivial. We first consider all the colorings, then select from among them the regular colorings, and from among the latter the coloring with the least number of colors.

At this point, it would be appropriate to get an idea of the scale of such a sorting process. Suppose that a graph consisting of n vertices may be colored in $Z(n)$ distinct ways. If we then consider a graph with one more vertex, in any coloring of the first n vertices of this graph we could color the new vertex in any of the n colors already used or we could use another color, i.e., the $(n+1)$th color. Thus, in the transition from a graph with n vertices to one with $(n+1)$ vertices, each coloring of the n-vertex graph generates $(n+1)$ colorings of the $(n+1)$-vertex graph, i.e., $Z(n+1) = Z(n) \times Z(n+1)$. If we assume that $Z(1) = 1$, we at once find that $Z(n) = n!$.

The author would be quite happy if at this point the critically attuned reader were to interrupt his reading and ask himself one or more of the following three questions with regard to this number.

1. How should colorings of $(n+1)$-vertex graphs in which the $(n+1)$th color is used more than once be counted?
2. The relation $Z(n+1) = Z(n) \times (n+1)$ is valid only whenever distinct colorings of n-vertex graphs lead (in accordance with the above construction) likewise to distinct colorings. Is this so? And, in general,
3. What is meant by distinct colorings?

These questions are especially pertinent in that it would be a far simpler matter to obtain yet one more estimate of the number of colorings given an n-vertex graph and n colors. Each vertex may be colored in any of n colors, i.e., in n ways. All the colorings may be obtained by combining together all the combinations of each coloring for each vertex. The total number $Y(n)$ of combinations is equal to

$$\underbrace{n \times n \times \ldots \times n = n^n}_{n \text{ times}}$$

Let us compare these two methods of estimation for the case $n = 3$. To estimate $Z(n)$, a method of obtaining the colorings follows automatically from the inductive relation between $Z(n)$ and $Z(n+1)$. The method of obtaining colorings for estimating $Y(n)$ becomes clear if we consider any coloring as the expression of an n-digit number in an n-ary system, where the positions in the number are the vertices of the graph and the digits are the colors. As a result, we obtain the following coloring (the vertices are distinguished by the letters a, b, and c, and the numbers 1, 2, and 3 represent the colors):

$Z(n)$:			$Z(3) = 6$	$Y(n)$:	$Y(3) = 27$
$n=1$: a	$n=2$: $a\ b$	$n=3$: $a\ b\ c$		$a\ b\ c$	$a\ b\ c$
1	1 1	1 1 1		1 1 1	2 3 1
	1 2	1 2 1		1 1 2	2 3 2
		1 1 2		1 1 3	2 3 3
		1 2 2		1 2 1	3 1 1
		1 1 3		1 2 2	3 1 2
		1 2 3		1 2 3	3 1 3
				1 3 1	3 2 1
				1 3 2	3 2 2
				1 3 3	3 2 3
				2 1 1	3 3 1
				2 1 2	3 3 2
				2 1 3	3 3 3
				2 2 1	
				2 2 2	
				2 2 3	

By comparing the different colorings, we find that method Y gives us many "redundant" colorings. We are not interested in all the colorings in and of themselves; for us, what is important is to be able to select a minimal coloring from among all the regular colorings. If we are able to color a graph with one color, it is of no importance whether this is color 1 or color 2. From this standpoint, we see that though method Z does not really give us all the colorings, it nevertheless contains all the "interesting" colorings, i.e., those colorings from which any coloring whatsoever may be obtained by means of a trivial re-coloring in which a single color is replaced by some other color not already present in the original coloring.

Let us correlate with each coloring in $Z(3)$ those colorings in $Y(3)$ that may be obtained by a sequence of such re-colorings:

$111 \to 111$	$121 \to 121$	$122 \to 122$	$123 \to 123$
222	131	133	132
333	212	211	213
$112 \to 112$	232	233	231
223	313	311	312
331	323	322	321
$113 \to 113$			
221			
332			

We let $C_{Z,n}$ and $C_{Y,n}$ denote the sets of colorings obtained using method Z and method Y, respectively. Let us prove that for any coloring $c \in C_{Y,n}$, there exists a coloring $c' \in C_{Z,n}$ that may be obtained from c by means of some trivial re-coloring.

Suppose that $c = k_1, k_2, \ldots, k_n$, and let $i_1, i_2, \ldots, i_t$ $(t \le n)$ be the colors enumerated in the order in which they are used. Consider the coloring

$$c' = k'_1, k'_2, \ldots, k'_n$$

obtained by replacing each i_l by l $(l = 1, \ldots, t)$. In such a coloring, the color k'_j (for each $j = 2, \ldots, n$) either coincides with one of the colors that color the vertices $k'_1, \ldots, k'_{j-1}$ or has ordinal number one greater than the maximal ordinal number of these colors. Hence it follows that $c' \in C_{Z,n}$.

Thus, the lemma is proved.   □

Recalling Stirling's formula for $n!$

$$n! \approx n^n e^{-n} \sqrt{2\pi n},$$

we see that method Z is roughly e^n times more economical than "blind" sorting of the colors in method Y. However, even this method creates a coloring with something "left over": of the six colorings only five are truly distinct (the reader is invited to think about what this really means), and colorings 112 and 113 reduce to each other by means of a re-coloring. A second cause of the redundancy is that we have generated not just the regular colorings, which we are of course interested in, but every coloring. It is already quite a complicated matter to compute the number of regular colorings. First, the number of colorings is no longer a function of just the number of vertices, but depends essentially on the graph. For a graph with n isolated vertices, method Z yields all $n!$ colorings (each of which is regular), but for a complete n-graph (n pairwise adjacent vertices) it yields just the single regular coloring

1, 2, . . . , n. Second, the estimate is not exact, but only asymptotic (like Stirling's formula), i.e., it approaches the exact formula as $n \to \infty$. In our discussion, it is not possible to prove this estimate, and we can only claim that the function e^n gives an asymptotic estimate of the number of regular colorings of connected graphs with n vertices.

This brief excursus into combinatorics, however superficial it may seem, suffices to demonstrate one result. Any attempt to search for a minimal coloring by means of direct sorting of all possibilities is destined to fail if we are interested in an effective solution of the storage packing problem.

The Need for a General Approach

Before proceeding on to a less trivial approach to the search for minimal colorings, we have to understand why it is even necessary to consider the problem in its full generality. Not to get carried away by yet another interesting mathematical problem, recall that within the framework of our study a coloring of the vertices of a graph is not essential in and of itself. All it does is to serve as a tool by means of which a minimal storage allocation schema is implemented. It may turn out that the incompatibility graphs that may be obtained for program schemas possess certain special properties that could help in the search for a minimal coloring. For example, it is known that no more than five colors are needed to color any planar graph. ([Shortly before publication of the original book, the problem was solved in its entirety: Four colors suffice to color any planar graph.—transl.)] Questions of this sort must be asked each time we reduce the specialized problem we are interested in— storage packing—to the general problem of coloring the vertices of a graph.

Unfortunately, in our case we arrive at a negative response to our question without much ado. Let us prove that for any undirected graph $T(Y, W)$, it is possible to construct a program schema whose incompatibility graph will be the graph $T(Y, W)$. We will try to derive the construction directly from the conditions of the problem. Suppose that $Y = \{y_1, \ldots, y_l\}$. Consider some edge of the graph $(y_i, y_j) \in W$. From the conditions of the problem, this edge necessarily represents the incompatibility of the two domains y_i and y_j. The incompatibility relation requires that the set

$$R(y_i) \cap R(y_j) \cup T(y_j) \cap R(y_i) \cup R(y_i) \cap T(y_j)$$

be nonempty. It is not difficult to contrive a fragment of program schema such that this set is nonempty. However, it is more important to do this as simply and uniformly as possible, and this basically means that in the ultimate program schema any constructed fragments must not be in competition nor should they create any sort of derived uncontrollable incompatibility not foreseen in the initial graph T. By the principle of economy of thought, it is most natural to create incompatibility by introducing into the schema a statement fij with two results, one of which is correlated with x_i and the other with x_j. (In this way, we at once have the memory $X = x_1, \ldots, x_l$ for a single variable x_i for each required liveness domain of y_i.) Note that in such a construction there are as many statements f_{ij} for each domain y_i in the schema as there are other vertices y_j adjacent to y_i, or—expressed in terms of the language of graph theory—as there are edges incident to y_i. If y_i is an isolated vertex of the graph T, it is nevertheless necessary to establish a domain for it, but not one connected to any other domain. For this purpose, it suffices to use a statement f_i with a single result x_i. Arcs must then be drawn from each statement f_{ij} that lead ultimately to some other statements that read x_i and x_j. Here it is important that all the results correlated with x_i occur in the same connectivity component of the data flow graph. Once again, this can be done most easily by correlating with each y_i a single statement gi with a single argument to which the variable x_i is correlated. Since it would seem that our

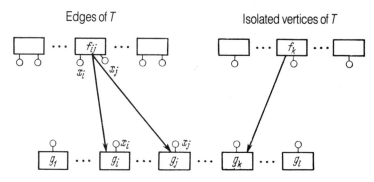

Figure 3.5. Any undirected graph T may be an incompatibility graph.

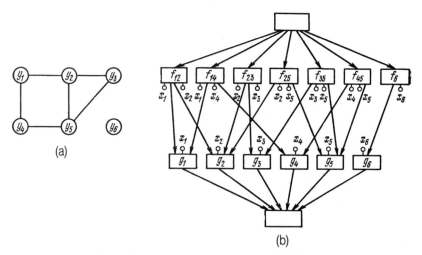

(b)

Figure 3.6. Constructing a program schema from a given incompatibility graph: (a) graph; (b) schema.

introduction of the statements fij ensures incompatibility, there is no need to introduce internal statements into the schema, and instead we may at once draw the arcs from statement fij to statements gi and gj. As a result, we obtain the configuration depicted in Figure 3.5. Formally speaking, this is already an entirely regular program schema, though it lacks the customary single entry and single exit statements. Of course, it costs us nothing to append these statements, as is shown in an example that makes the construction of Figure 3.6 more rigorous. Strictly speaking, our construction requires a converse line of reasoning to prove its correctness, though the author hopes the reader will be able to do this on his own.

Estimating the Complexity of an Algorithm

Now that the problem of coloring the vertices of a graph must once again be considered in its full generality in our search for the most effective algorithm for finding a minimal coloring, we will have to establish definite limits to this search. Let us explain what we have in mind. We have established that to solve the problem "in our minds," we must construct n colorings and for each coloring again use a number of operations that determines whether the coloring is correct and compute the number of colors used. This number of operations obviously is of order no greater than n^2. Thus, the total number of "elementary" operations in a complete sort will be of order $n^2 n!$ if by elementary operation we understand a simple manipulation with a single vertex or single edge of the graph.* (Note that the factor n^2 of $n!$ in the above product is nearly negligible by comparison with $n!$, since $n! \times n \times n < (n+2)!$. The presence of this factor could be thought of as equivalent to the construction of colorings for a graph that contains two more vertices than the original graph.) If we construct the colorings with more care, limiting ourselves solely to the regular colorings, by the estimate just given we will have used on the order of $n^2 e^n$ operations, understanding n^2 as an overstated estimate of the number of operations needed to obtain a regular coloring.

This is why there are two limits to consider when we speak of the scope of the search for an effective solution of a combinatorial problem. One limit is the lower limit of the estimate of the complexity of the algorithm. Here we are thinking of the mathematically provable assertion that a given problem may not, in principle, be solvable in less than some number of elementary operations (given by the lower limit). Obtaining reliable lower limits for particular algorithms is as a rule a rather difficult mathematical problem, though its solution is often based on extremely simple, though fundamental observations. For example, it is quite a simple matter to prove that in the general case it is impossible to compute a function of n variables in less than $(n-1)$ steps if on each step only binary operations may be executed, i.e.,

---

* Below we will speak of the "elementary" operations in more detail.

operations that compute a function of two variables. For the sake of simplicity, consider the case $n = 2^k$, and assume as an axiom the self-evident assertion that if a function depends essentially on each of n variables (i.e., a variation in each variable varies the values of the function), each of the variables must occur at least once in the algorithm itself; there must exist at least an indirect data path from this occurrence to the result of the function (the concept of an indirect data path is illustrated in Figure 3.7).

Thus, in a single step we may compute a single operation that implements a function of two variables. In two steps, i.e., by performing two operations, we may implement (as we just proved) a function of at most three variables. However, if we substitute four independent variables for the four possible arguments of the two operations, we would not be able to relate these operations to each other (see Figure 3.7(b)). If we perform three steps, we would be able to realize a function of four variables, moreover in two different ways, as shown in Figure 3.7(c). We will select a kind of balanced cascade circuit, as such a circuit at once suggests a general construction of a k-level tree of data paths that computes a function of 2^k variables in at most $1 + 2 + \ldots 2^{k-2} + 2^{k-1} = 2^k - 1$ steps (Figure 3.7(d)).

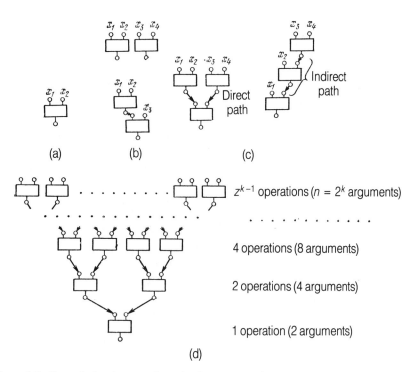

Figure 3.7. Cascade implementation of a function of 2^k variables: (a) one operation; (b) two operations; (c) three operations; (d) general construction.

Thus, we have arrived at the unfortunate conclusion that a rigorous solution of the minimal coloring problem for the vertices of a graph may not be obtained in any way other than by a "total search," i.e., in a number of steps comparable with the total number of all possible regular colorings. The term, *total search*, is used to indicate that the statement of this problem, like many other combinatorial problems, may be reduced to the following general assertion. Suppose we are given some finite set (in the current case, the set of all colorings). It is necessary to find an element in this set with a specified property (in this case, a minimal coloring). The problem of finding some element is said to be solved by a *total search* if the number of steps needed to find this element is comparable with the cardinality of the set.

Cross Section Problem

This doesn't mean that all combinatorial problems are as troublesome as to require a total search procedure. The author knows of one problem which, incidentally, is related directly to the general problem discussed in the first part of the book.

Let us turn to the discussion of Examples 6 and 7 in Chapter 1, where we computed x^{59} by means of the formula

$$x^{59} = (((x \times x^2) \times ((x^2)^2)^2 \times (((x^2)^2)^2)^2) \times ((((x^2)^2)^2)^2)^2),$$

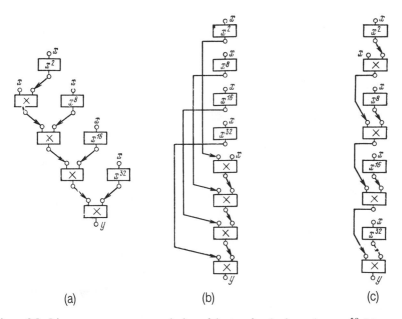

Figure 3.8. Linear program as an ordering of the tree for the formula $y = x^{59}$: (a) tree of formula; (b) inefficient ordering; (c) minimal ordering.

though the sequence of the computations was different. The difference in the sequence of the computations had a marked influence on the volume of memory required which, as we explained, is equal to the maximal width of the cross section of data paths in the case of linear programs. Let us update the form of the cross sections in each of the programs (Figure 3.8) and, at the same time, represent the data paths in the formula itself by deriving a cascade construction analogous to Figure 3.7. (For the sake of simplicity, we will compute the eighth, sixteenth and thirty-second powers by means of elementary operations.) A construction that represents a formula will be called a *cascade data flow graph*. It differs from an ordinary data flow graph in that it represents, not just the poles and data paths, but also the statements, and depicts the correspondence between poles and statements (the mapping V in the definition of a program schema). We consider the statements as the vertices of a cascade data flow graph. Then such a directed graph is a special type of graph, called a *tree*. It has a single vertex without any arcs emanating from it, called the *root* of the tree. It also has a series of *pendent vertices* or *leaves* which no arc enters. All the vertices other than the root have precisely one arc emanating from them. Finally, there is one and only one path from each leaf to a root. These three properties describe fully what it means to say that a graph is a tree.* If with each vertex v of a tree we consider its inverse transitive closure, we obtain a subgraph $T(v)$ that is also a tree with root v.

The data paths between the vertices of a tree of a formula define a partial order relation between the operations that are executed when evaluating a formula. That is, any vertex v must be executed after any vertex in $T(v)$. This order relation is partial in the sense that it prescribes an order of execution which is not complete. Vertices occurring in arcs that connect a leaf to a root must be executed strictly in the order in which they occur in this path; on the other hand, given two vertices v_1 and v_2 that compute the arguments of some binary operation w, any pair of vertices in the trees $T(v_1)$ and $T(v_2)$, respectively, may be executed in any order with respect to each other. It is precisely because the order relation between the vertices in the tree of a formula is a partial ordering that one and the same formula may be programmed in many different ways (two methods of programming a formula that evaluates x^{59} are shown in Figure 3.8(b) and (c)). Any program that evaluates a formula defines a complete ordering between the operations (i.e., between the execution of each of these operations) that comprise the formula. Here, however, there remains a partial ordering that establishes the data paths in the formula. Thus, a program that executes a formula may be in the form of a complete ordering of the operations of the formula that preserves the partial ordering inherent in it.

We see that the different versions of a program that computes some formula require different quantities of memory cells; to compute these quantities we

---

* A tree may also be defined such that the arcs have the opposite orientation from the root and leaves. The latter are also called the *terminal vertices* or simply *terminals*.

need only determine the maximal width of the "cross sections" of the data paths. The following combinatorial problem arises quite naturally: Find an ordering of the vertices of the tree of a formula that has least width of all orderings. (In speaking of the width of an ordering here, we are thinking of the maximal width of all the cross sections for a given ordering.) This problem is a typical example of what are known as "minimax" combinatorial problems, which are often encountered in mathematics. The section thus found is also called the *minimax cross section* of the formula.

Let us first estimate the total number of ways of ordering the vertices of a tree. For the sake of simplicity, we will take the case of a symmetric or, as is usually said, *balanced* k-level binary tree (Figure 3.7(d)) having 2^k arguments and $2^k - 1$ vertices, of which 2^{k-1} are leaves. We will attempt to complete the number of orderings by induction on the number of levels. Let us consider some terminal vertex w of the tree and its two predecessors v_1 and v_2. We have already remarked that each pair of vertices in $T(v_1)$ and $T(v_2)$, respectively, may be ordered arbitrarily under the condition that both of them precede w. Suppose that m is the number of vertices in the two trees $T(v_1)$ and $T(v_2)$ (The same for both trees, since they are symmetric) and let A and B be some ordering of the vertices in $T(v_1)$ and $T(v_2)$, respectively. Then for given A and B, we may obtain a series of orderings for the tree $T(w)$ in the following way. We merge together vertices from $T(v_1)$ and vertices from $T(v_2)$ in an arbitrary way, though making sure that the relative orderings in A and B between vertices of the same tree are preserved (we call this procedure an *ordered merging* of the sequences A and B), and insert w right after this ordering of length $2m$. Suppose that $R(p, q)$ is the number of all possible ordered mergings of two sequences of length p and q, respectively, and let M be the number of all possible orderings of the vertices of the trees in both $T(v_1)$ and $T(v_2)$. Then the number M' of all possible orderings of the vertices of $T(w)$ is given as

$$M' = M^2 \cdot R(m, m). \tag{1}$$

Let us now estimate the function $R(p, q)$. For the sake of brevity, we will refer to a sequence of length n as an *n-tuple*.

The ordered merging of a q-tuple with a p-tuple may be interpreted as asserting that some p "places" in a designated $p + q$ "places" are occupied by the p-tuple, while the remaining q places are occupied by the q-tuple. Obviously, any ordered merging may be characterized by a choice of some p places of the designated $p + q$ places and, conversely, the choice of the p places specifies some ordered merging in a unique way. Hence we at once find that

$$R(p, q) = C_{p+q}^{p} = \frac{(p+q)!}{p! \, q!}. \tag{2}$$

Suppose that M_k is the number of all possible orderings of a k-level balanced binary tree. Then (1) and (2) together yield the relation

$$M_k = M_{k-1}^2 \frac{(2^k - 2)!}{|(2^{k-1} - 1)!|^2}.$$

The numerator and denominator of the fraction are called the *rising factorial* and the *falling factorial*, respectively. The relation itself is denoted $F(k-1)$ and $(k-1)$ is called its order.

Let us substitute in M_{k-1} its expression in terms of M_{k-2}, i.e., we apply the relation $F(k-2)$:

$$M_k = M_{k-2}^4 \frac{[(2^{k-1}-2)!]^2}{[(2^{k-2}-1)!]^4} \cdot \frac{(2^{k-2})!}{[(2^{k-1}-1)!]^2}$$

$$= M_{k-2}^4 \frac{[(2^{k-1}-2)!]^2}{[(2^{k-1}-2)!(2^{k-1}-1)]^2} \cdot \frac{(2^k-2)!}{[(2^{k-2}-1)!]^4}$$

$$= \frac{M_{k-2}^4}{(2^{k-2}-1)^2} \cdot \frac{(2^k-2)!}{[(2^{k-2}-1)!]^4}.$$

Here is a rule for applying the relation $F(k-2)$, that is, reduce the rising factorial of $F(k-2)$ by the falling factorial of $F(k-1)$, leaving in the denominator an exponential factor with exponent 2 raised to a power equal to $(k-1)$ less the order of the relation. With successive application of the relations $F(k-i)$ $(i=1, \ldots, k-1)$ in the expression for M_k, the numerator will contain $M_{k-i}^{2^i}$ and the factorial factor $(2^k-2)!$ will remain, while exponential factors will accumulate in the denominator and a falling factorial, i.e., $[2^{k-i}-1)!]^2$, will be obtained. After applying $F(1)$, we obtain

$$M_k = \frac{M_1^{2^{k-1}}}{(2^{k-1}-1)^{2^1} \times \ldots \times (2^1-1)^{2^{k-1}}} \cdot \frac{(2^k-2)!}{[(2^1-1)!]^{2^{k-1}}}.$$

Since $M_1 = 1$, the final expression has the form

$$M_k = \frac{(2^k-2)!}{\displaystyle\prod_{i=1}^{k-1}(2^i-1)^{2^{k-i}}}.$$

Let us simplify this expression, replacing the right side by its lower bound and increasing the denominator by replacing 2^i-1 by 2^i:

$$M_k > \frac{(2^k-2)!}{\displaystyle\prod_{i=1}^{k-1}2^{i2^{k-1}}} = \frac{(2^k-2)!}{2^{\sum\limits_{i=1}^{k-1}i2^{k-i}}} = \frac{(2^k-2)!}{2^{2^k\left(\sum\limits_{i=1}^{k-1}i2^{-i}\right)}}$$

The terms in parentheses refer to the segment of a converging number series with sum (according to the problem book of B.P. Demidovich) equal to 2. Replacing a segment of the series by its sum strengthens the inequality, and recalling that $2^k-1=n$, where n is the number of operations in the tree, we obtain the following final estimate for M_k:

$$M_k > \frac{(n-1)!}{4^{n+1}}.$$

Thus, we have found that the number of distinct orderings of the operations of a formula that may be represented by a balanced tree with n vertices increases with increasing n somewhat more slowly than $n!$. At the same time, we may now show that given some (of course, simplified) method of computing a formula, the minimax cross section of this formula may be found by means of a very simple algorithm with number of steps on the order of only n. The simplification derives from the fact that the arguments of the formula are the sort of variables for which we might wish to economize on memory, and also the fact that if there are identical sub-expressions in a formula, they are programmed anew each time. In this case, the data paths in the formula actually form a tree, rather than any sort of more complicated graph (though we do not insist that the tree be strictly binary and balanced; in particular, it may contain unary operations, i.e., operations on a single argument).

Let us describe this algorithm by induction on the construction of the tree. In other words, in speaking of a tree $T(w)$ with root w, we consider two cases:

(a) w has a unique predecessor v which is a root of $T(v)$ (unary operation);
(b) w has two predecessors v_1 and v_2 which are the roots of $T(v_1)$ and $T(v_2)$, respectively (binary operation).

We will assume that the minimax cross sections of the three trees $T(v)$, $T(v_1)$, and $T(v_2)$ have been found and that they are equal to s, s_1, and s_2, respectively. The essence of the algorithm is revealed by the following auxilary assertion.

Theorem 3.2 *In the notation we have been using, the minimax cross section s' of a formula specified by a tree $T(w)$ is equal to s in case* (a), *and in case* (b) *is expressed by the formula*

$$s' = \begin{cases} \max(s_1, s_2) & \text{if } s_1 \neq s_2, \\ s_1 + 1 & \text{if } s_1 = s_2. \end{cases}$$

An ordering of the vertices of $T(w)$ that attains the minimax width (optimal ordering) is constructed in the following way:

In case (a), take the optimal ordering of $T(v)$ and then append w;

In case (b), take the optimal ordering of the tree with greatest minimax width (or any tree in the case of equal widths) and then append the optimal ordering of another tree, and finally append w.

Proof. Case (a) is trivial, since once we have an optimal ordering of some tree $T(v)$, we may augment it by means of the terminal vertex w in a unique way. The width of the added cross section is equal to unity and may not be greater than the minimax width already attained.

Let us consider case (b). In Figure 3.9(a), we have given a schematic outline of an ordering without merging of $T(w)$ of orders $T(v_1)$ and $T(v_2)$, and in Figure 3.9(b), an ordering with merging. Obviously, if $s_1 > s_2$, the ordering stipulated by the conditions of the theorem is optimal, since the data paths in the two trees $T(v_1)$ and $T(v_2)$ are not in competition in an ordering without merging and the attainable width, equal to $s_2 + 1$ in one cross section for computations in $T(v_2)$ does not exceed the width s_1, which is at once (by the

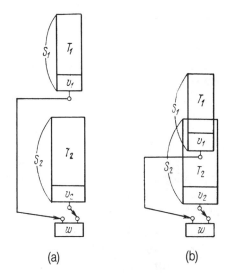

Figure 3.9. Proof of Theorem 3.2: (a) ordering without merging; (b) ordering with merging.

theorem) the minimax width of the entire formula. But if $s_1 = s_2$, then $s_1 + 1$ is the minimax width. Any other ordering with merging of orders $T(v_1)$ and $T(v_2)$ can only increase the width attained in the ordering given by the conditions of the theorem, since in this case not only is there a new path from v_1 to w, but some of the paths within $T(v_1)$ and $T(v_2)$ also turn out to be in competition.   □

With this theorem in mind, the optimal ordering algorithm assumes the following form. A width function is first constructed on the vertices of the tree by induction. In the case of leaves, the function is obviously equal to unity. Using the rule stated in the theorem, this function is then found for the next vertex of the tree, using the values of the width function of its predecessors already found. The tree is then ordered from the root to the leaves by taking a root, placing in front of it its unique predecessors (one-place statement). In the case of two predecessors v_1 and v_2, the vertex v_1 is placed in front of the root (if $s_1 < s_2$), and the variable v_2 is stored. The vertex v_1 then becomes the "root" and everything is repeated until a leaf is reached. Leaving the leaf as is, we take the last of the stored vertices as the "root". Figure 3.10 gives two results of such an optimal ordering process, the first for the tree of a formula for computing x^{59}, and the second for a more complicated formula (the Latin numbers represent the values of the width function, while the arabic numbers represent the optimal order in an inverse numbering).*

---

* Readers who wish to study the optimal ordering algorithm in its own right may be interested to learn that attempts to generalize it to linear programs with data paths more complicated than trees have encountered considerable difficulties.

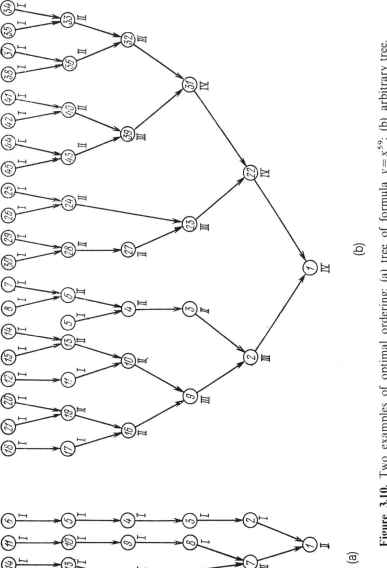

Figure 3.10. Two examples of optimal ordering: (a) tree of formula $y = x^{59}$; (b) arbitrary tree.

Estimating the Number of Steps

From the standpoint of the central theme of our presentation, this example is instructive by virtue of the form assumed by the algorithm that solves our combinatorial problem. The most important element of this algorithm is its overall line of development. On the one hand, it basically uses information incorporated in the tree of the formula which is the "substance" of our problem. Our task is to "traverse" each vertex and "process" each binary relation that forms a particular arc of the tree. We have already noted the difference between the leaves and the other vertices. On the other hand, in the operation of the algorithm we may discern a kind of unified orientation to its development, which proceeds at first from the leaves to the root in the course of constructing the width function, and then conversely, in the process of ordering. If we were also to set aside some of the vertices "in reserve" (storing vertices with greater values of the width function), we would do so systematically rather than hunt willy-nilly among them, always taking the vertex that stores the one previous to it. Such an intuitive representation of the effectiveness of our algorithm, which we have expressed using just the words, "sorting algorithm" and "directed algorithm," is not enough for a mathematical treatment, however. Estimates of the complexity of an algorithm, a subject we have alluded to previously, play the role of efficiency criteria. We are already well aware that every program may be characterized by the number of instructions it contains and the volume of memory it requires. Note that the number of instructions of a program may refer either to the number of instructions actually present in a program or to the number of instructions that have to be executed to run the program. In a number of branches of mathematics and computer programming, the first characteristic is also important, though program efficiency is characterized best in terms of the second indicator. There are analogous characteristics for algorithms. If we decide on a method of describing an algorithm (algorithmic language), and describe rigorously what sort of information is to be stored in memory, then by executing the algorithm on certain initial information it is possible to count or estimate quite accurately both the number of elementary steps involved in the execution of the algorithm and the number of units of information that must be present simultaneously in memory. If the initial information is characterized by some parameter (say, the order of a matrix, the number of vertices or arcs in a graph, the number of independent variables, etc.), the tabulated or estimated number of steps and volume of memory become functions of this parameter. These functions are also called the indicators or *estimates of complexity of the algorithm* (*program*). Estimates of the number of steps are referred to as *time estimates*, while estimates of the number of memory cells required by the program are called *memory estimates* or *storage estimates*.

Some natural number n related in some way to the volume of initial information of an algorithm is usually taken as the parameter of this information. Then the efficiency of an algorithm, understood in terms of its operational time, may be correlated to the rate of growth of the time estimate by mean of a function $F(n)$. Within this gradation of rates of growth we distinguish mainly the following functions:

$F(n) = n$ linear time,
$F(n) = n \log_a n$ logarithmic time,
$F(n) = n^2$ quadratic time,
$F(n) = a_0 n^k + a_1 n^{k-1} + \ldots + a_k$ polynomial time,
$F(n) = a^n$ exponential time,
$F(n) = n!$ factorial time,
$F(n) = n^n$ hyperexponential time.

Each of these functions in fact defines a whole series of estimates of a given rate of growth that may be distinguished from the expressions given above by the coefficients of n or by the function itself. If n characterizes the number of "independent variables" in the initial information, by the above line of reasoning the linear estimates characterize the most rapid algorithm, in which the number of operations required by each element of the initial information is bounded by some constant. Certain algorithms for ordering n numbers are examples of algorithms that operate in logarithmic time. Algorithms with polynomial (in the special case, quadratic) time are considered extreme cases of "operational" algorithms, whereas algorithms with higher estimates are applied only for low values of n, and in the case of higher values are replaced by "approximating" algorithms that give a kind of approximate solution of the given problem within an acceptable time (if possible, not more than in quadratic time).

The following line of intuitive reasoning may help explain the special role of quadratic time estimates. If some algorithm operates in linear time, this means that each of its input variables makes its own contribution to the result independent of the other variables. A typical example is the summation of a series of numbers. Here, what we have called the sense of directedness of an algorithm appears in pure form. Once several operations have been performed on the input variable, we no longer have need to resort to it again. Quadratic time appears whenever the contribution of each input variable to a result depends actually on its "interaction" with all or nearly all the other variables. The reader may find this strange, though he will not find it so easy a task to think of a problem that would basically require for its solution an algorithm with quadratic time, glancing back over these remarks, the first such problem we can think of is that of constructing a polynomial that takes n designated values. (Such polynomials are called *interpolational polynomials*; some readers may have heard of Lagrangian polynomials, a type of polynomial that satisfies this requirement.) Thus, wherever it is necessary to compute all the possible differences $x_i - x_j$ $(i, j = 1, \ldots, n)$ of given values of a polynomial $x_1, x_2, \ldots, x_n$, we are dealing with an algorithm with quadratic time.

Let us now return to our problem. To relate it to the discussion just concluded, we will have to decide what is it that characterizes the "independent variables," the number of such variables in the initial information, and the "unit of operation" in the coloring algorithms. We have already estimated the combinatorial volume of different colorings as a function of the number n of vertices of a graph. We would be able to give a complete description of the graph if we were able to indicate for each vertex the set of edges to which it belongs or, what is the same thing, the set of vertices adjacent to it. Such a description of the "environment" of a vertex or, as we will have occasion to say, a *first-order neighborhood*, we will think of as the "unit of information" in the definition of a graph. Of course, strictly speaking, in a very real sense it is not possible to discuss such a unit of information, since its volume may be highly varied. An isolated vertex has an empty first-order neighborhood, while a "star," i.e., the vertex of a graph adjacent to all the other vertices, contains in this neighborhood the vertices of the entire graph. The total volume of this information is also highly varied for fixed n, from zero edges in a graph consisting of isolated vertices, to $(n-1)$ edges in the simplest connected graph (open chain of n vertices), and, finally, $n(n-1)$ edges in an *n-complete graph* (a graph in which all n vertices are pairwise adjacent). Nevertheless, for the sake of heuristic reasoning about the efficiency of coloring algorithms, unless there are special additional stipulations about the methods used to represent a graph, such an interpretation of the unit of information suffices. And whenever we succeed in placing in discussion the number of edges of a graph p, there we will also use this number as a parameter of the problem.

In such an approach, it is natural to consider the set of operations related to a vertex and its first-order neighborhood as a "step" of the given algorithm. But if we require a greater degree of detail, a single step may be thought of as the "processing" of a single edge of the graph, involving, as an example, finding out the color of an adjacent vertex.

3.4. Coloring the Vertices of a Graph. The Search for an Algorithm

Let us begin the search for a practicable algorithm for coloring the vertices of a graph, bearing in mind that, in the general case, minimal colorings require an exponential number of steps. This means that we will have to approach the construction of the algorithm from a different starting point. Once we have given up finding obviously minimal colorings, we will prescribe some general guiding principle for the algorithm that will provide us with an acceptable time estimate, but within the framework of this principle we will try to act in some reasonable fashion by imparting a degree of rigor to the general principle of common sense that prescribes "proceeding as best as you can within the limits of the possible." The scope of what is possible and what is best—this is what constitutes the content of the concrete analysis of our problem which we will now attempt to undertake.

Heuristic Methods

Man in his daily activities is constantly compelled to deal with situations that, were they expressed mathematically, would look like the sort of combinatorial problems that entail exorbitant expenditures of time in a search for an absolutely optimal solution. It is this which makes it necessary to develop some kind of guiding strategy in a search for an admissible solution. Here are examples of rules for such a strategy:

do not go back on any decision once it has been reached;
in packing things in a suitcase, begin with the bulkiest objects;
in searching for the maximum in some function, proceed in the direction of
    the gradient;
a bird in the hand is worth two in the bush;
if you don't know what to do, go ahead anyway.

Let's suppose you aren't too embarrassed by the "unscientific" form of these maxims. In any rigorously described combinatorial problem, these rules may be clothed in the most refined mathematical formalism, but this does not change their essential nature, which—particularly at the initial stage in the search for an algorithm—is far better expressed in a form that penetrates directly to the subconscious, the vessel where man's creativity resides. Conjecture and intuition play just as great a role in the process of finding and formulating rules of this type as do rigorous knowledge and logical reasoning. It is no accident that rules for the approximate solution of combinatorial problems are referred to as heuristic rules, from the Greek work *Eureka*! (I found it !), which since the time of Archimedes has been among the most well-known catchwords in science. In any heuristic problem- solving method there will typically be what are known as counterexamples, that is, instances that demonstrate the ineffectiveness or unacceptability of this or that particular method discovered in the course of searching for an ideal solution. Though we are fully aware of what's involved here, we will reconcile ourselves to the existence of such counterexamples, trusting, first, that they will not spoil the general picture too much and, second, that any attempt to get around these special cases will cost more than it's worth. At the same time, the search for and analysis of such counterexamples must be an integral part of any serious investigation if we wish to grasp the power and range of applicability of heuristic methods.

Heuristics of the Coloring Process

In the problem at hand, our wish to find a coloring algorithm with at most quadratic time may be interpreted as meaning that we would prefer not spending more than around n steps to color a single vertex. In n steps we may take a look around any neighborhood of a vertex, except for one greater than the entire graph. With such an economy of operation, none of the vertices gets colored more than once by the algorithm, similarly after undertaking an analysis of the neighborhood of some vertex or, possibly, the entire graph, this vertex is colored with the understanding that we "don't go back on a decision once it's been made." This seemingly quite trivial approach already imposes a degree of discipline on the algorithm. To choose a color for some vertex, we must now decide what should be the order of scanning the vertices of the graph and what should our analysis be directed towards (a neighborhood or the entire graph).

"Color" and "vertex"—the fact that we are dealing with two entities suggests a dual approach to the general organization of the coloring process. The first approach is to take some color and use it to color vertices chosen arbitrarily until there is no vertex left with which this color might be associated. In the second approach—we are now simply repeating the end of the preceding paragraph—we consider the vertices in some order and select an appropriate color for the next vertex. We still don't have a very good understanding of the difference between the first and second approaches, and these restatements may very well seem like little more than playing with words to many readers. However, because of the demand for a logical analysis of any situation whatsoever, a demand which every mathematician senses, we find it necessary to "fool around" a bit with these versions.

Let us consider some intermediate state of the coloring algorithm in each of these approaches. To take the next step and color a succeeding vertex, we must, in particular, determine what are the constraints (i.e., what may not be done) and how many degrees of freedom there are (i.e., how can we arrange things). In the first approach we determine on each step the set V' of uncolored vertices with which the current color α may not be associated and the set V'' or uncolored vertices this color may be associated with. Obviously, V' consists of those vertices (and only those vertices) adjacent to at least one vertex colored with α. (We denote this set $V(\alpha)$.) Then V'' is $(V \setminus CV) \setminus V'$, where V is the set of all the vertices of the graph and CV is the set of vertices so far colored at the given moment. In particular, the condition for intermediate termination, i.e., a point at which all possibilities for any further application of color α is exhausted, may be stated thus: $V'' = \phi$, and the ultimate termination of the algorithm occurs when it is found that $V = CV$.

In the second approach, the analysis of the constraints must deal with the first-order neighborhood $R_1(v)$ of the current vertex v, which is the set of vertices adjacent to this vertex. None of the colors correlated with vertices in $R_1(v)$ can be used for v. There are two ranges over which the degrees of freedom for coloring v may vary, the first of which involves selecting a particular color from among those already used, and the second selecting a "fresh" color.

With these two paragraphs in mind, the difference between the two approaches becomes more tangible. The first algorithm would seem to be more goal-directed, in that on each step we simply select a vertex from V'' or, if V'' is empty, take a fresh color. However, more global operations on the graph are required to create V' and V'', e.g., manipulating $V(\alpha)$, all the first-order neighborhoods of its vertices, or the sets CV and V. The second algorithm localizes the analysis in the neighborhood $R_1(v)$, though it makes less rigorous alternatives available. Obviously, we must now focus our attention and try to see whether there isn't some way of improving the analysis in the first algorithm, which we might accomplish by exiting from $V(\alpha)$. Now $V(\alpha)$ is part of CV and, therefore, is, so to speak, a fully developed part of the graph. None of the vertices in $V(\alpha)$ are pairwise adjacent. For the subsequent solutions, we are interested only in the nature of the relations between the vertices of $V(\alpha)$ and the vertices adjacent to them. This situation may be represented in the form of a diagram (Figure 3.11(a)). With such a representation, the reader should be able to see (or so we would hope) that if the vertices of $V(\alpha)$ were to be "glued together" as shown in Figure 3.11(b), V' would become just a first-order neighborhood of the new vertex w. Surely there can be no doubt that this is now a whole lot better, but to glue together the vertices of $V(i)$ it is still necessary to first bring them together. But now we're finally beginning to do some quick thinking. On the preceding stages in which the color α was used, we were able to "hold in our hands" each of the vertices of $V(\alpha)$ in turn; thus, once we had a succeeding vertex v colored in α, we found the replacement v' in the family $V(\alpha)$, plucking it out of V''. It is at this moment that v and v' are glued together. We proceed this way always, the process of assigning a color to a vertex turning into a sequence of pairwise gluings of nonadjacent vertices. But we have not yet analyzed fully what it means to say that the process of gluing is based on a visual representation taken from a diagram, so let us now develop this idea in all its ramifications. Let us imagine how the process develops from the very start, i.e., working with the first color α_1. The set CV is

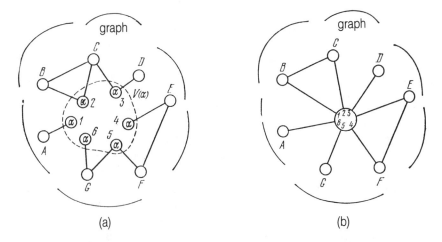

(a)   (b)

Figure 3.11. Gluing together the vertices of a graph: (a) before gluing; (b) after gluing:

empty at the initial moment. At each step of the gluing process, V'' $= (V \backslash R_1(v_1)) \backslash \{v_1\}$, where v_1 is the vertex to which we "glue" vertices colored in α_1. At the intermediate end-point $V'' = \varnothing$, whence it follows that $\{v_1\} \bigcup R_1(v_1) = V$, i.e., v_1 is now a *star*. If we then begin to work with another color α_2, once we have glued together all the vertices colored in α_2 to some vertex v_2 so that $v_2 \in R_1(v_1)$, the set $CV = \{v_1\}$ becomes automatically a subset of $R_1(v_2)$, whence we find that for v_2 as well, $V'' = (V \backslash R_1(v_2)) \backslash \{v_2\}$. If we think a bit about this, we find that the rule for selecting V'' and the intermediate termination condition (the next vertex after a series of gluings becomes a star) is preserved for any succeeding color. The termination condition for the algorithm itself now appears rather curious: For every vertex v of the graph $R_1(v) \bigcup \{v\} = V$, where, however, V is no longer the set of vertices of the initial graph, since every vertex of the resulting complete graph (recall its definition!) is a collection of glued and pairwise nonadjacent vertices of the initial graph.

Gluing Together Vertices

Now we must stop and think about what to do next. We have not simply found some graphic restatement of the first approach to the coloring algorithm, but actually introduced a completely new interpretation (in some sense) of the process of coloring the vertices. Instead of coloring the vertices, we undertake successive transformations of a graph G in which nonadjacent vertices are glued together. To *glue together* the two *vertices* v_1 and v_2 with neighborhoods $R_1(v_1)$ and $R_1(v_2)$ means eliminating these vertices from the graph along with the edges to which they are incident and adding the new vertex v and the edges incident to it so that $R_1(v) = R_1(v_1) \bigcup R_1(v_2)$. The resulting graph G' has one fewer vertex and may also have fewer edges. There are fewer edges since if we are given two vertices v_1 and v_2 for which there exists a third vertex v_3 adjacent to both v_1 and v_2, in place of the two arcs (v_1, v_3) and (v_2, v_3) in G' there remains only the single arc (v, v_3). This will happen if v_1 and v_2 are a distance 2 apart, measuring *distance between vertices in a graph* by the number of edges in the shortest path connecting these vertices. This may also be expressed in the following way: $v_2 \in R_2(v_1)$ and, conversely, $v_1 \in R_2(v_2)$, understanding by a second-order neighborhood of some vertex the set of all vertices a distance 2 from this vertex. Here v_3 is naturally referred to as the vertex that *separates* v_1 and v_2. The number of edges decreases by one for any vertex that separates v_1 and v_2. Thus, it may be concluded that the number of edges in a graph G can decrease only if we glue together all vertices a distance of 2 apart. In this case, the number of edges that vanish is equal to the number of separating vertices. Everything we have just said is nothing other than a rigorous observation of the process of gluing together vertices, an observation that will certainly be useful in what follows. For readers who like pictures, we have shown in Figure 3.12 two kinds of vertex gluings and for the careful readers we emphasize that our definition of

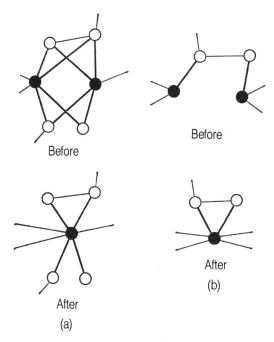

Before

Before

After
(a)

After
(b)

Figure 3.12. Examples of vertex gluing: (a) edges disappear; (b) without any edges disappearing.

the concept of separating vertex holds only for vertices that are a distance 2 apart.

Returning to the process of successive gluing, we find that the transformations of each succeeding graph G continue until there is no longer any pair of nonadjacent vertices, i.e., until G has become a K-complete graph. Obviously, a K-complete graph admits only a single trivial coloring in which each of the K vertices v is colored in its own color, which simultaneously happens to be the color of all the vertices in the initial graph that are linked to v. Since none of the vertices are pairwise adjacent, such a coloring its admissible; the order K of the resulting complete K-graph is equal to the number of colors. The problem of deriving a minimal coloring devolves to constructing a sequence of gluings of vertices of the initial graph* such that the order of the resulting K-complete graph is the least of all possible graphs, in other words equal to $\chi(G)$. (Recall that $\chi(G)$ is the chromatic number of the graph G.)

Continuing our analysis, we see that an interpretation of the coloring process as a pairwise gluing of vertices is also entirely suitable for the second

---

* One more remark for lovers of rigor: In speaking of a transformation of an initial graph G into a "new" graph G', we may nevertheless still "recognize" in the new graph the vertices of the initial graph, though it is not important in this case whether or not they are glued together.

approach to the coloring algorithm. Here we also search for a pair of nonadjacent vertices and glue them together. The only difference between the two approaches now is that in the first one we glue together as many vertices as possible to the same vertex until it is a star, whereas in the second one we start by assigning an order to the vertices and then proceed from one vertex to another, searching for an appropriate mate to glue to it.

In reducing the process of coloring the vertices of a graph to a successive gluing together of these vertices, we must verify that we do not thereby lose the ability to create a minimal coloring of the initial graph. Of course, if some minimal coloring consisting of χ colors is considered right away and if all the vertices colored in the same color are glued together, we end up with a χ-complete graph, though in fact we require a stronger assertion, which we now formulate as a theorem.

Theorem 3.3. *For every graph with chromatic number χ, there exists a sequence of pairwise glued vertices that reduce to a χ-complete graph.*

Proof. We say that two vertices of a graph G are *co-chromatic* if there exists a minimal coloring of the vertices of G in which these vertices are colored in the same color. $\qquad\square$

Lemma 1. *In any incomplete graph G there exists at least one pair of co-chromatic vertices.*

Suppose that there are n vertices in G. If no minimal coloring contains a pair of vertices colored in the same color, then $\chi(G) = n$. Since G is an incomplete graph, it contains at least one pair of nonadjacent vertices v_1 and v_2. Let us glue these two vertices together. The resulting graph G' has $(n-1)$ vertices, therefore $\chi(G') \leq n-1$. Let us consider any coloring of G' with $(n-1)$ or fewer colors. In this coloring, we may find a vertex to which v_1 and v_2 are glued. Once these two vertices have been unglued "in reverse order," with the colors from the coloring G preserved in their wake, we end up with a coloring of G that uses $(n-1)$ or fewer colors, which contradicts the assumption that $\chi(G) = n$. $\qquad\square$

Lemma 2. *If a graph G' may be obtained from a graph G by gluing together a pair of its co-chromatic vertices, then $\chi(G') = \chi(G)$.*

In fact, if we consider a minimal coloring of G in which these vertices are colored in the same color, and if the vertex of G' obtained after the gluing retains this color, and likewise the other vertices retain their colors, we obtain a coloring of G' using $\chi(G)$ colors. Hence, it follows that $\chi(G') \leq \chi(G)$. The inequality $\chi(G') < \chi(G)$, however, does not hold by the reasoning of the proof of Lemma 1. $\qquad\square$

By means of these two lemmas we obtain the required sequence of gluings. In the initial graph G we find a pair of co-chromatic vertices and glue them together. By Lemma 2, we have not "spoiled" the graph in the sense that its chromatic number remains the same. By Lemma 1, we may continue gluing together vertices until one of the succeeding graphs is a complete graph. Once again, by Lemma 2 it will have no more than $\chi(G)$ vertices.   □

With this we may consider our search for an overall guiding principle for the coloring algorithm to be complete. If we had been able to find the co-chromatic vertices without any trouble, we would then have a method of obtaining minimal colorings. We still do not have a direct approach to do so, though it is precisely this which shall now be the goal of our search for an appropriate heuristic for selecting pairs of vertices their can be glued together.

Co-chromaticity Theorem

Still one more digression is needed before concluding our analysis. The serious reader who has been able to grasp at once the basic definitions and the actual constructions of the algorithm that follow these definitions may think the preceding several pages an unintelligible jumble or just trivial rewordings that doesn't get us anywhere. But let me defend this part of the presentation. To the best of my abilities as a writer, I wish to bring to light the unseen effort underlying the mathematician's search for a solution to some problem. It is while looking at the same thing from different angles that ideas and observations for new plans of attack ripen, and this will at once lead to success once some algorithm or proof is found that strings together these preliminary findings along the pivotal axis of the reasoning or action. In fact, in our perhaps diffuse and repetitious presentation we have imperceptibly gathered together everything that might be needed to create effective coloring algorithms. Here are the crucial ideas and observations:

directionality of the coloring process (do not color any vertex more than once);

there is no guarantee that a minimal coloring may be obtained;

the concept of first- and second-order neighborhoods of a vertex;

the coloring process as a vertex gluing process;

separating vertices as the source of gluable edges.

Now we show how these ideas and observations together can help us solve the coloring problems. We begin by stating a rather remarkable theorem.

Theorem 3.4. *The neighborhood $R_2(v)$ of any vertex v of a connected graph G that is not a star has at least one co-chromatic vertex.*

Proof. Let us illustrate the reasoning of Figure 3.13, which depicts the vertex v and its two neighborhoods $R_1(v)$ and $R_2(v)$. The reader should have no

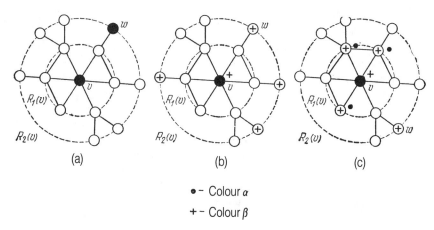

• – Colour α

+ – Colour β

Figure 3.13. Proof of Theorem 3.4 (three cases).

trouble seeing that if a vertex in a connected graph is not a star, its first- and second-order neighborhoods are not empty. Let us consider some minimal coloring of G in which v is colored in the color α. If some vertex w of $R_2(v)$ is also colored in α in this coloring (see Figure 3.13(a)), the theorem is proved.   □

Let us now consider the case in which none of the vertices of $R_2(v)$ is colored in α. In this case, we consider any vertex w from $R_2(v)$ colored in some color β and focus our attention on the neighborhood $R_1(v)$. Here once again there are two cases possible. If none of the vertices that belong to $R_1(v)$ is colored in β (Figure 3.13(b)), then nothing prevents us from recoloring v in β, which thereby means that the theorem holds.

Finally, consider the case in which there are several vertices in $R_1(v)$ colored in β. We denote this neighborhood of v by R'. Note that the following holds true of the sub-neighborhood of any vertex $u \in R_1(v)$ (see Figure 3.13(c)):

$$R_1(u) \subseteq \{v\} \bigcup R_1(v) \bigcup R_2(v),$$

Hence it is clear that given any vertex in R', v is the only vertex adjacent to it colored in α. Let us strip α off of v for a minute. Then there is nothing to prevent us from recoloring all the vertices in R' in α, thereby eliminating this color from $R_1(v)$. In this case we color u in β, obtaining a coloring that satisfies the premise of the theorem.   □

The importance of this theorem for our purposes is self-evident. It makes it possible to contract substantially the domain in which we have to search for co-chromatic vertices, ensuring thereby that a co-chromatic vertex may be found inside a second-order neighborhood of a given vertex. We have already obtained some sense of direction, in that even if we glue together the vertices in a graph in an entirely haphazard manner, we still have a greater chance for success if the randomness of the gluing is limited to second-order neighborhoods. The constraint that a graph be connected can hardly cause any confusion: We will simply color each component separately using the same colors.

The reader may at once verify the effectiveness of this heuristic (creating a gluing to an arbitrary vertex a distance 2 away) by drawing a series of graphs and coloring them this way. For the sake of orientation, in Figure 3.14 we present a graph colored some time ago by the author by guesswork; the only condition was that the coloring be planar.

Here we again digress to make a series of practical remarks regarding the search for examples that illustrate the process of coloring graphs. We would like to know how "good" are our colorings. In certain cases, we know of a greatest lower bound on the number of colors for graphs of a particular type. In particular, in the case of planar graphs, i.e., those which may be drawn in a plane without any of the edges crossing, it is known that the chromatic number is not greater than 5, but is not less than 4 (to bring these two bounds together is the subject of the well-known "four color problem"). Further, if a graph contains an n-complete subgraph, the number of colors can in no way be less than n.

Thus, if we consider the graph of Figure 3.14 and color it in accordance with the heuristic suggested by Theorem 3.4 (we will refer to this as the first heuristic), then, following the designated enumeration of the vertices (begin with the first vertex and glue it to the vertex with the least ordinal number in its neighborhood, denoting as the result of this gluing the lesser of the two ordinal numbers considered), we obtain a coloring of this graph using three colors, as shown in the figure by Latin letters.

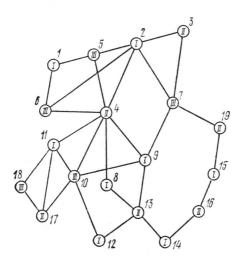

Figure 3.14. Successful application of first heuristic.

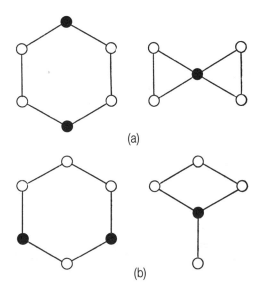

Figure 3.15. Example showing that the first heuristic is nontrivial: (a) triangles appear in the gluing process; (b) the chromatic number remains the same.

That this heuristic is nontrivial is demonstrated by the rather simple example of Figure 3.15. The initial graph is a hexagon with an even number of vertices and (recall Section 1.3) chromatic number equal to 2. If we link together vertices a distance 3 apart, we end up with triangles (Figure 3.15(a)) and, therefore, increase the chromatic number; whereas creating gluings in accordance with the rules of the first heuristic preserves the chromatic number (Figure 3.15(b)).

This example may also help us understand how to think about the theorem just proved. By assigning the color α to vertex v, we form a "dead zone" $R_1(v)$ about v in which α may no longer be used. To say that a coloring is minimal means that each color is applied to the "greatest" number of vertices. An increase in the number of vertices colored in a given color leads to a growth in the dead zones. Once these zones encompass the entire remainder of the graph, there is no longer any place where this color may be used. We will gain something if the dead zones spread about the graph overlap as much as possible. The dead zones of two nonadjacent vertices may overlap if and only if they are a distance 2 apart; the extent of the overlapping is determined by the number of separating vertices. Thus we arrive at the central idea of Theorem 3.4.

Anyone who remembers his childhood should be able to recall the analogous situation in the game of battleships. In that game, once a ship has been knocked out of the game, it displays to the opponent an analogous dead zone, in the form of contiguous cells no ships may enter. Any skillful player knows that if he spreads his ships far apart, i.e., far from the walls and from each other, his fleet will be rapidly knocked out of action, since even if both players have suffered equal losses at the start of the game, later on his opponent will have much greater space in his bay out of range of cannon fire from the other side's ships.

Estimating the Chromatic Number

The theorem we have proved gives us not only an encouraging heuristic, but also a simple estimate of the number of colors needed in a coloring using the first heuristic. This upper bound may be found as a function of the number of vertices n and edges p of a connected graph. The basis for this estimate is the fact that at least one edge vanishes from a graph if vertices a distance 2 apart are glued together (there is at least one separating vertex). It is easy to see that the number of edges p in a connected graph satisfies the inequalities

$$n - 1 \le p \le \frac{n(n-1)}{2}.$$

The maximal number of edges characterizes an n-complete graph. Let us now consider how vertices are glued together. We glue together the vertices one after the other until a k-complete graph ($k \le n$) is obtained. It will have $k(k-1)/2$ edges. Since at least one edge is removed from the graph in the process of gluing together vertices a distance 2 apart, in the final graph there are fewer edges than there were in the initial graph. The number of edges that vanish is given as $s = p - k(k-1)/2$. By the remark just made, $s \ge n - k$, where $n - k$ is the total number of gluings. Hence we obtain the inequality

$$p - \frac{k(k-1)}{2} \ge n - k,$$

which after some algebra assumes the form

$$k^2 - 3k - 2(p - n) \le 0. \tag{1}$$

The positive root of the equation is given as

$$k_+ = \frac{3 + \sqrt{9 + 8(p - n)}}{2}.$$

Hence we see that no positive number k that satisfies (1) can exceed the integral part of k_+, whence we derive the following estimate of the chromatic number $\chi(G_p^n)$ and number of colors $h_1(G_n^p)$ obtained in a coloring in accordance with the first heuristic (G_n^p is a connected graph with n vertices and p edges)

$$\chi(G_n^p) \le h_1(G_n^p) \le \left[\frac{3 + \sqrt{9 + 8(p - n)}}{2} \right]. \tag{2}$$

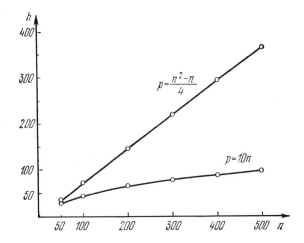

Figure 3.16. Efficiency of first heuristic.

In simplified form, showing only the rate of increase of the estimating function, the estimate has the form

$$h_1(G_n^p) \approx 3\sqrt{(p-n)}/2.$$

By means of this formula, it is possible to represent the estimated efficiency of the above coloring algorithm in the form of a graph. Since the estimate is a function of two variables, we give the graph h as a function of n (encompassing the range of more or less realistic scales of the coloring problem for the sake of storage packing from $n = 50$ to $n = 500$), taking for p the case of "dense" graphs, in which p is, say, less than half the number of edges in a complete graph ($p = (n^2 - n)/4$), and the case of less dense graphs in which the number of edges is proportional to the number of vertices, for example, $p = 10n$. The resulting graph (Figure 3.16) shows that the storage packing produced by coloring the incompatibility graph may be quite substantial indeed.

Vanishing Edges

Our application of the co-chromatic vertices theorem does not end here, however. The line of reasoning followed in deriving an upper bound on the chromatic number as a function of the number of vertices and edges of a connected graph allows us to once again glance at the coloring problem as a whole.

What does a coloring consist of after all? In a sequence of gluings of the vertices of a graph. At what point is it concluded? When a complete graph is obtained in the gluing process. How may it be described? By the maximal ratio of the number of edges to the number of vertices, which is equal to $(k - 1)/2$. This ratio is less in all incomplete graphs. Why is it that the process of gluing vertices together does not, as a rule, reach some limit? (Incidentally, what is this limit for a connected graph that has more than one vertex?) Because in the process of gluing vertices together, a graph becomes "denser" and the proportion of edges increases, reaching saturation ($k(k-1)/2$ edges for k vertices) at some point. Thereby, the better the different colorings obtained, the later on in the process of successive gluings is a complete graph formed. Let us analyze this in more detail. We represent the combined number

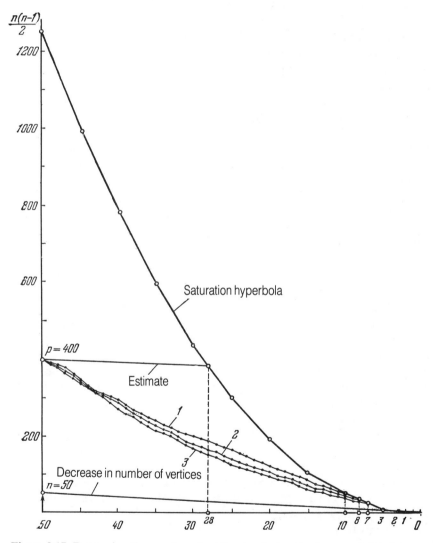

Figure 3.17. Decreasing the number of vertices and edges in the process of gluing together the vertices of a graph: (1) first heuristic; (2) second heuristic; (3) third heuristic.

of vertices and edges in a gluing of the vertices of a graph in the form of an x–y diagram. Along the x-axis (Figure 3.17) is laid out the number k of vertex gluings. The figure depicts first the number of vertices in the graph as a function of the number of gluings, which is none other than the function $\phi = n - k$. Then for each k we lay out along the y-axis the number of edges in a complete graph with $(n - k)$ vertices. This is the descending branch of the parabola $y = ((n - k)^2 - n + k)/2$, which intersects the y-axis at the point $n(n - 1)/2$ and the curve which plots the function of the number of vertices of the graph at the point $n - k = 3$. (Recall that in a triangle the number of vertices is equal to the number of edges.) Finally, we lay out along the y-axis the number of edges p of some connected graph G_n^p. In gluing the vertices together, we label the number of edges in the resulting graph for each k. We will have obtained a special kind of decreasing curve for the number of edges. As soon as this curve runs into the bounding parabola, the vertex gluing process comes to a halt; the saturation state has been attained. If in each gluing precisely one edge vanishes, the trajectory has the form of a line: $y = p - k$. The x-coordinate k^* of the point of intersection of this line and the "saturation parabola" yields an estimate of the number of colors, equal to ($n - k^*$), as guaranteed by the first heuristic. And this suggests the following assertion.

Theorem 3.5. *A minimal coloring of a connected graph G may be obtained by a sequence of gluings of vertices in which the total number of edges that have vanished is not less than this number for all other sequences.*

This conclusion is a good one for us, in that it yields an intelligible point for more effective heuristics. If we start by considering the neighborhood $R_2(v)$, we can't know for certain which of the vertices is a co-chromatic vertex. However, if we were to select a vertex w from $R_2(v)$ which, of all the vertices of $R_2(v)$, has least number of separating vertices with v, we will have achieved on this step the most accessible decrease in the number of edges. This algorithm we call the second heuristic. More precisely, the algorithm works as follows. Suppose we are given some order of the vertices of a graph. We consider the succeeding vertex, and in its second-order neighborhood find a vertex w with maximal number of separating vertices. We link u and w together, and consider the resulting vertex to be the next vertex. We continue in this vein until a succeeding vertex is a star, and then switch over to the sequentially next vertex which is not a star, and so on.

Figure 3.18 illustrates the case in which the second heuristic (Figure 3.18(c)) turns out to be more effective than the first one (Figure 3.18(b)) and in Figure 3.19 we illustrate the case in which a vertex selected in accordance with the second heuristic is not a co-chromatic vertex.

In the second heuristic we established the succeeding vertex and found a possible mate for a gluing that resulted in the maximal number of separating vertices. We may improve the algorithm by introducing a third heuristic that does not impose a rigid order on the vertices in the graph. This heuristic

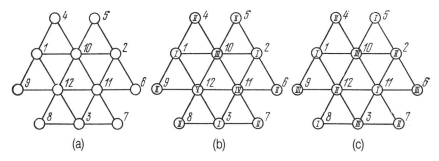

Figure 3.18. Successful application of the second heuristic: (a) graph; (b) first heuristic; (c) second heuristic.

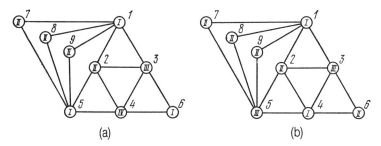

Figure 3.19. Unsuccessful application of the second heuristic: (a) second heuristic; (b) minimal coloring.

specifies that before each gluing we find a pair of vertices in the graph in which all pairs of vertices a distance 2 apart have the maximal number of separating vertices. The example of Figure 3.19 deprives us of any hope of obtaining a minimal coloring by means of this heuristic, though in general we are still confident it is more efficient than the first two heuristics. Of course, any possible improvement would require, in general, on the order of n^2 operations to accomplish the first gluing.

The author has analyzed a graph consisting of 50 vertices constructed on a computer entirely randomly except for the requirement that it be connected and contain 400 edges. In Figure 3.17 we have derived three descending trajectories of the number of edges in this graph obtained using the first, second, and third heuristics. They confirm our intuitive conception of the relative efficiencies of the three heuristics and of the proper "reserve capacity" of these algorithms by comparison with the estimate (2), which was derived for given n and p only in a rather special type of graph (precisely what kind of graph, that we leave for the reader to think about).

CHAPTER 4

Implementation

4.1. Introduction

In this chapter we will take one further step in our effort to impart a degree of rigor to our study and bring it to a conclusion. We will transform the algorithms defined over abstract objects found in the preceding chapter into fully executable procedures. Under our conditions, by the term, "fully executable," we will understand executable on a computer. That is, it must be possible to program the algorithms and to express them in an algorithmic language. We have already hinted in passing that this language will be ALGOL.

The first, and extremely important, stage in the programming process is to find appropriate representations for the abstract objects we have introduced previously for our problem (program schema, data graph, connectivity components of data flow graph, incompatibility graph, and the process of coloring an incompatibility graph). The choice of these representations is governed by two obvious constraints:

(1) the representations must be based on ALGOL objects (integers and real numbers, Boolean values, and all their possible compositions in an array);
(2) the representations must be "natural" for the particular abstract objects, in particular, it should be possible to "discern" the representations of the components of a compound object in the representation of this compound object.

Note that ALGOL (i.e., ALGOL 60) is rather impoverished in terms of the variety of its objects. In more recently devised languages, it is possible to select more natural representations for some of the abstract objects we are considering. Nevertheless, for our problem ALGOL 60 suffices for familiarizing us with one of the most universal methods of "arithmetization" of abstract objects, by which we understand the representation of abstract objects in the form of numbers and combinations of numbers.

Such an arithmetization of abstract objects is based on the assumption that all the sets we are considering are finite, moreover their cardinality is assumed known when we are working with them. In this case, all these sets are numbered, after which the ordinal number of a set is made the representation of an element of this set. That elements of the most highly varied sets are then represented by the same object (integer) as a result of this stipulation is nothing to be concerned about. It is assumed that at any moment a program is running, we know which number we are dealing with, i.e., the number of a variable magnitude, or the number of a statement, or the number of an argument. We will say "the element i" or "the ith element" whichever is more convenient, understanding in advance that we are speaking about the same thing in both cases.

The second universal rule specifies a method of representing sets that are subsets of some general denumerable set $M = \{m_1, \ldots, m_n\}$. In this symbolism, any $M' \subseteq M$ has the form $M' = \{m_{i_1}, m_{i_2}, \ldots, m_{i_k}\}$, where $k \geq 0$, $1 \leq i_k \leq n$. Then the representation may be in the form of a Boolean vector of length n in which each of the components with ordinal numbers $i_1, i_2, \ldots, i_k$ is equal to **true**, and all the other components are equal to **false**. In many problems, 1 and 0 are used in place of the logical values **true** and **false**. In the literature such vectors are sometimes called *Boolean scales*.

In certain instances, the representation of an element of a set must show what set a given representation is an element of. Suppose that these sets are $M_1, M_2, \ldots, M_k$. Then for these sets we form the numerical set $\{1, \ldots, k\}$, called the *index set*; its elements are called *indices*. An index is simply the ordinal number of one of the sets $M_1, \ldots, M_k$. Then the mth element of a set M_l is represented by the pair (l, m). A direct application of these rules of arithmetization will be demonstrated in the corresponding stages of programming.

We will demonstrate a programming technique, called "structured programming," that has become quite popular in recent years for program development. The term, "structured programming," is not the only term used. In the Russian literature alone, it is even possible to find the equivalents of such terms as "systematic programming," "stepwise programming," "top-down programming," and others that denote roughly one and the same method. We will explain the method of structured programming in the next section, and for now restrict ourselves to remarking on the kinds of programming difficulties this technique is designed to overcome.

In April 1975 The International Conference on Reliable Software was held in Los Angeles, California. One of the papers, by Harlan D. Mills, entitled "How to Write Correct Programs and Know It" (Sigplan Notices 10,363–371, 1975), set forth the essence of structured programming. To the sober-minded reader who is not all that familiar with routine programming, such a topic for a scientific report may seem quite naive and pretentious. However, this topic becomes quite understandable once one becomes more familiar with the programming process. To create a program, it is necessary to predict the behavior of a computer in every case in which the program might be used, whatever kind of input data may be encountered. If a programmer were to write a program consisting of, say, 1000 instructions that takes 1 minute to run on some computer (say the BESM-6), this means that in writing the text of this program (which occupies about 20 pages), he will have to conceive of and predict exactly the execution of 60,000,000 arithmetic and logical operations. And it cannot be said for any of these operations that "it doesn't matter what happens," in fact the programmer must specify the result of all these operations explicitly and unambiguously in advance.

Formally speaking, a program is a text consisting of letters, digits, and symbols. The process of writing a program may be thought of as a sequence of decisions, for example deciding which letter to write out, what sign to use, etc. Of course, a genuine attempt to write out a program as if it were simply a text consisting of, say, 10,000 characters, with the characters being written from left to right, letter after letter, each required character being selected for each spot from a set of several dozen possible characters, the entire process being repeated 10,000 times, may be considered only as an extreme, theoretical limit of a decision-making process. A programmer writes out a program by already starting out with some systematic knowledge about the problem he wishes to solve. However, there are many obstacles to overcome in the process of transmitting this knowledge to the computer. People acknowledged the difficulty of planning ahead long before the advent of computers; this difficulty has much in common with the combinatorial complexity of the problem of choosing between different alternatives alluded to in the preceding chapter. Such colloquial expressions as "Look before you leap," "Divide and conquer," "It looks good on paper, but it's another matter altogether when you get down to the nitty-gritty" have a host of purely programming interpretations.

Thus, the search for a better programming methodology is being directed increasingly towards making the programming process as goal-directed as possible, eliminating any sort of continuity in the process and creating logical interludes in the process of writing a program where the programmer can "stop and look around," separate global information from the "localized" details, and try to reduce the chance of typing mistakes or structural errors. The development of such purely linguistic tools as algorithmic languages and flow charts is only one element in the search for improved methods of programming.

We will not delve any deeper into these general lines of reasoning. Instead, in order to describe storage packing programs, we will briefly consider one such method.

4.2. Structured Programming

Towards the end of 1975 there appeared in bookstores in the Soviet Union (and very rapidly disappeared) the Russian translation of a book by O.-J. Dahl, E.W. Dijkstra, and C.A.R. Hoare, entitled *Structured Programming*. The book contained a fundamental article by E. Dijkstra, "Notes on Structured Programming." Dijkstra is generally acknowledged to be the computer scientist who has made the greatest contribution to the development and general acceptance of structured programming, though a similar technique had been developed by other writers (under different names, however) and its mathematical foundations in the algebra of recursive functions had been known for some time previously, without, however, having been used in practical applications. We will assume that any programmer must have studied this outstanding paper, and so will not bother repeating fundamentals. Instead we will describe (simplifying somewhat) the technique of structured programming with regard to ALGOL constructions.

The focus of *structured programming* is the "module," which is a program composed by a single programmer. Before he even begins a programmer possesses knowledge (to some extent, exhaustive knowledge) about the problem he wishes to solve, so that his task reduces to simply figuring out how to translate this knowledge into an ALGOL language construct. In particular, his knowledge suffices for defining in a rigorous manner the objects (input data and final results) that are needed to state the problem in the form of ALGOL declarations. A problem is programmed either in the form of a procedure (in which case its objects are the formal parameters of this procedure) or as a block (or compound statement), in which case its objects are global variables whose descriptions are in effect within this block. We will also assume that a problem has assigned to it some symbolic name (designator) that reveals its content to some extent.

In structured programming the solution of a *given* problem is always performed in a single step, the execution of which involves the selection of one of several alternatives. If a problem is so stated that it may be solved through the application of a single primitive statement of ALGOL 60 (assignment or procedure statement), the step consists in writing an object program, i.e., in correlating with the designator assigned to the problem the statement that executes it. In the opposite case, the step consists in a structurization of the problem, i.e., a one-time partitioning of the problem into a (small) number of other, simpler problems. It is assumed that because the programmer has complete knowledge about the problem, he is able to correctly decide at this step how to structure his problem, via concatenation, alternation (in logic, called exclusive disjunction), or iteration.

By *concatenation* we understand that a problem constitutes a successive solution of two other problems X1 and then X2. These two problems form a compound statement or block if problem X1 processes some new information that is then interpreted by problem X2. In this case, problem X1 is preceded by a declaration part in which the new variables localized in the given block are described. The programmer will think up some sort of reorganization that replaces summary knowledge about the initial problem by "segmental knowledge" about problems X1 and X2 (see Figure 4.1). The objects of the initial problem then become, either completely or in part, the global objects of problems X1 and X2. In selecting the names for local variables that relate X1

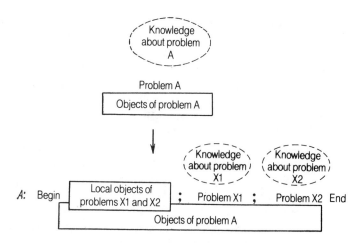

Figure 4.1. Concatenation.

and X2, The programmer has to be certain that these names do not conflict with the names of any of the global variables.

By *alternation* we understand that a problem constitutes a process of checking some condition *R* and, depending upon its truth or falsity, executing problem X1 or problem X2, respectively. Thus, condition *R* together with problems X1 and X2 forms an ALGOL conditional statement (see Figure 4.2). No local variables then arise in this type of structurization. Problem X2 may be absent, in which case we have the construction of an **if** clause lacking an **else** clause.

By *iteration* we understand that a problem constitutes a loop with respect to some parameter *i* with repeat condition *R* (which may be either a **while** type

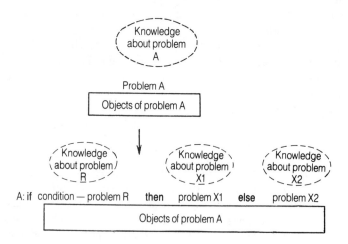

Figure 4.2. Alternation.

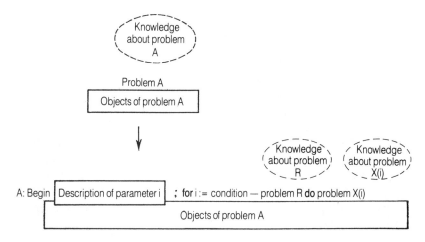

Figure 4.3. Iteration.

condition or the header of an incremental type of loop) in which the problem X(i), which forms the body of the **do** operator, is executed repeatedly (Figure 4.3).

The rules of structured programming are thus quite simple. Their overall intent is to keep the programmer from taking too great a leap in his program, and because of structural constraints complex data relations and overly complicated control transfers cannot appear. (Clearly, in such an approach there are, in general, no "goto" transfers.) No less important is the constant "reshuffling" and "filtering" of the programmer's knowledge about the initial problem as it is transformed into new subproblems. Incidentally, this associated work of the mind entails strenuous effort on the part of the programmer. Structurization does not make the programming process any simpler, indeed it may even make it more laborious. However, because of its systematic and demanding nature, it compensates by producing greater certitude in the results, which are now also easier to check.

As a preliminary illustration of structured programming, consider the process of constructing a program for what is perhaps the most traditional type of algorithm—an algorithm to find the greatest common divisor of two positive integers. Our presention of this problem will be somewhat dramatic, in that we shall emphasize the broad range of mental efforts the programmer must undertake, from an overall conception of the algorithm to careful reasoning about the method of interchanging two values. Moreover, we will introduce and elucidate a definite style of writing out a program which we will subsequently adhere to.

In the programming process, a program is written out in the form of paragraphs. Each paragraph describes a single act of structurization of the program and begins with the symbolic name of the structured problem. If a method of structurization of the problem is self-evident and does not require any explanation, the corresponding structure (concatenation, alternation, iteration) is written right after the name of the problem, separated from it by a colon. If the name of a problem is thought of as a label, and if braces are used to abbreviate the key words **begin** and **end**, the structural formula becomes an ALGOL construct. The only difference is that we allow the use of abbreviations of keywords (e.g., **int** for **integer**).

The structural formulas are numbered for reference. The number within oblique lines right after the name of the structured problem is the function reference to the formula where this problem is a subproblem. Conversely, the number within oblique lines right after the name of a subproblem just presented is the function reference to the structural formula that structurizes the given subproblem. These references are inserted only if the formula that introduces the subproblem and the formula that structurizes it do not succeed one another.

In the general case, a structural formula is preceded by some relevant discussion that reflects our knowledge about the problem. So as not to overly encumber the presentation, we will try to the brief, supposing that the fundamentals of our knowledge are supported by the preceding chapter. The central goal of the discussion is to make our choice of the structural formula for a given problem an obvious one. The discussion itself begins with the word **Comment** followed by the name of the problem, itself followed by a reference to the formula (within oblique lines) where the problem occurs as well as a list of the global variables that are used as the actual variables in solving the problem. A comment ends with ■.

In simple cases, we will sometimes combine several structurizations into a single formula so as to make our presentation resemble the writing of object programs.

FINDING THE GREATEST COMMON DIVISOR

Comment   Suppose that x and y are designated natural numbers and let z be their greatest common divisor. We construct the program as a description of a GCD procedure that has x, y, and z as its formal parameters ■.

(1) **proc**   GCD (x, y, z); **var** x, y; **int** x, y, z; BODY GCD

Comment   BODY GCD $/x, y, z/$. The problem is solved by reducing it to a simpler problem. Suppose that RES (A, B) is the residue from the integral division of A by B. If we know that RES $(A, B) = 0$, we then have $z = x$. But if x does not divide y, then, as is well known, GCD $(x, y) = $ GCD (RES $(y, x), x)$. By virtue of this relation, we are able to reduce the numbers we are considering until the residue is equal to zero. The problem is thereby divided into a sequence of two problems: reduction and extraction of an answer from the variable x. A procedure for finding the residue is used in this case. ■

(2)   BODY GCD: {int proc RES (A, B); var A, B; int A, B; BODY RES;
        REDUCTION $/4/$; $z := x$}

Comment   BODY RES $/A, B/$ consists of a single assignment statement that
                uses integral division. ∎

(3)   BODY RES: RES: $= A - (A/B) * B$

Comment   REDUCTION $/x, y/$. Obviously, the reduction is iterative. At
                each step, x and y are replaced by RES (y, x) and x, respectively;
                the iteration is controlled by the value of the variable $u =$
                RES (x, y). ∎

(4)   REDUCTION {int u; for $u := $ RES (y, x) while $u \neq 0$ do REPLACE}

(5)   REPLACE: {$y := x$; $x := u$}

To create a program from the structural formulas, we must undertake
systematic substitutions of the structural formula for the problem into
another structural formula in which a reference is made to this problem (as a
subproblem). Names for problems that remain are not needed in the program
as labels and may be discarded, since a structured program does not contain
any **goto** operators. It may nevertheless be useful to retain some of the labels in
the resulting program so as to retain meaningful reference points in the
program. Below we give the resulting program for finding a greatest common
divisor.

```
proc GCD (x, y, z); var x, y; int x, y, z;
                    begin int proc RES (A, B); var A, B; int A, B;
                    RES := A − (A ÷ B) * B;
                    REDUCTION: begin int u;
                    for u := RES (x, y) while u ≠ 0 do
                    begin y := x; x := u end
                    end;
                    ASSIGN z := x
                    end
```

4.3 General Organization of the Storage Packing Process

The entire text of the present chapter so far presented may very well recall the
illustrative example just presented. Perhaps it is not so difficult to read these
sections, though rather tedious. The reading would be a lot slower, though far
more interesting, if the reader were to attempt to structurize the storage
packing program on his own using the text of the present chapter as reference.
In that case, he would be competing with the author (of course, assuming he
has complete knowledge of the preceding chapters and some skill in ALGOL)
at nearly equal levels, since this chapter was the author's very first exercise in

structured programming, and the program itself is presented precisely in the form in which it was obtained (naturally, exclusive of the lines that had to be rewritten due to mistakes).

STORAGE PACKING IN A PROGRAM SCHEMA

comment   We begin by giving a rigorous definition of what is meant by the objects of the problem. In accordance with what we said in the introduction to the chapter, we will represent elementary abstract objects, chiefly natural numbers and sets of natural numbers, by segments of the series of natural numbers, and subsets by Boolean scales. To specify a set of statements, we need only designate **int** n as the number of statements. The control flow graph will be represented by the adjacency matrix **int array** $C[1:n, 1:n]$ in which $C[i, j]$ is equal to 1 if the jth statement is the successor of the ith statement, and 0 otherwise. Such a representation is useful for constructing transitive closures, since the ith row of C is the set of successors of statement i, while the jth column is the set of predecessors of statement j. The set of arguments and results together forms the set of poles. Since we will have to work in general with both poles and, in particular, with arguments and results, it will be useful for us to think of the set of poles as a segment of the series of natural numbers from 1 to $(p+q)$, where **int** p is the number of arguments, and **int** q the number of results. In this case, the ith result is represented by the number $(p+i)$. The allocation of poles may then be represented in a natural way by the vector **int array** $V[1:p+q]$, where $V[j]$ is the statement associated with the jth pole. The vector **int array** $L[1:p+q]$ specifies a storage allocation if $L[i]$ is understood as a variable allocated to the ith pole. Let us find **int array** $L1[1:p+q]$ for the program schema thus defined, which is a new, possibly minimal storage allocation. The program for storage packing in a program schema [SPPS] is constructed in the form of a description of an SPPS procedure with the formal parameters just enumerated.

(1)   **proc** SPPS $(n, C, p, q, V, L, L1)$; **var** n, C, p, q, V, L;
      int n, p, q;
      int array $C, V, L, L1$; BODY SPPS

comment   BODY SPPS $/n, C, p, q, V, L, L1/$. The key step in the storage packing process is the construction of the data flow graph, more precisely, the construction of the liveness domains of the graph. In fact, the result of the construction of the liveness domains are **int** l, the number of domains, and the canonical storage allocation **int array** $LK[1:p+q]$ in which variable i is associated with all the poles allocated to the ith domain. Storage packing is realized via the canonical allocation. ∎

(2) BODY SPPS: {**int** *l*; **int array** $LK[1:p+q]$; CANONICAL ALLO-CATION /7/; STORAGE PACKING}

comment STORAGE PACKING/*n*, *C*, *p*, *q*, *V*, *l*, *LK*, *L1*/. We wish to first structurize our program by distinguishing large segments that, in turn, form the content of the sections of the present chapter. STORAGE PACKING may be divided quite naturally into the creation of the incompatibility graph, followed by coloring of the graph: this also yields the desired storage allocation. We specify the incompatibility graph by its adjacency matrix **int array** $U[1:l, 1:l]$, in which $U[i, j] = 1$ if the *i*th and *j*th domains are incompatible, and $U[i, j] = 0$ otherwise. (This resembles the way in which a control flow graph is specified.) Obviously, *U* is a symmetric matrix. ■

(3) STORAGE PACKING: {**int array** $U[1:l, 1:l]$; CREATE INCOMPATIBILITY GRAPH /49/; COLORING AND FINAL ALLOCATION}

comment COLORING AND FINAL ALLOCATION /*p*, *q*, *l*, *LK*, *U*, *L1*/. The structurization of the problem is suggested by its name. It is simplest to represent the coloring of the vertices of *U* by taking into account the examples of mappings presented above; a coloring may then be represented by the vector **int array** $Q[1, l]$, where $Q[i]$ is the color correlated with the *i*th vertex of the incompatibility graph. It is assumed that the actual set of colors is represented, as before, by a segment of the series of natural numbers. ■

(4) COLORING AND FINAL ALLOCATION: {**int array** $Q[1:l]$; COLORING /75/; FINAL ALLOCATION}

comment FINAL ALLOCATION /*p*, *q*, *LK*, *Q*, *L1*/. We now bring to a close the concluding part of the program so that we may next turn our attention to the principal subproblems. To create a minimal final storage allocation, for each pole we have to find a color that may be correlated with its liveness domain, and then correlate this color with the pole itself. ■

(5) FINAL ALLOCATION: {**int** *j*; **for** *j*:= 1 **step** 1 **until** $p+q$ **do** ASSIGN ITS OWN COLOR TO *j*th POLE

comment ASSIGN ITS OWN COLOR TO *j*th POLE /*j*, *LK*, *Q*, *L1*/. We must determine the value of $L1[j]$. $LK[j]$ gives us the number of the domain with which the *j*th pole is associated. Since $Q[i]$ is the color correlated with the *i*th domain, the desired color is equal to $Q[LK[j]]$. ■

(6)   ASSIGN ITS OWN COLOR TO jth POLE: $L1[j] := Q[LK[j]]$

Thus we have found the three principal subproblems with which we shall be concerned in what follows. These are:

CANONICAL ALLOCATION

CREATE AN INCOMPATIBILITY GRAPH

COLORING

4.4 Canonical Storage Allocation

comment   CANONICAL ALLOCATION $/(2)$ $n, C, p, q, V, L, l, LK/$ begins by assuming that, in accordance with Section 3.1, each pole belongs to a connectivity component "of its own" in the data flow graph. In other words, there occurs a maximal ungluing of the storage allocation that specifies the initial value of the vector LK. The direct construction of the liveness domains then follows. ■

(7)   CANONICAL ALLOCATION: {UNGLUE THE POLES; CONSTRUCT LIVENESS DOMAINS $/9/$}

comment   UNGLUE THE POLES $/P, Q, LK/$ is performed in an obvious way by means of an iterated allocation of variable i to the ith pole $(i = 1, \ldots, p+q)$

(8)   UNGLUE THE POLES: {**int** i; **for** $i := 1$ **step** 1 **until** $p+q$ **do** $LK[i] := i$}

comment   CONSTRUCT LIVENESS DOMAINS $/(7)$ $n, C, p, q, V, L, l, LK/$. In addition to constructing the canonical storage allocation LK, it is also necessary to compute the number of liveness domains l. ■

(9)   CONSTRUCT LIVENESS DOMAINS: {FIND $LK/11/$; COMPUTE NUMBER OF DOMAINS}

comment   COMPUTE NUMBER OF DOMAINS$/LK, l/$. By the rule for merging current liveness domains together, we always leave in the schema a variable with lesser ordinal number. In this way we are able to determine the number of domains by taking the maximal element of the vector LK. ■

(10)   COMPUTE NUMBER OF DOMAINS: {$l := 0$; {**int** i; **for** $i := 1$ **step** 1 **until** $p+q$ **do if** $LK[i] > 1$ **then** $1 := LK[i]$}}

comment   FIND $LK/(9)$ $n, C, p, q, V, L, LK/$. By Section 3.1, for each result of the schema, this is performed by means of an iterated construction of the restricted transitive image of a statement. In the course of constructing the image, the current connectivity components are merged whenever necessary. ■

(11)   FIND *LK*: {**int** *I*; **for** *i* := 1 **step** 1 to *q* **until** TRANSAM OF FIRST RESULT}

comment   TRANSAM OF FIRST RESULT /*n, C, p, q, V, L, LK, i*/. The construction of a restricted transitive image requires some preparatory effort prior to execution of the basic iteration loop for traversing the arcs of the graph. We have to specify the initial values of the start and augmented sets *S* and *T* and also construct the restricting set *R*. To merge current liveness domains together, it is necessary to establish points where we reach statements that read the variable correlated to the *i*th result in the routine course of operation. These statements form the "argument" set A. We represent all these sets in the form of Boolean scales of length *n*. That these sets must be introduced is self-evident; this is little more than a superficial observation.

The next step in the structurization of the problem, however, gives us useful information that helps in understanding why correct structurization and timely introduction of new objects requires truly exhaustive knowledge of the problem and a well-defined representation of how to proceed in the inner layers of the program.

In that case, we are concerned with the mechanism by which current connectivity components are merged once we end up at a statement from the argument set A in the process of constructing the transitive closure. Once we find that there is some statement *j* in *T* that belongs to *A*, we must find the argument of this statement with which the variable $L[p+i]$ is associated and combine the current connectivity component of this argument with the connectivity component of the *i*th result. Recall (Section 2.2) that in the general case a statement may have several such arguments, though such cases will be quite rare in an initial schema. Since $L[p+i]$ and the statement *j* that reads in $L[i]$ are given, the search for the arguments, i.e., for *k* such that $V[k]=j$ and $L[k]=L[p+i]$, may be performed by scanning the argument segment of the vector *L*. If distinct variables are always allocated to the arguments of each statement, the argument set *A* could then have a second vector **int array** $a[1:n]$ in which $a[i]$ would be equal to the argument *k* of *j* such that $L[k]=L[p+i]$. Such a vector could be constructed in the preparatory stage. This is a tempting proposition, especially as such situations are encountered quite often. Nevertheless, we cannot overlook the general case in which a statement may have an arbitrary number (as many as *p*) of arguments all with the same variable. However, by means of some algebra, we may combine the utility of creating a list of arguments *a* with the generality of an algorithm. For this purpose, we distinguish in *A* statements in which $L[p+i]$ is interpreted once versus statements in which it is interpreted more than once. The point is to prevent 1's from being inserted into the necessary component of A when assigning a statement to the argument set, and instead to add them. This is done as many times as $L[p+i]$ is associated to the arguments of this statement. If a statement reads a variable more than once, for the sake of definiteness the argument with least ordinal number is placed in a. The other arguments will be in L, which will be indicated by the value of a criterion that specifies the membership of a statement to A (it will equal not 1, but some larger number). ∎

(12)   TRANSAM OF FIRST RESULT: {**int array** $S, T, R, A, a[1:n]$; PRE-PARATION; MOVEMENT ALONG ARCS /22/}

comment   PREPARATION /$n, p, q, V, L, i, S, T, R, A, a$/. Let us think a bit about the methods of specifying the sets S, T, R, A, and a. The set S contains the single vector $V[p+i]$. The set T is empty. The sets R and A are special types of "level lines," i.e., sets of statements correlated to their own variable $L[p+i]$ in the allocation of the poles. Let us imagine how they might be obtained. In traversing L we might recognize the desired variable $L[p+i]$ from among its components and, using the ordinal number of component j, extract the desired statement $V[j]$, labeling with 1 the component in R numbered $V[j]$ and adding 1 to the analogous component of A. The other components of A and R must be 0. Thus before undertaking the proper creation of S, R, A, and a, we must annihilate all of them (naturally, T as well.) ∎

(13)   PREPARATION: {INITIALIZE; COMPLETE /15/}

(14)   INITIALIZE: {**int** j; **for** $j := 1$ **step** 1 **until** n **do** $T[j] := S[j] := R[j] := A[j] := a[j] := 0$}

(15)   COMPLETE /13/: {$S[V[i+p]] := 1$; COMPLETE REMAINDER}

(16)   COMPLETE REMAINDER: COMPLETE R; COMPLETE A /19/

comment   COMPLETE R /n, p, q, V, L, i, R/. In accordance with (13), we traverse L (more precisely, the part of L associated with the results: $L[p+1:p+q]$), and using V, find the desired statement. ∎

(17)   COMPLETE R: {**int** j; **for** $j := 1$ **step** 1 **until** q **do** TEST NEXT RESULT

(18)   TEST NEXT RESULT **if** $L[p+j] = L[p+i]$ **then** $R[V[p+j]] := 1$

comment   COMPLETE A /(16) n, p, V, L, i, A, a/. This step is in analogy with the completion of R, except for the fact that the argument segment of L is traversed and the set of argument poles a is also completed by the method indicated in (12). ∎

(19) COMPLETE A: {**int** j; **for** $j := 1$ **step** 1 **until** p **do if** $L[j] = L[p+i]$ **then** LOAD COMPONENT}

comment LOAD COMPONENT $/V, A, a, j/$. This may be done in various ways, depending on whether or not the desired argument is found the first time. If $V[j]$ is already in A, the multiplicity of the argument is increased by 1. But if $V[j]$ is still not in A, not only is it not labeled in it, but the corresponding argument is assigned to a. ■

(20) LOAD COMPONENT: **if** $A[V[j]] = 0$ **then** ASSIGN TO A **else** $A[V[j]] := A[V[j]] + 1$.

(21) ASSIGN TO A: $\{a[V[j]] := j;\ A[V[j]] := 1\}$

comment TRAVERSE ARCS $/(12)\ n, C, LK, i, S, T, R, A/$. In accordance with the rules for the construction of a transitive closure (Section 3.1), we traverse the arcs once the start set is nonempty. We formulate as a logical procedure function the condition that a set represented by a Boolean scale of some length is nonempty, since we will be encountering such tests repeatedly. After the entire program has been constructed, we determine an appropriate level of localization of this procedure to make its description accessible to all calls. ■

(22) TRAVERSE ARCS: {**int** j; $j := 0$; **for** $j := j+1$ **while** NONEMPTY (S, n) **do** MOVE AND MATCH $/28/$}

comment NONEMPTY $/S, n/$. Within the framework of structured programming, the search for the first nonzero component in a Boolean scale requires some algebra as there are no labels (a property of structured programming). For this purpose, movement along the scale is programmed in a loop, and we introduce into the procedure a local variable that stores the fact that a nonzero component has been found. Once we exit from the loop, we determine the result of the procedure as a function of the value of the variable. ■

(23) **boolean proc** NONEMPTY (A, m); **var** m; **int** m; **int array** $A[1:m]$; BODY NONEMPTY

(24) BODY NONEMPTY $/A, m/$; {**boolean** p; $p :=$ **true**; TEST}

(25) TEST: {SCAN A; CHECK P $/27/$}

(26) SCAN A: {**int** i; $i := 0$; **for** i $:= i+1$ **while** $i \leqslant n$ & p **do** $p := A[i] = 0$}

(27) CHECK P $/25/$: NONEMPTY $:= \neg p$

comment MOVE AND MATCH $/(22)\ n, C, LK, i, S, T, R, A/$. Recall the algorithm for constructing the liveness domains given in Section

3.1. Let us analyze in more detail the induction step. From the start set S we find $\Gamma(s)$, which in our representation is a logical sum $(1 \vee 1 = 0 \vee 1 = 1 \vee 0 = 1; 0 \vee 0 = 0)$ of all the rows of matrix C with ordinal number corresponding to the nonzero components of S. To build up $\Gamma(S)$ we require the local vector **int array** $\Gamma[1:n]$ with which the initial empty variable is specified. Once Γ has been created, we add it to the augmented set T and routinely check whether the next element of Γ is in the argument set A. If so, it is then necessary to check (using LK) whether the ith result and corresponding argument of the statement from A belong to the same current component, and merge them together if this is not so. In this loop, in which we traverse Γ, we may extract from it elements of the next start set. That is, an element of Γ is in the next S only if it is not in the preceding T and does not process $L[p+i]$, i.e., is not in R. ∎

(28)   MOVE AND MATCH: $\{$**int array** $\Gamma[1:n]$; FIND ΓS; USE ΓS /35/$\}$

(29)   FIND ΓS /n, C, S, Γ/: $\{$CREATE ΓS; SUM ΓS /31/$\}$

(30)   CREATE ΓS: $\{$**int** i; **for** $i := 1$ **step** 1 **until** n **do** $\Gamma[i] := 0\}$

(31)   SUM ΓS /(29) n, C, S, Γ/: $\{$**int** i; **for** $i := 1$ **step** 1 **until** n **do** TEST $SI\}$

(32)   TEST SI: **if** $S[i] \neq 0$ **then** ADD CI

(33)   ADD CI /n, C, Γ, i/: $\{$**int** j; **for** $j := 1$ **step** 1 **until** n **do** ADD $CIJ\}$

(34)   ADD CIJ: **if** $C[i,j] = 1$ **then** $\Gamma[j] := 1$

comment   USE ΓS /(28) n, LK, i, S, T, R, A/. This is basically the loop for the next application of elements of the start set. ∎

(35)   USE ΓS: $\{$**int** j; **for** $j := 1$ **step** 1 **until** n **do** PROCESS NEXT ELEMENT$\}$

(36)   PROCESS NEXT ELEMENT: $\{$COMPUTE START SET; ADD TO AUGMENTED SET /38/$\}$

comment   COMPUTE START SET /n, S, T, R, Γ, j/. By Section 3.1, a statement does not occur in S if it does not occur in Γ. But if a statement occurs in Γ, *then* we exclude the case in which it belongs to T or R. ∎

(37)   COMPUTE START SET: **if** $\Gamma[j] = 0$ **then** $S[j] := 0$ **else if** $T[j] \neq 0 \vee R[j] \neq 0$ **then** $S[j] := 0$ **else** $S[j] := 1$

comment   ADD TO AUGMENTED SET /(36), $n, p, V, L, i, T, A, a, j$/. This depends mainly on whether or not statement j occurs in Γ. ∎

(38)   ADD TO AUGMENTED SET: **if** $\Gamma[j] \neq 0$ **then** PROCESS ELEMENT IN Γ

(39)   PROCESS ELEMENT IN Γ: $\{T[j]:= 1;$ POSSIBLE MATCH$\}$

comment   POSSIBLE MATCH $/n, p, V, L, i, T, A, a, j/$. This step begins by testing whether j belongs to the argument set. ■

(40)   POSSIBLE MATCH: **if** $A[j] \neq 0$ **then** MATCH

comment   MATCH $/p, V, L, i, A, a, j/$. By what was said in (12), MATCH is performed in two ways, for the first argument of j and then for any other arguments. The first argument is extracted from the set of argument poles a, and the others, if they exist, are found in the argument segment of L. This means that the process of merging the current connectivity components of the ith result and the argument just found will occur at two points in the program. For this reason, it is best to program the merge as a procedure with two formal parameters, the result r and the argument a. ■

(41)   MATCH: $\{$**proc** MERGE (r, a); **var** r, a; **int** r, a; BODY OF MERGE; FIRST ARGUMENT $/46/$; OTHER ARGUMENTS $/47/\}$

comment   BODY OF MERGE $/p, q, LK, r, a/$. If r and a belong to the same component, i.e., if $LK[p+r] = LK[a]$, then LK remains unchanged. In the opposite case, the variables are identified: all occurrences of MAX $(LK[p+r], LK[a])$ in LK are replaced by MIN $(LK[p+r], LK[a])$. ■

(42)   BODY OF MERGE: $\{$**if** $LK[p+r] \neq LK[a]$ **then** EQUATE$\}$

(43)   EQUATE: $\{$**int** min, max; FIND MIN MAX; REPLACE MAX BY MIN$\}$

(44)   FIND MIN MAX: **if** $LK[p+r] < LK[a]\}$ **then** $\{$min$:= LK[p+r];$ max$:= LK[a]\}$ **else** $\{$min$:= LK[a];$ max$:= LK[p+r]\}$

(45)   REPLACE MAX BY MIN: $\{$**int** $i;$ **for** $i:= 1$ **step** 1 **until** $p+q$ **do if** $LK[i] = $ max **then** $LK[i]:= $ min$\}$

(46)   FIRST ARGUMENT $/41/$: MERGE $(a[j], i)$

(47)   REMAINING ARGUMENTS $/41/$; **if** $A[j] > 1$ **then** SCAN ARGUMENTS

comment   SCAN ARGUMENTS $/p, V, L, i, A, a, j/$ consists in a sequential scanning of the argument segment of the set of poles. Since $a[j]$ stores the first required argument, it is natural to begin the scanning with the ordinal number $a[j] + 1$. Once an argument has been found such that $L[k] = L[p+i]$, we then further check whether it is associated with the given statement j. In this case k together with i is transmitted to the merge procedure so as to merge their current connectivity components together. ■

(48)   SCAN ARGUMENTS: $\{$**int** k; **for** $k := a[j] + 1$ **step** 1 **until** p **do if** $L[k]$ $= L[p+i]$ & $V[k] = j$ **then** MERGE $(k, i)\}$

4.5. Creating the Incompatibility Graph

Comment   CREATING   THE   INCOMPATIBILITY   GRAPH/ (3) n, C, p, q, V, l, LK, U /. By Section 3.2, the final stage in the direct definition of incompatibility of two liveness domains d and d' involves the sets $R(d)$, $R(d')$, $T(d)$, and $T(d')$, where $R(d)$ is the set of statements that process the variable x and are correlated to d, and $T(d)$ is the set of internal statements of all the routes of all the data pairs realized by x (recall that now we are dealing with a cannonical storage allocation). In turn, $T(d)$ is obtained from the intersection of the two sets $E(d)$ and $L(d)$, where $E(d)$ is the transitive image of $R(d)$, indeed bounded by it, and $L(d)$ is the transitive pre-image of the set $A(d)$ of statements that read in x, which here is strongly restricted by $R(d)$.

Recall that we enumerated the basic intrinsic objects that arise in the construction of the incompatibility graph all together. Since the incompatibility relation must be computed pairwise for all variables (of course, taking symmetry into account), we must first have R and T for all l variables before computing U. Since each set is a scale of length n, we arrive at a description of these sets in the form of matrices **int array** R, $T[1:l, 1:n]$, and also obtain a natural structurization of the problem. ■

(49)   CREATE INCOMPATIBILITY GRAPH: $\{$**int array** $R, T[1:l, 1:n]$; COMPUTE R and T /55/; COMPUTE $U \}$

Comment   COMPUTE $U/n, l, U, R, T/$ by analogy with the computation of the sum of three products of a matrix: $U = R' * R + R' * T + T' * R$; here the prime denotes the transpose. Recall that the element $[i,j]$ of a matrix that is the product of two matrices A and B is equal to the scalar product of the ith row of A by the jth column of B, i.e., the sum of the paired products of their components. Since we must compute the sum of three products, in the summation loop we may at once add together three pairwise products of the components of the necessary combinations of rows and columns of R and T. Finally, though we need the matrix U, which consists of 0's and 1's, we may replace Boolean products and sums by arithmetic products and sums, normalizing the subsequently computed element of U by replacing any nonzero value of the element by 1. To this we might recall that we will in fact compute only the "upper triangle" of U, assigning the computed element of U to both entries $[i,j]$ and $[j,i]$ and setting the diagonal elements equal to 0 without performing computations. ■

(50) COMPUTE U: {DIAGONAL ELEMENTS; OTHER ELEMENTS /52/}

(51) DIAGONAL ELEMENTS: {**int** i; **for** $i := 1$ **step** 1 **until** l **do** $U[i, i]$ $:= 0$}

(52) OTHER ELEMENTS: {**int** i; **for** $i := 1$ **step** 1 **until** $l - 1$ **do** {**int** j; **for** $j := i + 1$ **step** 1 **until** l **do** COMPUTE AND SUBSTITUTE}}

(53) COMPUTE AND SUBSTITUTE: {**int** u; COMPUTE ELEMENT; $U[i,j] := U[j,i] := $ **if** $u = 0$ **then** 0 **else** 1}

(54) COMPUTE ELEMENT: {$u := 0$; {**int** k; **for** $k := 1$ **step** 1 **until** n **do** $u := u + R[i,k] * R[j,k] + R[i,k] * T[j,k] + T[i,k] * R[j,k]$}}

Comment   COMPUTE R AND T /(49) $n, C, p, q, V, l, LK, R, T$/. This computation will be performed in turn for all the variables of the canonical storage allocation. ∎

(55) COMPUTE R AND T: {**int** i; **for** $i := 1$ **step** 1 **until** l **do** PROCESS NEXT DOMAIN}

Comment   PROCESS NEXT DOMAIN /$n, C, p, q, V, LK, R, T, i$/. Following the comment appended to (49), $R(d)$ is created before $T(d)$. ∎

(56) PROCESS NEXT DOMAIN: {CREATE R; CREATE T /60/}

Comment   CREATE R /n, p, q, V, LK, R, i/ constitutes a scanning of the result segment of the storage allocation LK. Once the variable i has been found at the $(p+j)$th place, 1 is transmitted to the $V[p +j]$th component of the ith row of R. Before undertaking the scanning, the ith row is "annihilated." ∎

(57) CREATE R: {ANNIHILATE; SCAN RESULTS /59/}

(58) ANNIHILATE /n, R, i/: {**int** j; **for** $j := 1$ **step** 1 **until** n **do** $R[i,j] := 0$}

(59) SCAN RESULTS /(57) p, q, V, LK, R, i/: {**int** j; **for** $j := 1$ **step** 1 **until** q **do** **if** $LK [p+j] = i$ **then** $R[i, V[p+j]] := 1$}

Comment   CREATE T /(56) n, C, p, V, LK, R, T, i/. This requires the computation of the sets E and L, which in their intersection yield T. ∎

(60) CREATE T: {**int array** $E, L[1:n]$; COMPUTE E AND L /62/; INTERSECTION}

(61) INTERSECTION /n, T, i, E, L/: {**int** j; **for** $j := 1$ **step** 1 **until** n **do** $T[i,j] := E[j] * L[j]$}

(62) COMPUTE E AND L /60/: {COMPUTE E; COMPUTE L /69/}

Comment   COMPUTE E /n, C, R, i, E/ becomes a standard problem in finding a restricted transitive image. We need only introduce the start set S with its initial value equal to R and specify the initial empty value of the augmented set E. ∎

(63)   COMPUTE E: {**int array** $S[1:n]$; INITIALIZE; MOVE ALONG ARCS/65/}

(64)   INITIALIZE $/n, R, i, S, E/$: {**int** j; **for** $j := 1$ **step** 1 **until** n **do** {$S[j]$ $:= R[i,j]$; $E[j] := 0$}}

Comment   MOVE ALONG ARCS $/(63)$ $n, c, R, i, E, S/$ by analogy to step (22) in the construction of a canonical storage allocotion. ■

(65)   MOVE ALONG ARCS: {**int** j; $j := 0$; **for** $j := j + 1$ **while** NONEMPTY (S, n) **do** MOVE}

(66)   MOVE $/n, C, R, i, E, S/$: {**int array** $\Gamma[1:n]$; FIND Γ; USE Γ /68/}

Comment   FIND Γ $/n, C, S, \Gamma/$. To illustrate the principle of economy of thought, we rewrite formulas (29)–(34), which solve this problem, in condensed form. ■

(67)   FIND Γ: {{**int** i; **for** $i := 1$ **step** 1 **until** n **do** $\Gamma[i] := 0$}; {**int** i; **for** $i := 1$ **step** 1 **until** n **do if** $S[i] \neq 0$ **then** {{**int** j; **for** $j := 1$ **step** 1 **until** n **do if** $C[i,j]$ $= 1$ **then** $\Gamma[j] := 1$}}}

Comment   USE Γ $/(66)$ n, R, i, E, S, $\Gamma/$. This step is performed by analogy to (35)–(39), except for the fact that there is no match. ■

(68)   USE Γ: {**int** j; **for** $j := 1$ **step** 1 **until** n **do** {COMPUTE START SET: if $\Gamma[j] = 0$ **then** $S[j] := 0$ **else if** $E[j] \neq 0 \lor R[i,j] \neq 0$ **then** $S[j] := 0$ **else** $S[j] := 1$; ADD TO AUGMENTED SET: **if** $\Gamma[j] \neq 0$ **then** $E[j]$ $:= 1$}}

Comment   COMPUTE L $/(62)$ $n, C, p, V, LK, R, i, L/$ constitutes the problem of calculating a strongly restricted transitive pre-image. We let the set A of arguments with which the variable i is associated in LK be the initial value of the start set. The initial value of the augmented set L is empty. The ith row of R is a strongly restricting set. ■

(69)   COMPUTE L: {**int array** $A[1:n]$; {{**int** i; **for** $i := 1$ **step** 1 **until** n **do** $A[i] := L[i] := 0$}; FIND A}; MOVE IN DIRECTION OF ARCS /71/}

Comment   FIND A $/p, V, LK, i, A/$ is performed by moving along the argument segment of the storage allocation $LK[1:p]$. Once the variable i is found in the jth component, we place 1 in the $V[j]$th component of A. ■

(70)   FIND A: {**int** j; **for** $j := 1$ **step** 1 **until** p **do if** $LK[j] = i$ **then** $A[V[j]]$ $:= 1$}

(71)   MOVE IN DIRECTION OF ARCS $/(69)$ $n, C, R, i, L, A/$: {**int** j; $j := 0$; **for** $j := j + 1$ **while** NONEMPTY (A, n) **do** ADVANCE}

(72)   ADVANCE $/n$, $C, R, i, L, A/$: {**int array** $\Gamma\{1:n\}$; COMPUTE Γ; APPLY Γ /74/}

Comment   COMPUTE $\Gamma/n, C, A, \Gamma/$. In computing Γ, we must recall that we move from elements of the start set to their predecessors, which form the columns of C. ∎

(73)   COMPUTE Γ: {{**int** i; **for** $i := 1$ **step** 1 **until** n **do** $\Gamma[i] := 0$}; {**int** i; **for** $i := 1$ **step** 1 **until** n **do if** $A[i] \neq 0$ **then** {**int** j; **for** $j := 1$ **step** 1 **until** n **do if** $C[j,i] = 1$ **then** $\Gamma[j] := 1$}}}

Comment   APPLY $\Gamma/(72)$ $n, R, i, L, A, \Gamma/$. This is performed in the same way as in (68), but in making an addition to the augmented set we may add only an element in Γ that does not belong to the restricting set. ∎

(74)   APPLY Γ: {**int** j; **for** $j := 1$ **step** 1 **until** n **do** {COMPUTE A: **if** $\Gamma[j] = 0$ **then** $A[j] := 0$ **else if** $L[j] \neq 0 \lor R[i,j] \neq 0$ **then** $A[j] := 0$ **else** $A[j] := 1$; ADD TO L: **if** $\Gamma[j] \neq 0$ & $R[i,j] = 0$ **then** $L[j] := 1$}}

4.6. Coloring the Vertices of a Graph

Comment   COLORING· $/(4)$ $l, U, Q/$ It is first necessary to determine the overall organization of the coloring algorithm in light of the representations we have selected for the objects and the different heuristics proposed in Section 3.4. If the initial graph is a complete graph, nothing can be done with it, and our result is the trivial coloring in which each vertex of the graph has assigned to it a color of its own. Then the coloring algorithm is structured so as to specify an initial trivial coloring and a graph reduction loop (linking vertices a distance 2 apart) that is repeated until the graph has been reduced to a complete graph (a process that is not executed at all if the graph is a complete graph). In the reduction process, the coloring Q is adjusted such that all occurrences of color J are replaced by color I ($I < J$), where I and J are the colors of a pair of vertices glued together. In reducing an initial graph, the ordinal numbers of the vertices and their colors coincide. This result is useful, in that we want to be certain that this property is preserved in any intermediate reduced graph. At the same time, in systematizing the algorithm it is important that the vertices of the graph be numbered sequentially. This means that if two vertices I and J ($I < J$) are glued together, all vertices beginning with the $(J+1)$th vertex have their ordinal number reduced by 1. The same adjustment must be done in the current state of coloring Q of the initial graph.

　　Now let us see what the graph reduction condition looks like. By the rules of ALGOL, the condition must be in the form of a Boolean expression (which is **true** if the graph is not a complete graph and **false** otherwise). Since it is impossible to write out the process of checking this condition in the form of an expression containing only basic ALGOL operations, we create the Boolean procedure function INCOMPLETE GRAPH (n), where n is the number of vertices in the graph, and treat U as a global object, computing (if U is not complete) the ordinal numbers I and J of the glued vertices at the same time. This sequence of application of the algorithm is especially useful, as it serves to distinguish the two processes of reduction and recoloring from the method of determining pairs of vertices that may be glued together. ∎

(75)   COLORING: {**boolean proc** INCOMPLETE GRAPH (n); **var** n; **int** n; INCOMPLETE GRAPH BODY /83/; **int** I, J; INITIAL COLORING; REDUCTION LOOP /77/}

(76)   INITIAL COLORING /l, q/: {**int** i; **for** $i := 1$ **step** 1 **until** l **do** $Q[i] := i$}

(77)   REDUCTION LOOP /(75) l, U, Q, I, J/: {**int** i; $i := 0$; **for** $i := i + 1$ **while** INCOMPLETE GRAPH $(l - i + 1)$ **do** REDUCTION}

Comment   REDUCTION /l, U, Q, I, J, i/ concludes in a gluing of the Ith and Jth vertices of the graph, a renumbering of the vertices, begining with the $(J + 1)$th vertex, and a corresponding adjustment of the coloring Q. Note that before the ith reduction the graph has $(l - i + 1)$ vertices. ∎

(78)   REDUCTION: {GLUING; ADJUSTMENT /82/}

Comment   LINKING /l, U, I, J, i/ consists in adding the Jth row to the Ith row (together with a symmetric transformation of the Ith column. Then occurs the actual reduction of the graph, a process that consists in converting the "peripheral" portion of the adjacency matrix as shown in Figure 4.4. ∎

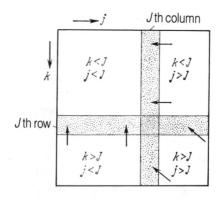

Figure 4.4. Reduction of the adjacency matrix of a graph.

(79) GLUING: {ADDITION; TRANSFER /81/}

Comment   ADDITION /l, U, I, J, i/. In linking the Jth column to the Ith column, we simultaneously assign the result to the Ith row, taking into account the symmetricity of the matrix. Recall that the adjacency matrix of an undirected graph has 0's along its diagonal (graph without loops). Since we are adding together columns of nonadjacent vertices, after the addition there will be 0's on the diagonal. ■

(80) ADDITION: {**int** k; **for** $k := 1$ **step** 1 **until** $l - i + 1$ **do** $U[k, I]$ $:= U[I, k] := U[k, I] + U[k, J]$}

Comment   TRANSFER/l, U, I, J, i/consist in a transfer loop for all the columns of the matrix, beginning with the $(J + 1)$th column. By virtue of the ALGOL rules we do not have to treat the case $J > l - i$ any differently, since the loop then is not executed at all. Components of columns beneath the Jth row are moved one position to the left and simultaneously placed at the symmetric position of the matrix. Components of columns above the Jth row are moved one position to the left and up. ■

(81) TRANSFER: {**int** j; **for** $j := J + 1$ **step** 1 **until** $l - i + 1$ **do** {**int** k; **for** k $:= 1$ **step** 1 **until** $l - i + 1$ **do if** $k < J$ **then** $U[k, j - 1] := U[j - 1, k]$ $:= U[k, j]$ **else if** $k > J$ **then** $U[k - 1, j - 1] := U[k, j]$}}

Comment   ADJUSTMENT /(78) l, Q, I, J/recalls the process of merging the current connectivity components in (42)–(45). Since by the condition $I < J$, all the components of the vector Q equal to J must be replaced by I. Moreover, all the components greater than J must be decreased by 1 because of the renumbering of some of the vertices of the reduced graph. ■

(82) ADJUSTMENT: {**int** i; **for** $i := 1$ **step** 1 **until** l **do if** $Q[i] = J$ **then** $Q[i] := I$ **else if** $Q[i] > J$ **then** $Q[i] := Q[i] - 1$}

Comment   INCOMPLETE GRAPH BODY /(75) U, I, J, n/. As a heuristic for searching for potential vertices to be rendered co-chromatic (see Section 3.4), we select a more cumbersome, though more efficient procedure for finding a pair of vertices I and J ($I < J$) a distance 2 apart that possesses the greatest number of separating vertices. The organization of the algorithm is straightforward. We create a variable d initially with a negative value. This variable will store the largest separating vertex from among those found. We then sort all the vertices of the graph, checking whether any of them is a star. If some vertex is not a star, we begin to select vertices a distance 2 away which are not adjacent to the vertex and which have greater ordinal number. If the current number of separating vertices is greater than d, it is replaced by the preceding number, and the ordinal numbers of the vertices are stored in I and J. If d turns out to be negative after all the vertices have been scanned, this means that the graph is a complete graph.

This rule is designed for connected graphs (here incompleteness automatically ensures the existence of a pair of vertices a distance 2 apart). The algorithm must yield a required pair of vertices no matter what, regardless of whether the particular graph is connected. However, if a graph is a collection of isolated complete subgraphs, it may be impossible to make any reasonable assignment of values to I and J. For this special case, we must introduce an additional rule for gluing some vertex I of one subgraph to a vertex J of another subgraph. We leave it as an exercise for the reader to establish that, whatever the initial gluing of two complete subgraphs, the gluing algorithm described above always yields a minimal coloring, i.e., it prescribes that a subgraph of lower order that formerly had been glued after a subgraph of higher order is now to be "glued" inside the latter, the process to continue until a larger subgraph absorbs a smaller subgraph without thereby becoming greater in size.

In the present case, we proceed in the following manner. The moment some succeeding vertex encounters a vertex that is not adjacent to it, it computes the number of separating vertices according to a general rule that yields 0 if the vertices are not a distance 2 apart. If d is nevertheless negative, its value is replaced by 0, and I and J are assigned the ordinal numbers of these nonadjacent vertices. Any "equivalent" pair of vertices with one or more separating vertices then replaces this pair, but if this does not happen, we obtain a gluing of two complete subgraphs. ∎

(83) INCOMPLETE GRAPH BODY: {{**int** d,i; $d := -1$; **for** $i := 1$ **step** 1 **until** n **do** SORT VERTICES}; RESULT /87/}

(84) SORT VERTICES $/U, I, J, n, d, i/$: {**int** j; **for** $j := i+1$ **step** 1 **until** n **do if** $U[i,j] = 0$ **then** PROCESS NONADJACENT VERTEX}

Comment   PROCESS NONADJACENT VERTEX $/ U, I, J, n, d, i, j /$. In this case the representation of a graph by an adjacency matrix is rather convenient, in that the number of vertices that separate the ith and jth vertices is simply equal to the scalar product of the ith and jth rows of U. If the vertices are more than a distance 2 apart the product is equal to 0. ∎

(85) PROCESS NONADJACENT VERTEX: {{**int** s; $s := 0$; {**int** k; **for** k := 1 **step** 1 **until** n **do** $s := s + U[i,k] * U[j,k]$}}; SELECT MAXIMUM}

(86)   SELECT MAXIMUM $/I, J, d, i, j, s/$: **if** $s > d$ **then** $\{d := s; \{I := i; J := j\}$

(87)   RESULT $/(83)$ $d/$: INCOMPLETE GRAPH $:= d \geqslant 0$

This, the eighty-seventh step, completes the process of programming the storage packing problem in a program schema.

CHAPTER 5

Concluding Analysis

5.1. The Relationship Between Theory and Practice

On the Study of Applications

Even Socrates had noted that the true test of wisdom is an understanding of its limitations. So now that we have completed the programming of our problem, let us return to its general analysis, viewing it in light of the knowledge we have gained.

Though this book is entitled, "Introduction to Theoretical Programming," we declared in the Preface that we will be considering the storage packing problem as an example of research into applications. Let us try to see what is "theoretical" in the study we have so far undertaken, and what is an "application." Of course, in such a literal formulation the question sounds a bit naive. A study of the relationship and differences between theoretical research and research into applications is among the most profound methodological problems of modern science in general, not just mathematics. Moreover, depending upon a given context, one and the same component of a study may seem to have been created incidental to the study as a tool for achieving a particular goal, while at the same time generating a "permanent record" of the theoretical foundations of an entire branch of science. For example, at one point (Section 2.3) the data flow graph seemed a useful, if auxiliary and ancillary construction that had no place in the ultimate program. Nevertheless, it is one of the basic concepts of theoretical programming, serving as an invariant of many useful transformations of programs, as well as constituting an independent, explicit construction that is applied in an important class of program schemas. In emphasizing the absurdity of any absolute dichotomy between theory and applications, Academician S.L. Sobolev has stated more than once that "There is no such thing as pure mathematics or applied mathematics, rather there is mathematics and its applications."

However, we will not delve too deeply into the dialectics that underlies a unity of opposites and instead extract from our study certain random observations, which we should note are scarcely comparable, in terms of significance, with serious studies on the methodology and history of mathematics. Nevertheless, in view of the introductory nature of our book as a whole, we will not worry if some of our thoughts seem unsophisticated. Instead we will try to make our interpretation of the theoretical and applied aspects of the storage packing problem somewhat concrete.

A study of applications is, more than anything else, goal-oriented, directed towards obtaining a pre-assigned result. The well-springs of a problem are usually outside mathematics proper, more precisely, they are external to the particular method of solution employed. The process of solving any one problem usually proceeds within some realistic framework that asserts the capabilities and constraints of the various methods of solution, which must also be thought of as given in advance.

In speaking of the differences between theoretical research and applied studies, we should not forget that, as a rule, applications are by nature more universal. The relationship between a study of applications and the "real world" is far richer and far more multi-dimensional than are the explicitly demarcated premises of theoretical research, which are also usually kept to the least number possible. No matter how paradoxical this might sound, a theory is always somehow specialized and therefore limited in scope, despite the exhaustive degree of completeness of the logical analysis it involves. Any theory is kept deliberately isolated from assertions or conditions that are not part of its system of primitive definitions or premises. Incidentally, one of the most common methodological errors in studies at the interface between theory and applications is due precisely to overlooking this truism.

With these general remarks in mind, let us return to our problem. At the outset would like to emphasize something the reader is probably well aware of. We are still only studying a problem of applications, not solving it. As an example of a complete solution, our presentation has neither a beginning nor an end, though the various stages through which we have passed in the first four chapters are an integral and principal part of the book. In speaking of storage packing as a problem of applications, we must first imagine the actual process in which the particular problem might arise, whether or not it involves human intervention. In our case, this might be the design of a compiler from some algorithmic language in which it would be desirable for storage requirements in compiled programs to be minimized automatically. Another example might be the design of a particular program library for airborne computers, where the small size of the internal memory necessitates maximal economy.

Relationship to Real Programs

To analyze the process of solving the storage packing problem, we first have to learn how to construct program schemas, starting from those types of programs whose schema requires an economical allocation of storage for the variables used in the programs. In the case of a compiler, this would be either the initial form of some program expressed in a source algorithmic language, or some intermediate form of the internal representation of a program during compilation or, finally, the symbolic form of the machine-language program discussed in Section 1.1. For each of these forms, we would have to find rules for identifying the statements and the arguments and results of the statements together with the variables created by them, as well as labels of all potential control transfers from one statement to another. We touched on these topics very superficially in the examples presented in the first chapter. In fact, the corresponding rules must be defined rigorously and programmed much like the actual storage packing algorithms.

A study of this problem would at once demonstrate how limited is our theory. There are two main flaws that have to be overcome. In real programs there are variables with subscripts that denote components of vectors, matrices, and, in general, multi-dimensional arrays. We might ask what might be the arguments and results of the statement

$$c[i, j] := c[i,j] + a[i, k] \times b[k,j] \tag{A}$$

One answer to this question turns on whether it is possible to figure out what are the values of the subscripts. If we cannot do so and if this is of no importance, we just assume that all the arrays altogether are arguments and results of the given statement, i.e., we treat the statement as if it had the form

$$c := F(c, a, b). \tag{B}$$

Without delving too deeply into the essential nature of the problem, let us merely remark that the storage packing problem becomes considerably more complicated if there are arrays to be manipulated. Here are two trick questions:

(1) Suppose we are given an array M consisting of 30 memory locations and two arrays K and L with 10 locations apiece. K and L are not compatible, though each is compatible with M. If storage packing is performed by gluing together the vertices of the incompatibility graph, after gluing, say, K and M, L will be incompatible with M. At the same time, there is an obvious economizing step, in which K and L are superimposed upon different segments of M, each with 10 locations. How should we take account of specific types of combinations of arrays of different lengths we would naturally not wish to overlook?

(2) An assignment to a variable x, i.e., finding that it is the result of a statement, has a dual purpose in a program schema. The assignment will have to interrupt some route, since x "obtains new life," and perhaps the variable begins a new route. This property of the assignment plays a fundamental role throughout the entire theory. If we were to apply this interpretation of the assignment literally to statement (B), which in our schema would be the image of statement (A) taken, say, from a matrix multiplication program, we would be committing a serious error. In fact,

though an assignment of an array c to some component $c[i,j]$ asserts that c becomes something "different," nevertheless it does not become so different as to interrupt the data paths from certain previously computed components of this array to components studied later on.

A second flaw in our theory is that there are subroutines running under different calls (moreover with different variables) that have to be taken into account. In Example 11 of Section 1.4, we extricated ourselves from this muddle by using two calls with the same actual parameter $F(x)$ in the procedure call **real proc** $F(r)$. If we had attempted to begin immediately with the general case, we would have encountered considerable difficulties.

Consolidating the Statements

There is a second source of discretion available in rules for identifying statements, arguments, and results if we look at our study from yet another viewpoint, i.e., the actual implementation of the storage packing algorithms. An elementary analysis of the final program demonstrates that there is a rather large number of computations in the storage packing process. To compute the adjacency matrix $U[1:l, 1:l]$ of an incompatibility graph from given matrices of initial $R[1; l, 1:n]$ and internal $T[1:l, 1:n]$ statements (Section 4.5), it is necessary to perform $l^2 \times n$ operations, where l is the number of domains and n the number of statements. Similarly, $q + 2l$ transitive closures must be computed to find a canonical storage allocation and construct the sets of internal statements. At the same time, if we are counting machine code instructions, there may be as many as several hundred primitive statements in a symbolic program, and so the combined total of all computations is a matter of tens and hundreds of millions of machine operations. It is therefore desirable to turn from program instructions to schema statements in a somewhat less direct fashion by *consolidating* the statements and reducing, as much as possible, the number of variables to be subjected to storage packing throughout the entire algorithm.

Without going into details, let us once again consider the various ways of consolidating statements. If we consider a well thought-out and, so to speak, realistic program, we can always find in it segments where the computations are executed one after the other, without being interrupted by any control transfers. These segments are also called *linear segments* of the program. In the abstract treatment of a program expressed as a control flow graph, the corresponding chains of vertices are called the *linear components* of the graph. More precisely, a linear component is a chain of vertices in a graph not contained entirely in any other chain. We consider any such component and divide all the poles related to it into three categories. The *arguments* of a linear component l are those arguments a such that there exist routes of data pairs of the form (r_i, a) that contain at least one statement not in l. Analogously, the *results of a component l* are those results r such that there exist routes of data pairs of the form (r, a_j) that contain at least one statement not belonging to l. For all other poles, the routes of data pairs are contained entirely within l. It is natural to call such data pairs *intermediate* or *internal data pairs*, and the variables associated with them *internal* or *local variables*. It is entirely obvious that the local variables within a single linear component may be identified by means of the far simpler rules considered in Section 1.2. Once we have implemented such an internal packing of the local variables of each component, we may then allocate a single segment of memory for all these variables,

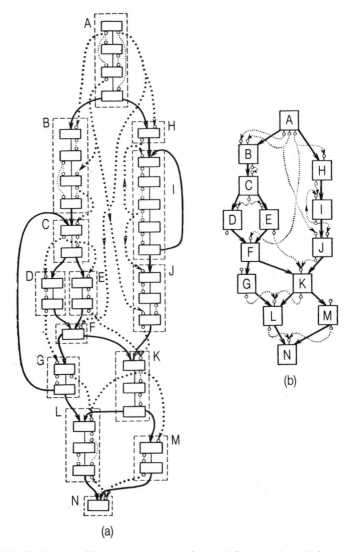

(a)

(b)

Figure 5.1. Reduction of linear components of control flow graph: (a) before reduction (35 statements, 26 domains); (b) after reduction (14 statements, 10 domains).

where the length of this segment is equal to the maximal width of the data paths of the internal variables within the components. Then the program schema is subjected to a process of reduction in which each linear component *l* is replaced by a single operator whose arguments and results are the arguments and results of the component *l* just determined. Naturally, in such an approach it is essential to reduce the number of statements and the number of poles that compose the program schema. As an example, Figure 5.1 shows the reduction of the linear components of an initial program schema into consolidated statements.

Factorization

Factorization of a program schema into so-called *hammocks* is an immediate generalization of this approach. A *hammock* is a subgraph *g* of a graph *G* (in this case, a transition graph) such that there exist two vertices that belong to it, *a* (input) and *z* (output) possessing the following properties:

all arcs from *a* enter the hammock;
any path entering a hammock from the outside passes through *a*;
all arcs to *z* emanate from the hammock;
any path emanating outward from a hammock passes through *z*.

A hammock is interesting in that it may be "contracted" to a single vertex without violating the adjacency relations between the other vertices of the graph. It is even possible to define a minimal hammock as one that does not contain any other hammock. Just as in the case of linear components, we may determine the arguments, results, and intermediate variables of a hammock.

By distinguishing hammocks and linear components, it is possible to decompose (factorize) the global storage packing problem within an entire program schema into several stages. We first identify the linear components in the schema within each of which the local variables may be minimized in accordance with the above simplified rules. Next the minimal hammocks in the schema are identified; the linear components just processed have already been reduced relative to these minimal hammocks into primitive components with respect to the hammocks of the vertex. For each hammock, the storage packing problem is solved separately with respect to its local variables, after which these first-order hammocks are reduced to vertices, which are primitive statements with respect to the rest of the schema. In the resulting schema the linear components are again identified and, consequently, the two-part stage is repeated anew.

This process is repeated until the schema is transformed into one or more isolated vertices after some succeeding reduction. Thus, the process of solving a storage packing problem for large memories reduces to a sequence of subproblems, each of which involves a far smaller number of computations. Since the complexity of storage packing algorithms is at least proportional to the square of the number of vertices in the control flow graph, such a

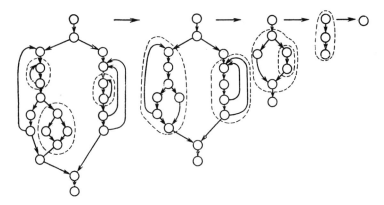

Figure 5.2. Factorization of a control flow graph.

factorization, even though it involves the solution of several problems rather than just one, may yield a considerable saving in time, possibly, however, at the expense of a somewhat poorer allocation of storage. Figure 5.2 presents as an example a factorization of a program schema.

Push-Down Storage Allocation

Both methods of reducing the size of the storage packing problem presume that parts of the problem within which may be found the routes of data paths we are interested in may be identified with some degree of reliability. It is no accident that we have referred to variables that implement such internal data paths as local variables. We may even recall that precisely such a term is found in ALGOL; the "local variables" in a block are those whose declarations are found at the head of the particular block. Abstracting, for the sake of simplicity, from the concept of procedures in ALGOL, we may note after a little reflection that, from the position of the declaration of a variable in some block, it follows at once that all the routes of data pairs implemented by means of this variable pass through statements that form the given block exclusively. Two blocks of an ALGOL program are said to be *parallel* if neither may be embedded one within the other in the text of the program. In this light, it is self-evident that the local variables of parallel blocks are never in competition and, therefore, may be placed in the same segment of memory.

Hence follows a rather simple method of achieving a minimal storage allocation for ALGOL programs with block structure. We assume that the memory locations allocated for storage of variables are arranged from the top down, with a filled segment of memory placed above, and an empty segment below, and that the filled and empty segments are demarcated by a *location counter*. The location counter is first at the top, at which point the entire memory is empty. Storage is allocated by means of step-by-step movement

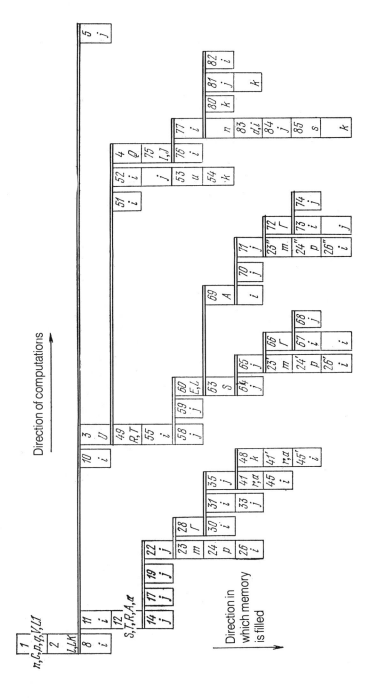

Figure 5.3. Push-down storage allocation in the SPPS program.

from left to right through the text of the program. The rule for allocation of storage may be stated thus: Suppose in traversing a program we encounter a left brace in block B and suppose that *l* locations are required to allocate the variables local to this block. Then, at the moment we encounter a left brace, we shift the location counter *l* locations down and allocate the local variables of block B to the segment of memory just filled. When we encounter the right brace of block B, we move the location counter up by the same number of locations (*l*). In such an approach, the segment of memory filled last is emptied first. It is precisely for this reason that this method of allocating storage is referred to as *push-down storage allocation* from the word, "store," in the field of firearms, where it is precisely the cartridge inserted last into the store which is fired first. Figure 5.3 depicts a push-down storage allocation in our SPPS program (program with fully developed block structure). The segments of memory in the store are labeled by the numbers of the blocks to which they refer. The body of each of the procedures has been duplicated and inserted wherever they are called.

Schemas and Programs

There is one further problem that arises when applying storage packing algorithms to actual programs, a problem that, while touched upon in the semantic analysis, nevertheless falls outside the realm of theory. By definition, our theory preserves the set of routes of data pairs in any re-allocation of memory, but says nothing as to whether the program (the program, not the schema!) obtained from the initial program by means of this type of transformation will run just as successfully as does the initial one. It is worth noting that, like you, dear reader, we have no doubt that this is so, but only because we are certain that the problem has been stated correctly and that the basic definition of computability of one schema by another (Section 2.2) is well-formed. Nevertheless, we do not have a rigorous proof that the concept of storage allocation for programs is well-formed. In fact, such a proof is, in principle, impossible within the scope of our presentation.

Let us briefly analyze what we are missing. First of all, we have no definition as to what constitutes a program, what a program run means, and what we mean when we say that a program run is preserved upon transformation of the program. In searching for such definitions, we will essentially have to enlarge our theory and subject these concepts to mathematical examination. Obviously, such an extension of the theory would have to be closely related to the rigorous definitions we have already introduced if, that is, we want to be able to see in the formal program the associated program schema without any trouble. Conversely, once some assertion has been established for a schema, it should be possible for us to readily imagine to which types of programs this assertion would be applicable.

The last sentence helps to understand how the two concepts of program and program schema are related. Man writes a program, and the computer executes it. But the programmer cannot simply hand over a program to the computer without having first written it out, i.e., without imparting to it some external textual form. And the text of a program is, in and of itself, still insufficient for solving the problem responsible for the very creation of this program. Only in the computer is there a device that confers such a meaning, or as is usually said, *interprets*, say the operation symbol "+" in a program or relates a definite meaning to the symbol for the variable x. Thus do we breathe life into the text of a program simply by conferring upon it some interpretation which is satisfied relative to the constituent elements of the program in and of itself and individually by virtue of the computer's ultimate control units or at least another "master program," in the form of a rigorous description of the operating rules of these devices. This division of our knowledge of programs—into text and meaning of text—finds its reflection in the division of the description of algorithmic languages into syntax (the study of text) and semantics (the study of meaning).

Returning once again to program schemas and programs, we arrive at an indisputable observation. A schema is a kind of abstraction of the text of a program. It contains something by means of which it is possible to understand and read through the text of a program without having to execute it. Our program schemas contain the names of statements and variables, along with a list of possible control transfers from one statement to another. To turn the schema into a program, it is necessary to give an interpretation of the formal symbols of the schema. In our case, to give an interpretation of the variables means describing the set of values of each variable (i.e., specifying its object domain), and to give an interpretation of a statement means giving the values of its results and a method of selecting its successor (the statement executed right after the given statement) as some actual function of the values of its arguments. By means of such an interpretation, it is possible to describe the process by which a program is executed in a rigorous fashion; the arguments and results of a program may also be determined. The execution of a program may then be defined in a natural way by asserting that it computes its results as the resultant function of its asguments. If two programs operate identically, this will mean that they compute one and the same function.

Here we have a juncture in the relationship between the theory of program schemas and programs themselves. Suppose we are given some assertion F about schema G. The first thing we must find out is, given some interpretation I that transforms G into a program $P = (I, G)$, how to interpret F as an assertion (I, F) about P. Our assertion about G is also of interest in general if, given that F is valid, it follows that every (I, F) is valid, no matter what the interpretation I is. In our case, if we take as our "schema assertion" the claim that one schema is computable by another $(G' \succ G)$, we would then like to have as corollary to the above assertion the claim that the two programs (I, G') and (I, G) will always compute the same function no matter what interpretation I we use.

We will not bother developing our line of reasoning any further, as we will be doing so for a different class of program schemas in the second part of the book. To reassure the reader, let us merely note that it is precisely in this way that an evaluation of our theory of storage packing may be said to hold.

It remains for us to add some commentary of a purely programming nature relative to the parts of the study we have completed so far. The program we have written is entirely realistic, though because of various features of structured programming and the scant resources afforded in ALGOL-60, we have made the feature of naturalness, or more exactly, straightforwardness, of implementation our primary feature. What are the other factors that must be taken into account to program correctly?

First, structured programming, at least in the formalism we have selected, creates far too many blocks. In certain ALGOL compilers the process of programming input into a block involves far more overhead than would be justified for the sake of describing, for example, a single loop parameter or some other temporary variable. Once the actual construction of a program is complete and the program tested, the structured programming process could perhaps then be accompanied by a systematic transformation of the program to reduce the number of blocks.

Second, we would have to analyze in more detail the relationship between consumption of storage and consumption of time in the process of storage packing. Each problem has its own lower bounds as regards time or capacity, for example, an operating time that cannot be decreased or a volume of storage that cannot be reduced. Except for these absolute bounds, however, it is possible to minimize one at the expense of the other. For example, there is no reason at all to create matrix R (Section 4.5) by extracting the required set of primitive statements from an allocation of poles every time it seems necessary. In constructing a canonical storage allocation (Section 4.4), on the other hand, for each of the primitive variables $x_1, \ldots, x_m$ we could have constructed in advance a set of statements that reads it, thereby forming a matrix of order $m \times n$ from the corresponding Boolean scales and reducing the time spent on the construction of the sets of arguments by a factor of q/m (each time for each variable instead of each time for each result). In this way, questions of structure could be solved with respect to each environment within which the storage packing algorithm is applied.

Finally, even within the context of algorithm organization, there are any number of ways of increasing efficiency. There is one ploy we have not retained, however—where a vector of argument poles a has been constructed for the most frequent case (a single occurrence of a variable in a statement as argument). For example, we could have reduced the time needed for the construction of the incompatibility graph quite a bit by specifying as the initial value of the components of the graph not zeros, but rather the result of multiplying the sets R_i and R_j together, where R_i is the set of primitive statements of the ith variable of a canonical statement. In a number of cases, we wouldn't even have to begin checking whether intersections of sets such as

$R \cap T$ are nonempty. The very process of pairwise multiplication of sets could be interrupted the moment a nonzero product of components is found.

It is these types of improvements that many programmers sense as the most exciting element of the programming process, an element that reflects the inventive and creative nature of programming itself. But it is only a matter of feasibility, which if understood properly, becomes a basis for reaching a decision in internal disputes as to whether to complement the "basic" flow of computations with special techniques. In every case, it is desirable to assess the improvement in a program's indicators for different special cases. A true sensitivity to such a measure in terms of real simplicity and less reliable refinement can be achieved only with experience and maturity, as in every form of endeavor.

5.2. Historical Survey

In our discussion of the storage packing problem, we have subordinated the method of presentation to didactic goals in an attempt to combine exhaustiveness of presentation with naturalness in the development of the topic. And though the solution of the problem is, on the whole, elementary, it relies on a number of nontrivial notions that are not so simple a matter to think about. Over 10 years passed from the first effective statement of the problem to the creation of the complete theory in its most natural form. The generalization of the theory to more complicated classes of program schemas continues to this very day. We will conclude our discussion of the storage packing problem by reviewing the studies that led to its solution, taking them in the sequence in which they first appeared. This historical survey will not be complete, but will be limited to studies that have had a direct influence on the creation of the theory or that have made direct use of its results.*

Shtarkman's Algorithm

The first work that discussed storage packing as an independent stage in the programming process was an article by V.S. Shtarkman, entitled "Minimization Unit for Working Cells in PP-2," published in the famous first issue of the journal *Problemy Kibernetiki* (Moscow, Fizmatgiz, 1958; translated in *Problems of Cybernetics*). This article laid the foundations for the development of the scientific foundations of programming in the Soviet Union. Essentially, it solved the storage packing problem for internal variables in linear segments of a program. The problem was considered within the context of the operation

---

* Readers may also wish to consult an early review in English: R.A. Di Paola, *A Survey of Soviet Work in the Theory of Computer Programming* (Rand Memorandum PM-5424-PR, October, 1967) (trans.).

of a compiler (at that time, called a programming program, thus PP) that generates the linear segments of a computer program for a three-address computer used to translate the arithmetic operators of some initial program. The idea of the algorithm is set forth in this paper so clearly that we will simply give the author's own words here in translation:

... The working locations in PP-2 are those intended for storage of internal results, i.e. results used in the given operator* but not used in any other operator. From the very definition, it obviously follows that locations that are working locations for one operator may be successfully used as working locations in another operator as well. It is entirely obvious that the total number of working locations needed in a program is equal to the maximal number of working locations in all operators of the particular program. Hence it follows that minimizing the number of working locations in a program means minimizing the working locations for each operator separately . . . .

The *domain* in which an intermediate [internal] result exists will be understood to refer to a set of instructions in the course of whose execution no location that stores a particular intermediate result may be used to store another result. Such a set obviously begins with an instruction that generates some result and concludes with an instruction that is executed before the last of all the instructions that use this result. Similarly, intermediate results with disjoint domains may be placed in the same memory locations without producing any adverse effects . . . .

The process of minimizing the number of working locations . . . is carried out in a single 'scan' of an operator* in the following way. All the instructions in an operator are successively sorted from bottom up, beginning with the last instruction and ending with the first one. In the sorting process, a table (T) is created; on each stage the *conditional numbers* [symbolic notation—Author] of intermediate results whose domain contains the next command to be 'scanned' are listed. This is done in the following way. If the conditional number of an intermediate result of some instruction occurs in address III [result address—Author], the line in T containing it is found and cleared. But if the conditional number occurs in addresses I and II and a 'scan' of T shows that it is not there, the uppermost empty line of T is located and the selected conditional number entered there. Only when there are no more empty lines in T is another line with the selected conditional number adjoined to T.

In such a system, conditional numbers of intermediate results with disjoint domains occur in each line of T; conventional numbers of results with disjoint domains will, of necessity, occur in distinct lines; finally, in the process of scanning T, the number of lines in T will increase from zero, in the end becoming equal to the number of working locations required . . . .

Shtarkman's principal achievement has to do with minimizing the number of working locations by scanning the instructions of a statement in reverse order. The route of each variable is thereby reviewed, beginning with its most recent application. This is fully in accord with the requirements of the general theory. That is, within any one route a given variable is in competition with

---

* Here Shtarkman is using the term, "operator," to refer to a piece of object code consisting of machine instructions that implement a particular statement of the source programming language.

the results of all the internal statements of the route. In the general case, the set of internal statements $T = E \cap L$, where E are the direct transitive closures and L are the inverse transitive closures. Obviously, $T = L$ for a linear program, which is what Shtarkman assumed.

Shtarkman's algorithm was improved upon in the design of yet another early translator, described in a book by the present author (*Programming Program for the BESM Computer*, translated by A. Nadler, edited by J.P. Cleave. New York, Pergamon, 1959). This compiler provided a conceptual implementation of an explicit specification of data paths within a single linear segment of a program, though this was not done entirely intentionally. In terms of three-address instructions, the process is as follows. If in the process of constructing the instructions of a linear segment, a succeeding instruction is placed in the kth sequentially ordered location, the third address of the instruction is left empty. The number k is entered into those (first or second) addresses of succeeding instructions which the result of the kth instruction would have to use. In this way it is possible to implement storage packing not just by renaming the internal variables, but at once by assigning working cells to the results and arguments of its instructions.

With this description of the data paths, the Shtarkman algorithm has the following form. The table T is expressed as a Boolean scale, so that $T[i]$ corresponds to the ith working location. In scanning the next instruction in

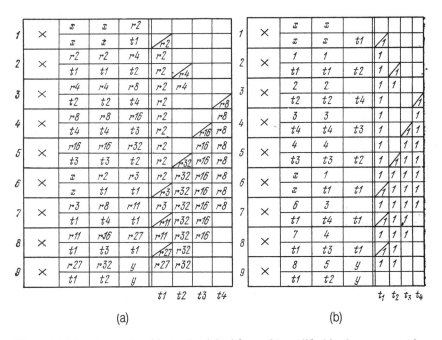

(a)   (b)

Figure 5.4. Shtarkman algorithm: (a) original form; (b) modified in the programming for the BESM computer.

T, the currently filled working cells are labeled with units. To survey the argument address A, we use the third (result) address R of the instruction whose ordinal number is in A. If empty, we search for the first nonzero digit in T; its ordinal number then designates a working location, which is entered in both R and A. If R is not empty, this means that the working location specified there has already been assigned to it, and this location is also placed in A. In surveying the result address of a current instruction, the working location occurring there is labeled empty in T. Figure 5.4 shows how the Shtarkman algorithm works for a linear program that computes $y = x^{59}$ (Example 5, Section 1.2) in both the original form and in a modified form (the external variables x and y do not coincide with the working locations). The succeeding instruction and table T are represented twice on each stage of the scanning process, the instruction with its old and new notation and the table both before and after the result address has been scanned.

The problem of storage packing in linear programs was studied further in a paper by the present author, entitled "On Programming of Arithmetic Operators." published in *Doklady Akademii Nauk SSSR* (Vol. 118, No. 3, 1958; translated in *Comm. ACM*, Vol. 1, No. 7, pp. 3–6). This paper introduced the concept of the width of a data path in a designated section of a program (discussed in Chapter 1), and showed how to order a tree with least width in the special formulation discussed in Section 3.3.

Closed Lavrov Schemas

A major contribution to the solution of the storage packing problem was made by S.S. Lavrov in his paper, "Storage Packing in Closed Program Schemas," published in 1961 in the fourth issue of the journal, *Zhurnal Vychislitel'noi Matematiki i Matematicheskoi Fiziki* (translated in *USSR Comput. Math. Math. Phys.*). Lavrov introduced the concept of a program schema, interpreted different types of storage allocations as equivalent transformations consisting in a renaming of variables, and introduced the concepts of route, canonical storage allocation, and incompatibility graph. But the theory he created lacked certain components, and so he was unable to solve the storage packing problem for the general case.

Lavrov's paper may be thought of as a kind of attempt to generalize Shtarkman's algorithm at once to the most general case. Let us now turn to the algorithm presented in Figure 5.4(a). It is clear that there are two parts to the algorithm's operation: Fill table T and select new notation for the variables by studying the table. From constructive considerations, both these parts are combined in a single scanning of a program, though they could also be considered separately. Let us transform T somewhat so that it could be considered separately from the program. For this purpose, we need only enter the ordinal number of an instruction at some position in the table instead of using it as the ordinal number of a line of the resulting matrix. In this way, the table is transformed into a set of pairs of the form (instruction, variable), and the states of the table "before execution" and "after execution" of an instruction are distinguished. For this to be possible, we consider the pairs (x, K) and (K, x) in turn, where K is an instruction and x is a variable, obtaining as a result a set of pairs (Figure 5.5), which Lavrov called the *load set* M. The meaning of an assignment of pairs to load sets is self-evident: $(x, K) \in M$ asserts that the value of x must be retained at the moment preceding execution of K, whereas (K, x) makes the same assertion for the moment following execution of K.

Even in our case of a linear program, there are a number of properties of the load set which may be formulated, understanding it as the constructive foundation of the theory of storage allocation.

1. The set M is constructed by traversing the program in the direction of control transfers. We begin to enter pairs containing x into M once x appears as an argument and halt the process once x appears as a result.
2. Each pair in T corresponds to one of the newly named variables; in other words, a new storage allocation is determined as a function defined on M.
3. The load set possesses a kind of constant structure relative to all the different storage packing functions; subsets may be found in the load set in which any "actual" function L must retain its value.
4. We assign to such subsets mainly the route chains, or sequences of pairs

$$(K_1, x)(x, K_2)(K_2, x) \ldots (x, K_{n-1})(K_{n-1}, x)(x, K_n)$$

such that K_1 computes x; $K_2, \ldots, K_{n-1}$ do not compute x; K_n reads in x; and any K_i in the program is a successor of K_{i-1} $(i = 2, \ldots, n)$.

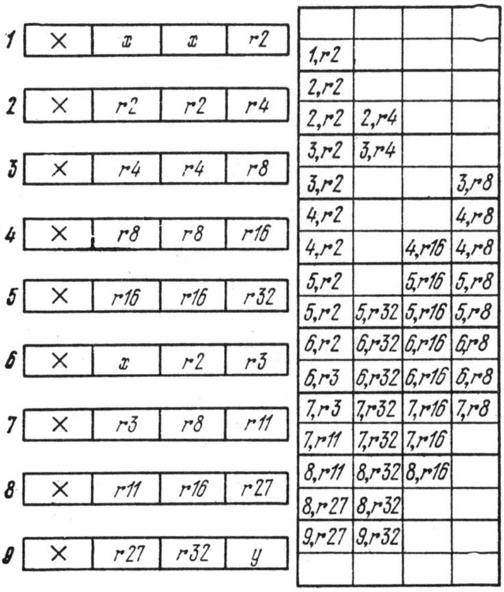

1: X | x | x | r2			
1,r2			
2: X | r2 | r2 | r4			
2,r2			
2,r2	2,r4		
3: X | r4 | r4 | r8			
3,r2	3,r4		
3,r2			3,r8
4: X | r8 | r8 | r16			
4,r2			4,r8
4,r2		4,r16	4,r8
5: X | r16 | r16 | r32			
5,r2		5,r16	5,r8
5,r2	5,r32	5,r16	5,r8
6: X | x | r2 | r3			
6,r2	6,r32	6,r16	6,r8
6,r3	6,r32	6,r16	6,r8
7: X | r3 | r8 | r11			
7,r3	7,r32	7,r16	7,r8
7,r11	7,r32	7,r16	
8: X | r11 | r16 | r27			
8,r11	8,r32	8,r16	
8,r27	8,r32		
9: X | r27 | r32 | y			
9,r27	9,r32		

Figure 5.5 Load set in program for $y = x^{59}$.

5. Route chains that contain the same variable are combined into bundles characterized (in the case of linear programs) by a common initial pair (K, x). The storage allocation function must remain constant on all pairs relative to any one bundle, which Lavrov refers to as a liveness domain.

6. We associate with distinct domains the same value of the storage allocation function if and only if the domains do not have any pair with the same direction and the same instruction. A storage allocation whose function assumes distinct values on distinct domains Lavrov termed *canonical*.

Once these properties of the load set had been established, Lavrov then searched for a class of program schemas that would ensure the well-formedness of a storage allocation in accordance with the above rules. It turns out that the first property suffices for these purposes; in fact, this property holds automatically for linear programs. That is, the property asserts that any statement from which some other statement that reads in x would be reachable would itself be reachable from some statement that computes x. Program schemas that satisfy this property are said to be *closed*.

A route chain with variable x is nothing other than information that specifies the initial, internal, and terminal statements of some route that implements a data path by means of x. Lavrov did not have to state exactly which result and which argument x was associated with, since in his definition of a program schema no variable is encountered more than once in any statement as argument or result.

Property (5) may clearly be formulated in more general form by declaring two route chains m and m' to be *connected* if there exists a sequence of chains

$$m, m_1, \ldots, m_k, m',$$

such that any two neighboring chains share a common initial or common final pair.

Let us compare the sixth property with the incompatibility criterion for domains given in Theorem 2.4 (Section 2.3). Suppose that two variables x and x' are correlated with two domains in a canonical storage allocation. We let $R(x)$ be a statement that computes x, we let $A(x)$ be a statement that reads in x, and we let $T(x)$ be an internal statement on routes whose data paths are implemented by x.

For closed program schemas, Lavrov's incompatibility criterion asserts that the set

$$(R(x) \bigcup T(x) \bigcup A(x)) \bigcap (R(x') \bigcup T(x') \bigcup A(x')) \backslash (R(x) \bigcap A(x') \bigcup R(x') \bigcap A(x)) \tag{*}$$

is nonempty.

In this notation, the compatibility criterion for the general case asserts that the set

$$(R(x) \bigcup T(x)) \bigcap (R(x') \bigcup T(x')) \backslash (T(x) \bigcap T(x')) \tag{**}$$

is nonempty.

It is a rather simple matter to prove that (∗∗) follows from (∗) for closed schemas. In fact, suppose that S is a statement that belongs to each of two routes $M_1(x)$ and $M_2(y)$ as internal or final statement. We select from the beginnings of these routes the statement H_1 closest to S. Suppose it is at the beginning of $M_1(x)$. Statement X is either itself the end K of $M_2(y)$ or is an internal statement of $M_2(y)$, i.e., the terminus K of this route is reachable from it. Then, obviously, K is also reachable from H_1. By virtue of the closure property, there exists a route $M(y)$ in which H_1 is either an initial or internal statement. Hence it follows that x and y are incompatible.

Thus, we have established that Lavrov's definition of a domain is in total agreement with the definition of a connectivity component of a data flow graph, while his incompatibility criterion is equivalent to the general criterion imposed on a set of closed program schemas.

Lavrov did not introduce any invariant that might be preserved under "well-formed" reallocations of storage, postulating instead properties of "well-formed" storage reallocation functions. For Lavrov, two schemas are equivalent if there exists a well-formed renaming of variables that converts one schema into another. In fact, to define well-formedness Lavrov had to implicitly require that the set of all routes of the initial schema be invariant. In well-formed transformations of closed program schemas, the set of routes does not change, so that all reallocations of storage prove to be reversible. Note that in the semantic analysis of the problem (Section 1.4), an open schema is encountered only at the very end (Example 11).

A procedure for the construction of the load set of a program schema partitioned into domains was Lavrov's constructive expression of the storage packing theory.

General Case.

The first version of the storage packing theory for the general case may be found in an article by the present author in *Doklady Akademii Nauk SSSR* (Vol. 142. No. 4, 1962; translated in *Soviet Mathematics*, Vol. 3, pp. 163–165) entitled, "Reduction of the Problem of Memory Allocation in Programming to the Problem of Coloring the Vertices of Graphs." Here a schema was defined in the same way as in Lavrov's paper, including concepts such as sets of statements and variables, a control flow graph, a binary matrix of arguments $\|a_{ij}\|$ ($a_{ij}=1$ if the ith variable is an argument of the jth statement), and an analogously constructed result matrix.

The theory still lacked poles, data paths, and the notion of a data flow graph. A carrier, consisting of the set of all routes (a route was defined in the same way as in Lavrov's paper, as having to do with variables, rather than with data paths), was made an invariant of the admissible storage allocations. Those allocations whose carrier could not be contracted were also made admissible storage allocations. A domain was defined as a connectivity component of a carrier in which a symmetric relation of connectivity was defined between routes. Such an approach formally required a proof (of course, trivial) that the number of domains is finite. An incompatibility criterion for domains was formulated in the paper (Theorem 2.4, Section 2.3), and a procedure for finding the set of internal statements was described as prescribing two transitive closures (sets E and L). Recursive formulas were presented for computing these closures.

An effort was made to solve the storage packing problem for programs containing arrays. For this purpose, a "weight," or integer indicating how many sequentially arranged memory locations were needed to store a given variable, was assigned to the variable. The weight of a variable was never taken into account at any stage of the theory right up through the coloring process. At the same time, in view of the problem touched upon in the summary analysis (second question at the start of Section 5.1), for each result in a program schema it was assumed known whether it is computed either "completely" or only partially. Only statements that recompute a variable as a whole could begin the route of that variable. Statements that did not compute variables completely could only be internal statements of routes.

In 1968, the present author published a paper in the journal *Kibernetika* (translated in *Cybernetics*) entitled, "Operator Schemas on Common and Distributed Memory." This paper introduced the concept of a data flow graph whose vertices were poles (arguments or results) of a schema, and whose arcs denoted data paths from results to arguments. In particular, it was proved that Lavrov's domains were the connectivity components of a data flow graph.

With this, the development of the general theory of storage packing in program schemas essentially concludes. An up-to-date presentation of the theory, virtually identical to the content of Section 2.3, was given by the present author in an article entitled, "Axiomatics of Storage Allocation," published in the symposium, *Theory of Languages and Methods of Constructing Programming Systems* (*Teoriya yazykov i metody postroeniya sistem programmirovaniya*) (Kiev-Alushta, Institute of Cybernetics, Ukrainian Academy of Sciences, 1972; see also *Acta Informatica*, 1976, Vol. 6, No. 1, pp. 61–75).

Programmers began to have an interest in graph theory once it became clear that the storage packing problem could be reduced to the problem of coloring the vertices of a graph. One of the first results in this area was a joint paper by the present author and G.I. Kozhukhin entitled, "Estimates of the Chromatic Number of Connected Graphs (*Dokl. Akad. Nauk SSSR*, Vol. 142, No. 2, 1962; translated in *Soviet Mathematics*, Vol. 3, pp. 50–53). It is of some interest that Kozhukhin came to this study from an interest in coloring theory in and of itself. He proved the co-chromatic vertex theorem (Theorem 3.4, Section 3.4) and derived an upper bound on the chromatic number as a function of the number of vertices and edges in a graph. The present author's contribution consisted of the derivation of a lower bound and of the application of an interpretation (due to A.A. Zykov) of the coloring process as one involing a successive gluing of the vertices of a graph.

In an article entitled "Minimal Storage Allocation," published in 1962 in the third issue of the journal, *Zhurnal Vychislitel'noi Matematiki i Matematicheskoi Fiziki* (translated in *USSR Comput. Math. Math. Phys.*) V.V. Martynyuk described the construction of a program schema for an arbitrary incompatibility graph (as described here in Chapter 3), and also proposed a heuristic procedure for combining together arrays with different weights. Also in the same year, L.K. Trokhan conducted a series of experiments on coloring graphs of order 45 on a computer using all three heuristic procedures discussed in Section 3.4, thereby proving the practicality of even the simplest heuristic procedure.

The design of the ALPHA compiler, a compiler which translates into machine code programs written in ALPHA (a language which is an extension of ALGOL), provided experience in the practical application of the theory of storage packing in the design of compilers. This experience was described in a paper by the present author together with L.L. Zmievskaya, R.D. Mishkovich, and L.K. Trokhan, entitled, "Storage Economization and Allocation in the ALPHA Compiler," published in the collection, *The ALPHA Autonomic Programming System* (Novosibirsk, 1967; in English translation, London–New York, Academic Press, 1971).*

Linear segments of a machine program, as well as hammocks with a simple structure, were made the statements of the schema. The body of a procedure was interpreted in such a way that its first statement became the successor of every call of the particular procedure, and all statements occurring after the calls in the program became the successors of the exit statement from the procedure. If some statement had as argument the formal parameter x, all variables that could be substituted in calls in place of x were considered arguments of the statement. Results were treated analogously.

Connectivity components were not constructed, though the features of nonconnectivity and noncompetitiveness of routes of variables described in parallel blocks were taken into account. In other words, if the descriptions of two arbitrary variables x and y occurred in parallel blocks, they were considered distinct compatible variables in the schema.

Arrays (vectors) as well as scalars (specifying a single memory location) were considered as variables. An incompatibility graph was specified by its adjacency matrix and was colored in accordance with the first heuristic. Arrays of the same length were made to coincide entirely "one inside the other." If an array A of lesser length was placed inside a longer array B, an attempt was made to place other variables compatible with B but not with A in the remainder of B.

By the time this book was being written, there were already several dozen titles in the literature on the theme of storage packing. These studies develop

---

* See also A.O. Buda, A.A. Granovsky, and A.P. Ershov, "Implementation of the ALPHA-6 Programming System," in: *Proc. International Conf. Reliability of Software 1975* (New York, IEEE/ACM, 1975), pp. 382–394 (trans.).

the algorithmic methodology of storage packing (construction of transitive closures, coloring and array coincidence heuristics), discuss storage packing in the context of the broadest transformations of programs, and extend the theory to the most all-inclusive classes of program schemas and programs. The very concept of a program schema and the various properties or entities that may be extracted from it continue to be the focus of theoretical investigations. We will have occasion to speak of some of these investigations in Part II, but otherwise the further development of the topic is a subject for a special study outside the scope of the present discussions.

Part II   Transformations of Yanov Schemas

CHAPTER 6

Brief Review of Mathematical Logic

6.1. Logical Formulas and Boolean Functions

Subject of Logic

Logic is a mathematical discipline like arithmetic and geometry which man must willy-nilly deal with from the very first years of his conscious existence. Perhaps it might be more correct to say that the laws of correct reasoning about objects and phenomena, together with the properties of the shapes of objects and the quantitative relations between them, are the principal content of mathematics, if we are thinking of its contribution to man's everyday existence. It is of no little interest, however, that logic, while it has served as an organizing element in human society far longer than has mathematics, did not itself become the subject of mathematical study until quite recently, in earnest only at the end of the nineteenth century. This fact is even more paradoxical, in that mathematical logic is somewhat simpler than many other branches of mathematics. There is an explanation for this paradox, but this we cannot go into here as exhaustively as the subject deserves. We only wish to note that for some time and, indeed, in general, mathematicians have successfully relied on a common sense approach in the application of the laws of logical reasoning as long as the particular mathematical discipline (foundations of mathematical analysis, paradoxes of set theory, non-Euclidean geometry) did not lead them to study the logical foundations of mathematics itself. On the other hand, it was necessary to reason at a high level of abstraction and to maintain a special kind of faith in symbolism in order to arrive at a proper understanding of the initial abstractions of logical arguments and be able to have faith in the universal applicability of the formally derived laws of logic expressed in symbolic form.

In this review chapter we will give a brief survey of one branch of mathematical logic—algebraic logic together with the propositional calculus—which, we believe, possesses quite a number of remarkable properties. The subjects of this theory and the problems related to it are comparatively simple; at the same time, the properties and theorems proved in algebraic logic and the propositional calculus are profound and significant, and are applicable to many phenomena of the real world and explain much in it. The theory, which is constructed in an extremely elegant and natural way, simultaneously comprises, as if in embryo, the general structure of many rich and complex theories of modern mathematics.

One of the goals of logical reasoning is establishing truth, i.e., the possibility of confirming or refuting some proposition in a reliable way. In this one sentence, there is already both an observation and a constraint. Man reasons, enunciating sentences in a human or, as is usually said, natural language. The constraint is that we consider only those sentences of natural language (propositions) about which it is meaningful to assert that they are correct or incorrect, true or false. The observation suggests that the properties of truth or falsity are mutually complementary; in other words, natural language is structured so that if we are given some false proposition ("Moscow is the capital of France"), it is always possible to express its negation, which is a true proposition ("It is false that Moscow is the capital of France"), and conversely. In this transition from an assertion to its negation, it is possible to perform a simple reconstruction of the sentence without having to penetrate to its actual meaning. From this standpoint, the transition from the false proposition, "Moscow is the capital of France," to the true proposition, "Paris is the capital of France," or "Moscow is the capital of the USSR" does not so much illustrate a rule for passing from an assertion to its negation (by means of the auxiliary construction, "It is false that . . .") as it constitutes a semantic substitution of one proposition for another carried out outside the formal laws of logic.

In analyzing propositions that form a chain of logical reasoning, we may find in the chain what are usually called the initial assertions, i.e., the simplest judgments whose truth or falsity is established in advance or, more precisely, by means of tools that fall outside the scope of the given logical argument. From these initial assertions, more complicated, deduced propositions are then created using the rules of natural language. As in the case of the negation rule, we check to see if there exist rules for constructing compound propositions in which the property of a proposition to be true or false depends solely on the truth or falsity of its constituent initial assertions and on whether they may be combined together into a compound proposition. In natural language, these rules serve to couple together two or more propositions by means of the following (here capitalized) words:

IT IS FALSE THAT: (IT IS FALSE THAT Moscow is the capital of France)—a negation;

AND: (It was raining AND two students left)—a conjunction;

OR: (He is drinking OR he is smoking)—a disjunction;

IMPLIES: (Crime IMPLIES punishment, elder in a garden IMPLIES uncle is in Kiev, the whistle of a crayfish IMPLIES goatsmilk, $2 \times 2 = 4$ IMPLIES the Volga flows into the Caspian Sea, but IT IS FALSE THAT true IMPLIES false)—an implication;

EITHER . . . OR: (EITHER he stole the overcoat OR he was robbed of an overcoat)—an exclusive or;

IS THE SAME AS: (x is a prime number IS THE SAME AS x is divisible only by itself and unity)—an identity.

We have taken the opportunity here to present several commonplace expressions as examples so as to emphasize as clearly as possible that one may speak rigorously about the truth or falsity of compound propositions without so much as a thought to their semantic import, provided that the rules for comprehending the particular connectives and locutions (called *logical connectives*) are stipulated once and for all.

These rules of usage become particularly clear if they are represented, as is usually done, in symbolic form, in which the initial assertions are represented as independent logical variables that take two values **f** (false) and **t** (true), and if the logical connectives are represented as logical operations with two arguments, thus:

$x \& y$ conjunction (also denoted $x \wedge y$);

$x \vee y$ disjunction;

$x \supset y$ implication (also denoted $x \to y$; x is called the *premise* and y the *conclusion* of the implication);

$x + y$ exclusive or (in programming, called alternator);

$x \equiv y$ identity;

and if we are also given an operation defined over a single argument:

$\neg x$ negation (also denoted $\bar{x}$).

The logical operations have the same two values of **f** and **t**. Thus, these operations are completely described by means of tables of values of the operations, called *truth tables*.

x	y	$x \& y$	$x \vee y$	$x \supset y$	$x + y$	$x \equiv y$	x	$\neg x$
f	f	f	f	t	f	t	f	t
f	t	f	t	t	t	f	t	f
t	f	f	t	f	t	f		
t	t	t	t	t	f	t		

In looking over these truth tables and the logical connectives they specify, we may observe that if a compound proposition is at all comprehensible, its meaning will not contradict the truth value obtained by means of the rules for computing the logical operations. It is precisely this observation (which is not a theorem!) which gives us a basis for trusting in the usefulness of the theory as developed further.

Logical Formulas

Thus, let us undertake the first stage in the construction of the theory, introducing some symbolism to create the *logical formulas*.

Logical formulas are constructed from the following symbols:

f or **t**	logical constants (truth values);
$A, B, C, \ldots, X, Y, Z$	logical variables;
(,)	parentheses;
$\vee, \&, \supset, +, \equiv$	two-place logical operations;
$\neg$	one-place logical operation.

(Henceforth, for the sake of brevity we will sometimes omit the word "logical".)

A constant or variable is a primary.
If Φ is a formula, (Φ) is a primary.
If Φ is a primary, Φ is a secondary.
If Φ is a secondary, $\neg \Phi$ is a secondary.
If Φ is a secondary, Φ is a conjunction.
If Φ_1 is a conjunction and Φ_2 is a secondary, $\Phi_1 \& \Phi_2$ is a conjunction.
If Φ is a conjunction, Φ is a disjunction.
If Φ_1 is a disjunction, and if Φ_2 is a conjunction, $\Phi_1 \vee \Phi_2$ or $\Phi_1 + \Phi_2$ is a disjunction.
If Φ is a disjunction, Φ is an implication.
If Φ_1 is an implication and Φ_2 is a disjunction, $\Phi_1 \supset \Phi_2$ is an implication.
If Φ is an implication, Φ is a formula.
If Φ_1 is a formula and Φ_2 an implication, $\Phi_1 \equiv \Phi_2$ is a formula.
There are no other formulas.

These definitions, while rather pedantic, nevertheless may be put to good use by providing an entirely rigorous explication of the logical formulas, at the same time establishing rules of precedence in the application of the logical operations. In the language of high-school algebra, we may say that operations within parentheses are executed first, followed by (in order of execution) negation; conjunction; disjunction and exclusive or; implication; identity.

Hopefully, this appeal to the reader's experience will suffice to verify that, for example, symbolic text such as the following

$$X \& \neg Y \vee Z \supset \neg X \equiv Y \vee \neg Z \& V \supset Z \equiv Y \& \neg X \qquad (*)$$

is a correct formula in which the arguments are identified in a unique way for each operation, that is

$$((((X \& (\neg Y)) \vee Z) \supset (\neg X)) \equiv ((Y \vee ((\neg Z) \& V)) \supset Z)) \equiv (Y \& (\neg X)).$$

Formal Syntax

It is now a good time to depart somewhat from the main thread of the presentation. The inductive definition of the logical formulas just given is in fact based on a general technique which is so important in programming that not speaking about it, now that we have occasion to do so, would be inexcusable.

Let us first note that for such inductive constructions there is a simple symbolism that helps make the definition more compact and graphic. From a general standpoint, our inductive definition successively defines increasingly broader classes of formulas, beginning with the "atomic formulas," in terms of "monomials," "conjunctions," "disjunctions," "implications," and so on through the general concept of a "formula." Moreover, we have introduced the intermediate literal notation Φ, Φ_1, and Φ_2 to demonstrate how to actually construct a particular class of formulas. The first rule of the symbolism, which we now introduce, allows us to use in place of the literal notation the actual names of the constructions we have created, enclosed within angular brackets for the sake of clarity. Thus, in place of the sentence, "if Φ_1 is an implication and Φ_2 is a disjunction, $\Phi_1 \supset \Phi_2$ is an implication," we may write more concisely,

$$\langle\,\text{implication}\,\rangle ::= \langle\,\text{implication}\,\rangle \supset \langle\,\text{disjunction}\,\rangle,$$

where the sign $::=$ denotes "equal by definition." Just like any other initial verbal definition, this notation gives a method of specifying a set of formulas, called "implications," in terms of the set of "implications" itself and the set of "disjunctions" in the following way. We consider an arbitrary "implication," assign the sign $\supset$ to it, after which we place an arbitrary "disjunction." The resulting line of text is, by definition, an element of the set of "implications." Note that in our system of rules there is no vicious circle, since there is another definition for the initial set of implications, which reads as follows:

"if Φ is a disjunction, Φ is an implication"

or, in the new symbolism,

$$\langle\,\text{implication}\,\rangle ::= \langle\,\text{disjunction}\,\rangle.$$

Thus we have two alternative definitions of an implication, which may be combined together by means of a vertical line on the right side of the construction to separate one alternative from the other:

$$\langle\,\text{implication}\,\rangle ::= \langle\,\text{disjunction}\,\rangle | \langle\,\text{implication}\,\rangle \supset \langle\,\text{disjunction}\,\rangle.$$

The construction itself is called a *metalinguistic formula*, and all the constructions we have defined are called *metalinguistic variables*. (Note that the elements of the constructed set of feasible objects, in our case, the logical formulas, are the values of these variables.)

All the rules for the complete set of logical formulas have the following form:

$\langle\,\text{constant}\,\rangle ::= \mathbf{f}\,|\,\mathbf{t},$

$\langle\,\text{variable}\,\rangle ::= A\,|\,B\,|\,C\,\ldots\,|\,X\,|\,Y\,|\,Z,$

$\langle\,\text{primary}\,\rangle ::= \langle\,\text{constant}\,\rangle\,|\,\langle\,\text{variable}\,\rangle\,|\,(\langle\,\text{formula}\,\rangle),$

$\langle\,\text{secondary}\,\rangle ::= \langle\,\text{primary}\,\rangle\,|\,\neg\,\langle\,\text{secondary}\,\rangle,$

$\langle\,\text{conjunction}\,\rangle ::= \langle\,\text{secondary}\,\rangle\,|\,\langle\,\text{conjunction}\,\rangle\,\&\,\langle\,\text{secondary}\,\rangle,$

$\langle\,\text{disjunction}\,\rangle ::= \langle\,\text{conjunction}\,\rangle\,|\,\langle\,\text{disjunction}\,\rangle$
$\qquad\qquad\qquad \vee\,\langle\,\text{conjunction}\,\rangle\,|\,\langle\,\text{disjunction}\,\rangle + \langle\,\text{conjunction}\,\rangle,$

$\langle\,\text{implication}\,\rangle ::= \langle\,\text{disjunction}\,\rangle\,|\,\langle\,\text{implication}\,\rangle \supset \langle\,\text{disjunction}\,\rangle,$

$\langle\,\text{formula}\,\rangle ::= \langle\,\text{implication}\,\rangle\,|\,\langle\,\text{formula}\,\rangle \equiv \langle\,\text{implication}\,\rangle.$

In this interpretation, the rules of specifying formulas recall the grammar of natural language, where the metalinguistic variables play the role of parts of speech. This analogy is no accident, indeed in mathematics any regular method of specifying objects that form some set L of words in a designated alphabet is often called a language. More precisely, a *language* is understood to refer to the actual set L, and the method of specifying L is called its *formal grammar*.

A rigorous description of a formal grammar itself requires some symbolism, usually described in some other language, called a *metalanguage*, which is used to describe L. In our case, we are describing the language of logical formulas using the metalanguage of metalinguistic formulas. A list of metalinguistic formulas is called the *syntax* of the particular language.

The concept of a formal grammar for natural languages was created in its most complete form in the 1950s by the American linguist and mathematician Noam Chomsky. The apparatus of metalinguistic formulas was suggested in 1959 by the American mathematician and programmer John Backus and used by his Danish colleague Peter Naur in 1960 to describe ALGOL 60. In their honor, grammars that may be described by means of metalinguistic formulas are called BNF (Backus–Naur form) grammars. This apparatus has since been extensively applied to describe programming languages, and has recently made its appearance in purely mathematical studies.

Now that we have a rigorous method of describing the logical formulas, we are now able to say more precisely what it means to assert that "the arguments for each operation are identified in a unique way."

Suppose we are given some logical formula. By the rules of a BNF grammar, we find that it is either an implication or is constructed from another logical formula, the operation sign $\equiv$, and some implication. The reader may verify that in this analysis a particular alternative is chosen in a unique way. The uniqueness of the choice is an important property of any successfully compiled BNF grammar. Thus, for each logical formula we may construct one or the other of the following two graphs:

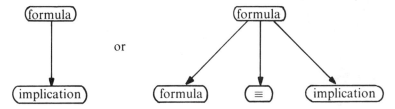

Here we have not only selected the alternative in a unique way, but have also partitioned the text of the initial formula into parts formed by metalinguistic variables on the lower level in a unique way. This means that for each of the *immediate constituents* of the initial formula we have thus identified, we may in turn select in a unique way the subformulas they consist of, so that the graph grows downward by one more layer of metalinguistic variables or symbols of the initial alphabet. This process of "dismantling" or "parsing" a formula continues until a symbol of the initial alphabet is reached along each path of the resulting graph (which is, naturally, a tree); each such symbol of the initial alphabet is then made a terminal character of the tree. The resulting graph, which is constructed in a unique way for the particular logical

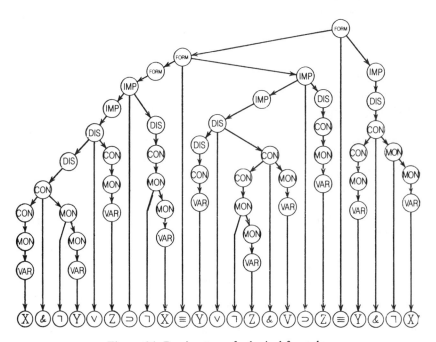

Figure 6.1. Parsing tree of a logical formula.

formula, is called the *parsing tree* of the logical formula. The symbols of the initial alphabet and the metalinguistic variables are its vertices. For the sake of brevity and generality, the former are referred to as the *terminal symbols* of the BNF grammar, and the latter as *nonterminal symbols*. The parsing tree for the above logical formula (∗) is presented in Figure 6.1.

Boolean Functions

Here it is pertinent to recall why this formalism has been presented. We have introduced the logical formulas as a tool for the rigorous description of compound propositions (logical formulas) whose truth may be established on the basis of the truth of the initial assertions (logical variables) using the semantic properties of the logical connectives (logical operations) as specified by their truth tables.

To justify our language of logical formulas, we must now provide them with a proper interpretation, i.e., show how to judge the truth or falsity of a logical formula once the truth values of the initial assertions (logical variables of the formula) are known. If we use the parsing tree, the "moment of truth" is reached by means of the following inductive procedure.

Basis of induction: Certain truth values are assigned (made inherent) to the terminal symbols, or variables (logical constants).

Inductive step: If a nonterminal symbol n has a unique constituent with truth value σ assigned to it, n is assigned the truth value σ;.

if a nonterminal symbol n is a monomial of the form $\neg n'$ and the symbol n' is assigned the truth value σ, n is given the truth value $\neg \sigma$ (from the truth table);

if a nonterminal symbol n is a construction of the form $n' \rho n''$, where ρ is one of the logical operations $\vee$, $+$, $\supset$, $\equiv$, and the symbols n' and n'' have been assigned the truth values σ_1 and σ_2, respectively, n is given the truth value $\sigma_1 \rho \sigma_2$ (from the truth tables).

Ultimately, by traversing all the layers of the parsing tree, we will have assigned a truth value to the root of the tree, and thus, along with the root, the entire logical formula. And just as a parsing tree is constructed from a formula in a unique way, so does the actual computation of the truth value yield a unique result.

Thus, our interpretation of the logical formulas consists in associating in a unique way some function of an arbitrary number of arguments (possibly no arguments at all) with each formula. The truth values **t** and **f** then become the truth values of both the arguments and of the function itself. For this reason, the functions are called *logical functions*, or functions of algebraic logic, or *Boolean functions*, in honor of the English mathematician John Boole, the first person to study them. If we wish our further analysis to be successful, we will have to become a bit more familiar with these functions.

We first find that every Boolean function may be specified in the form of a finite truth table. If we stipulate the order in which the truth values of the arguments of a function are computed (it is the same as the alphabetic order from **f** to **t**), every function may be completely described by means of the column of its values. Below we give a list of all the Boolean functions of two variables (of which there are 16).

$2^n = 4$

								$+$		$\&$	$\equiv$		$\supset$			$\bigvee$	
x_1	x_2	F_1	F_2	F_3	F_4	F_5	F_6	F_7	F_8	F_9	F_{10}	F_{11}	F_{12}	F_{13}	F_{14}	F_{15}	F_{16}
f	f	f	t	f	t	f	t	f	t	f	t	f	t	f	t	f	t
f	t	f	f	t	t	f	f	t	t	f	f	t	t	f	f	t	t
t	f	f	f	f	f	t	t	t	t	f	f	f	f	t	t	t	t
t	t	f	f	f	f	f	f	f	f	t	t	t	t	t	t	t	t

$n = 2$ $\qquad\qquad\qquad 2^{2^n} = 16$

Reflecting on this table leads us to the following observations:

Theorem 6.1. *A Boolean function of n variables has 2^n distinct sequences of truth values of its arguments.*

Theorem 6.2. *There is a total of 2^{2^n} Boolean functions of n variables.*

It is often convenient to replace the truth values **f** and **t** by 0 and 1, respectively. In this case, the Boolean functions become arithmetic binary functions. In such an interpretation, conjunction turns into ordinary multiplication, the exclusive disjunction into addition modulo 2, and negation into subtraction from 1.

Let us turn once again to the tabular representation of the Boolean functions. Suppose that Ω is a complete set of sequences of truth values of the arguments of a function of n variables, which will be assumed to be ordered in some way once and for all. In the arithmetic interpretation, each such sequence is a binary vector of length n. For every function f we consider the set of sequences T_f on which it is true (truth set) and the set F_f on which it is false. Obviously, $T_f \bigcup F_f = \Omega$. It is also obvious that if $T_{f_1} = T_{f_2}$, then $f_1 = f_2$, and conversely, if $f_1 = f_2$, then $T_{f_1} = T_{f_2}$ likewise. We are then able to identify the Boolean functions of n variables with their truth sets. This identification yields an interesting and useful interpretation of certain logical operations. The reader should have no trouble verifying that if g and h are Boolean functions with the same number of variables, then

Theorem 6.3. *If $f = g \vee h$, then $T_f = T_g \bigcup T_h$;*
if $f = g \& h$, then $T_f = T_g \bigcap T_h$;
if $f = \neg g$, then $T_f = \Omega \backslash T_g$;
if $f = g \supset h$, then $T_f = \Omega$ if and only if $T_g \subseteq T_h$.

Suppose that σ is a truth value. We let X^σ denote the logical formula X if $\sigma = \mathbf{t}$, and $\neg X$ if $\sigma = \mathbf{f}$. Suppose that $\sigma_1, \ldots, \sigma_n$ is an arbitrary sequence of n

logical values. We say that the logical formula

$$X_1^{\sigma_1} \& X_2^{\sigma_2} \& \ldots \& X_n^{\sigma_n}$$

is an *elementary conjunction*. It defines $F^{\sigma_1 \cdots \sigma_n}(x_1, \ldots, x_n)$ as a Boolean function which is true on the unique sequence of truth values of its arguments,* that is whenever

$$x_1 = \sigma_1,$$
$$x_2 = \sigma_2,$$
$$\ldots$$
$$x_n = \sigma_n.$$

In other words,

$$T_{F^{\sigma_1 \cdots \sigma_n}} = \{(\sigma_1 \ldots \sigma_n)\}.$$

Obviously, if $f = F^{\sigma_1 \cdots \sigma_n}$ and if $g = F^{\tau_1 \cdots \tau_n}$, where τ_i is also a truth value, then

$$T_{f \vee g} = \{(\sigma_1, \ldots, \sigma_n)\} \bigcup \{(\tau_1, \ldots, \tau_n)\}.$$

Hence follows at once the following very important assertion.

Theorem 6.4. *If* $f(x_1, \ldots, x_n)$ *is a Boolean function that takes the value* **t** *on at least one sequence of arguments, the logical formula*

$$\bigvee_{(\sigma_1 \ldots \sigma_n) \in T_f} X_1^{\sigma_1} \& X_2^{\sigma_2} \ldots \& X_n^{\sigma_n}$$

defines the function $f(x_1, \ldots, x_n)$.

Such a formula, in which the terms of the (for the sake of definiteness) conjunction are ordered in accordance with a fixed order of the sequences $(\sigma_1 \ldots \sigma_n)$ is called the *principal (disjunctive) normal form* of the function f. It is said to be a *normal* form because of its standardized form (a disjunction of several conjunctions), and is a *principal* form because of the following, also obvious assertion.

Theorem 6.5. *Two Boolean functions* f *and* g *are equal if and only if their principal normal forms coincide letter by letter.*

The last two theorems make direct use of the property that a Boolean function may be uniquely represented by its truth set.

The interpretation of the logical formulas associates with every formula some Boolean function. Theorems 6.4 and 6.5 demonstrate that even some

---

* Here and below we will distinguish between the formal variables X (letters of the alphabet of logical formulas) and the abstract variables x (arguments of a Boolean function). There is an obvious correspondence between them, but they are not the same objects.

smaller collection of logical formulas (principal normal forms) already suffices to specify an arbitrary Boolean function. By Theorem 6.2, there is a total of 2^{2^n} distinct Boolean functions of n variables. The number of distinct logical formulas in a BNF grammar which uses n distinct variables is, however, obviously infinite. Thus, there is an infinite number of formulas that specify the same function or, as we will say from now on, there is an infinite number of equivalent formulas. This assertion is hardly very surprising in and of itself, though it entails a serious response to the following two questions:

How do we know if two formulas are equivalent?

Is it possible to construct an algebra of logical formulas, i.e., methods for the systematic transformation of one formula into other formulas equivalent to it?

We won't waste time showing how important these questions are. They are the sort of questions which mathematics must respond to in one way or another in the development of any well-defined symbolic system. We only wish to note that in mathematical logic these questions are answered exhaustively, moreover by means of a variety of methods which, as we have already emphasized, recall many of the more highly evolved mathematical theories.

Let us note right now that for the first question there is at least one kind of affirmative answer that requires a direct, though cumbersome procedure. We consider functions specified by formulas and sort all sequences of truth values of the arguments one after the other. We then compute the truth values of the functions on these sequences, compile truth tables, and compare. Let us keep this possibility in mind, but for now deal with the second question.

6.2. Algebraic Logic

System of Identities

We have no doubt that the reader has sufficient preparation to understand that identity relations between formulas are the basic tool for equivalence transformations, i.e., transformations that preserve equivalence constitute the identity relations between formulas. The "baggage" we carry with us from high school already contains a vast arsenal of identities for the arithmetic operations, e.g.,

$$a+b = b+a,$$

$$a(b+c) = ab+ac,$$

$$a(bc) = (ab)c,$$

the algebraic identities,

$$(a+b)^2 = a^2 + 2ab + b^2,$$

$$(a^2 - b^2) = (a+b)(a-b),$$

the trigonometric relations

$$\sin^2 x + \cos^2 x = 1,$$

$$\sin(a+b) = \sin a \cdot \cos b + \cos a \cdot \sin b,$$

and so on.

We may find a large number of important relations that reflect the properties of Boolean functions by directly reviewing the simplest logical formulas and the logical operations. Some of them are trivial, while others are unexpected and of interest, and when originally discovered constituted a major contribution to the development of logic.*

The first group of relations expresses what are thought of as the properties of the logical operations. Note that the implication is neither commutative nor associative.

$$\neg \neg x = x, \tag{1}$$
$$x \vee y = y \vee x, \tag{2}$$
$$x \vee (y \vee z) = (x \vee y) \vee z, \tag{3}$$
$$x \& y = y \& x, \tag{4}$$
$$x \& (y \& z) = (x \& y) \& z, \tag{5}$$
$$x \supset (y \supset z) = y \supset (x \supset z), \tag{6}$$
$$x \equiv y = y \equiv x, \tag{7}$$
$$x \equiv (y \equiv z) = (x \equiv y) \equiv z. \tag{8}$$

The next group of relations demonstrates certain combinatorial properties of the operations:

$$x \& (y \vee z) = x \& y \vee x \& z. \tag{9}$$

Interestingly, conjunction and disjunction are mutually distributive:

$$x \vee (y \& z) = (x \vee y) \& (x \vee z). \tag{10}$$

Implication is also mutually distributive with respect to disjunction:

$$x \supset (y \vee z) = (x \supset y) \vee (x \supset z), \tag{11}$$
$$x \vee (y \supset z) = (x \vee y) \supset (x \vee z), \tag{12}$$
$$(x \vee y) \supset z = (x \supset z) \vee (y \supset z), \tag{13}$$

though there is only one type of distributivity for implication and conjunction:

$$x \supset (y \& z) = (x \supset y) \& (x \supset z). \tag{14}$$
$$x \equiv y = \neg x \equiv \neg y. \tag{15}$$

---

* In the presentation which follows we will leave aside the comparatively rare use of the exclusive or operation $(+)$.

The next group of relations gives the properties of the operations when certain constraints are imposed on their arguments:

$$x \vee x = x, \tag{16}$$

$$x \vee \neg x = \mathbf{t}, \tag{17}$$

$$x \vee \mathbf{f} = x, \tag{18}$$

$$x \vee \mathbf{t} = \mathbf{t}, \tag{19}$$

$$x \& x = x, \tag{20}$$

$$x \& \neg x = \mathbf{f}, \tag{21}$$

$$x \& \mathbf{f} = \mathbf{f}, \tag{22}$$

$$x \& \mathbf{t} = x, \tag{23}$$

$$x \supset x = \mathbf{t}, \tag{24}$$

$$x \supset (y \supset x) = \mathbf{t}, \tag{25}$$

$$\mathbf{t} \supset x = x, \tag{26}$$

$$\mathbf{f} \supset x = \mathbf{t}, \tag{27}$$

$$x \supset \mathbf{t} = \mathbf{t}, \tag{28}$$

$$x \supset \mathbf{f} = \neg x, \tag{29}$$

$$x \equiv x = \mathbf{t}, \tag{30}$$

$$\mathbf{t} \equiv x = x, \tag{31}$$

$$\mathbf{f} \equiv x = \neg x. \tag{32}$$

The final group of relations express certain operations in terms of others:

$$x \vee y = \neg(\neg x \& \neg y), \tag{33}$$

$$x \vee y = (x \supset y) \supset y, \tag{34}$$

$$x \& y = \neg(\neg x \vee \neg y), \tag{35}$$

$$x \supset y = \neg y \supset \neg x, \tag{36}$$

$$x \supset y = \neg x \vee y, \tag{37}$$

$$x \supset y = \neg(x \& \neg y), \tag{38}$$

$$x \equiv y = (x \supset y) \& (y \supset x). \tag{39}$$

However impressive this list of identities might seem, it may leave the critical reader unsatisfied simply because of how arbitrarily it is put together. In fact, it is just as easy to expand this list as shorten it. For example, we might add an interesting identity such as

$$x \supset (y \supset z) = (x \supset y) \supset (x \supset z),$$

or eliminate, say, the identity

$$x \supset y = \neg(x \,\&\, \neg y),$$

because it may be easily derived from the relations

$$x \supset y = \neg x \lor y,$$

$$x \lor y = \neg(\neg x \,\&\, \neg y),$$

$$\neg\neg x = x.$$

also, questions arise with less obvious answers, for example, can an identify such as $\neg \mathbf{f} = \mathbf{t}$ be derived from these 39 relations?

Thus, once we have found some system of equivalence transformations we must constantly ask ourselves whether this system suffices for deriving any formula equivalent to a given formula, and whether there are any redundant relations in this system, i.e., relations that may be deduced from other relations in the system. Of course, we speak of relations as being "redundant" only in the theoretical sense, since relations that may be deduced from other, fundamental relations may be extremely useful in and of themselves.

Returning to our problem of elucidating the notion of equivalence and finding an algebra of logical formulas, we may note in advance that if we had found a complete system of identities in the logical formulas, we would have obtained one more method of recognizing equivalence.

In fact, suppose that A and B are two logical formulas that specify the Boolean functions f_A and f_B. These two functions have the principal normal forms $K(f_A)$ and $K(f_B)$. By construction, A is equivalent to $K(f_A)$ and B is equivalent to $K(f_B)$. Since our system of identities is complete, we may systematically "derive" $K(f_A)$ from A and $K(f_B)$ from B. If we obtain the same principal normal forms from these two deductions, this will mean that A and B are equivalent (by Theorem 6.5).

Formula Schemas

Let us now rigorously describe the algebra of logical formulas. To the alphabet of the language of logical formulas we add the letters $A, B, C, \ldots$, to denote *metavariables*; logical formulas are the values of the metavariables. Applying the rules of the formal grammar to the expanded alphabet of variables, we find other formulas besides the ordinary logical formulas; the metavariables occur in these new formulas. To distinguish each such formula, we call it a *schema* (of a logical formula). A schema does not denote a formula, rather a set (as a rule, indeed an infinite set) of formulas that may be obtained as a result of replacing each metavariable every time it occurs by either one of its truth values (though the same one each time). The use of schemas in place of actual constructions is an ordinary mathematical device for the formulation of general assertions. By saying that a schema possesses some property, we are thereby making a general assertion about all the actual constructions that may be derived from it. A construction C may be obtained from a schema S if there exist truth values of the metavariables in S such that if they are replaced by these values, S turns into C. For example, if we declare that the schema $A \lor \neg A$ is identically true, we in fact are making the general assertion that there is an infinite list of formulas of the form

$$X \lor \neg X,$$

$$((A \lor B) \supset C) \lor \neg ((A \lor B) \supset C),$$

$$\neg A \lor \neg \neg A,$$

and so on, where all such formulas specify an identically true function. In a number of instances, in speaking of schemas we decide which constraints to impose on the metavariables. For example, the above assertion about the schema $A \lor \neg A$ is valid only if A is a monomial.*

Let us state more precisely what we have in mind when we say that a logical formula specifies a Boolean function. Suppose we are given several logical formulas $\Phi_1, \Phi_2, \ldots, \Phi_t$. We specify an arbitrary number of logical variables $x_1, \ldots, x_n$ provided that there are at least as many such variables as there are distinct variables in these formulas, and correlate with each variable from the formulas one of the logical variables x_i. This is done to make it possible for us to formally consider in some equivalence transformation, such as

$$x \supset (y \supset x) = \mathbf{t},$$

an identically true value $\mathbf{t}$ of a function of the two variables x and y. After this correspondence has been established, we determine as above the inductive process of computing truth values as a function f_i of the variables $x_1, \ldots, x_n$ for each of the formulas Φ_i. The resulting Boolean functions $f_1, \ldots, f_t$ are referred to as a (joint) *interpretation of the formulas* $\Phi_1, \ldots \Phi_t$.

Concept of a Calculus

A word of the form

$$A \sim B.$$

is said to be an *equivalence*, where A and B are logical formulas. An equivalence is said to be an *identity*, and two formulas are said to be *equivalent to each other*, if in any consistent interpretation the corresponding Boolean functions f_A and f_B are identically equal. Using schemas of logical formulas in place of the formulas themselves, we obtain an equivalent schema for which

---

* In every case, we must warn the reader not to confuse the metavariables $A, B, C, \ldots$ just introduced with the notation for arbitrary, but fixed formulas of the form A, B, C, ..., which are informally used in the text. These latter also constitute a special type of metavariable, though in a different metalanguage, namely Russian (or English), the language in which the present book is written.

we may also define an identity property for the methods already explained above. Replacing the equality sign (which we have reserved for semantic use) in the above identities (1)–(39) by $\sim$, we obviously obtain a series of identity equivalences. To generalize these equivalences to schemas, we must replace the symbols x, y, and z by metavariables, for example, A, B, and C, and for each schema show which formulas are possible as their values. For example, the equivalence (34)

$$x \vee y = (x \supset y) \supset y$$

may be transformed into the schema

$$A \vee B \sim (A \supset B) \supset B,$$

where A and B are conjunctions.

Further, by a *rule of inference* we understand a compound construction consisting of two parts, a *premise* and a *conclusion*. The premise is a set of schemas of logical formulas and equivalences, and the conclusion an equivalence or equivalence schema.* When printed out, a rule of inference has the form of a fraction whose numerator is the premise and whose denominator the conclusion, for example,

$$\frac{X \supset Y \sim \neg X \vee Y, \; X \vee Y \sim \neg(\neg X \& \neg Y), \; \neg \neg X \sim X}{X \supset Y \sim \neg(X \& \neg Y)}.$$

A list of rules of inferences and equivalences (or equivalence schemas) is called a *calculus*. Understood as a constituent element of a calculus, an equivalence is called an *axiom* (*axiom schema*). Let us now give an important inductive definition.

An equivalence or equivalence schema R is said to be *deducible* in a calculus T if any one of the following assertions is true:

(1) it may be obtained from an equivalence schema deducible in T;
(2) it is an axiom in T;
(3) it may be obtained from an axiom schema in T;
(4) if there is a rule of inference in T for which there exist deducible premises that define R as a conclusion of this rule.

It is by means of this definition that the meaning of a calculus becomes manifest. Indeed, the concept of a calculus is among the most fundamental of all mathematical concepts. In the general case, a calculus is a tool for systematically obtaining some set of constructive entities starting with some

---

* We hope the reader is not too embarrassed by our two uses of the words "premise" and "conclusion" within the same chapter to denote both the arguments of an implication as well as the constituent parts of a rule of inference. This sharing of terminology was not done haphazardly.

primitive designated set, here the axioms. Each rule of inference constitutes an inductive definition of a new construction (conclusion) expressed in terms of constructions given in its premise. For each construction that may be derived in the calculus, it is possible to specify its deductive history, starting with the axioms. In a schematic representation this history has the form of a tree whose terminals are the axioms and whose other vertices the conclusions of the rule of inference; arcs entering such a vertex specify the source of the premise, and arcs emanating from it, the point where the conclusion is used as the premise of a succeeding rule. Such a tree is called the *deduction tree* of the construction in the calculus.

However, a calculus does not, in and of itself, impart any meaning to the constructions deducible in it. For this purpose, we require a number of additional definitions.

An equivalence calculus is said to be *well-formed* if any equivalence that may be deduced in it is an identity. A calculus is said to be *complete* if any identity equivalence may be deduced in it. The axioms and rules of inferences of a complete calculus are said to be *independent* if the calculus becomes incomplete once any one of them is eliminated.

Calculus of Equivalences

Now we may show how to construct an algebra of logical formulas by finding a well-formed and complete calculus of equivalences consisting of independent axioms and rules of inference.

For the sake of brevity, we introduce some more notation. We will say that monomials, conjunctions, disjunctions, implications, and formulas proper are formulas of the first (highest), second, third, fourth, and fifth orders of priority, respectively. Analogously, the operations $\&$, $\vee$, $\supset$, and $\equiv$ are assigned second through fifth priority. The letters F^n and ρ^n denote a formula and operation of priority n, respectively. $\mathscr{F}\langle \mathscr{F}_1^n \rangle$ is a formula of $\mathscr{F}$ in which a single occurrence of the subformula $\mathscr{F}_1$ of priority n is isolated. $\mathscr{F}\langle X \rangle$ is a formula in which all occurrences of the variable X are isolated.

Calculus of Equivalences of Algebraic Logic (Calculus T)

Axioms and Axiom Schemas

(A1)	$\neg t \sim f$	negation.
(A2)	$\neg \neg X \sim X$	double negation.
(A3)	$X \vee Y \sim Y \vee X$	commutativity
(A4)	$X \vee Y \vee Z \sim X \vee (Y \vee Z)$	associativity.
(A5)	$X \vee X \sim X$	absorption.
(A6)	$X \vee \neg X \sim t$	law of excluded middle.
(A7)	$X \vee f \sim X$	disjunction with false.

(A8) $\neg(X \lor Y) \sim \neg X \& \neg Y$ distributivity of negation.

(A9) $X \& (Y \lor Z) \sim X \& Y \lor X \& Z$ distributivity of conjunction.

(A10) $X \supset Y \sim \neg X \lor Y$ implication.

(A11) $X \equiv Y \sim (X \supset Y) \& (Y \supset X)$ equivalence.

(A12) $(F^n) \rho^n X \sim F^n \rho^n X$ redundant parentheses of left operand.

(A13) $X \rho^n (F^{n-1}) \sim X \rho^n F^{n-1}$ redundant parentheses of right operand.

(A14) $(F) \sim F$ redundant parentheses of formula.

In (A12)–(A14), $n = 2, 3, 4, 5$.

Rules of Inference

(I1) $$\frac{\mathscr{F}_1 \langle X \rangle \sim \mathscr{F}_2 \langle X \rangle, F_3}{\mathscr{F}_1 \langle (F_3) \rangle \sim \mathscr{F}_2 \langle (F_3) \rangle}.$$

(replacement of variable*)

(I2a) $$\frac{\mathscr{F}_1^{(n)} \sim \mathscr{F}_2^{(m)}, \mathscr{F}_3 \langle \mathscr{F}_1^{(n)} \rangle \sim \mathscr{F}_4, m \le n}{\mathscr{F}_3 \langle \mathscr{F}_2^{(m)} \rangle \sim \mathscr{F}_4}.$$

(equivalent substitution)

(I2b) $$\frac{\mathscr{F}_1^{(n)} \sim \mathscr{F}_2^{(m)}, \mathscr{F}_3 \langle \mathscr{F}_1^{(n)} \rangle \sim \mathscr{F}_4, m > n}{\mathscr{F}_3 \langle (\mathscr{F}_2^{(m)}) \rangle \sim \mathscr{F}_4}.$$

That this calculus is well-formed may be established without any difficulty. By means of axiom schemas A12–A14, it is possible to eliminate redundant parentheses in transformations. The language of logical formulas admits formulas of the form $((A \lor B))$ or even $(A \& B) \equiv C$. There is no other way of asserting such obvious identities as

$$((A \lor B)) \sim A \lor B,$$

$$(A \& B) \equiv C \sim A \& B \equiv C$$

other than by introducing special axioms.

The formula F_3 substituted in place of the variable X in rule I1 must obviously be computed before executing any operations from $\mathscr{F}_1$ and $\mathscr{F}_2$ in which X is an operand. For this purpose, $\mathscr{F}_3$ is enclosed in parentheses, thereby giving it the highest priority. Naturally, redundant parentheses may be introduced, though this will be "noticed" by axioms A12 and A13. The priority conditions in rule I2 also guarantee that the priority of any formula inserted in place of $\mathscr{F}_1^{(n)}$ is not greater than n, so as not to corrupt the selection tree for $\mathscr{F}_3$.

---

* We are distinguishing between the metavariables F which may take as their values any formulas whatsoever, and the metavariables $\mathscr{F}$ which may take as their values only formulas that form deducible equivalences used as a premise of a rule of inference.

Note that once we have created a "tool" for identity transformations of logical formulas, our calculus then plays still one more role, indeed an extremely important one in and of itself. Every axiom and every rule of inference depends on some property of the formulas or functions that may be specified by formulas. In executing a transformation that may be described by an axiom or rule of inference, we must have a clear understanding of which property of a formula or function we are applying. The ability of a calculus to stipulate, or as is usually said, *postulate* or *formalize* various properties of abstract objects (in our case, Boolean functions) accounts for their central position in mathematical methods of reasoning. Basically, every mathematical discipline, based as it is on an axiomatic method, is, in its rigorous description, nothing more than a calculus with a language of constructions of its own that represents, or *denotes*, the abstract objects of the axioms, and postulates properties of the objects and rules of inference by means of which chains of reasonings are realized. The calculus itself may also be described in some metalanguage, which even if not introduced explicitly, is nevertheless logically present in every mathematical work. Such properties of a calculus as well-formedness, completeness, and independence are not just "serious characteristics," so to speak, but also reflect the appropriateness, completeness, and nonredundancy of the theory formalized by the particular calculus.

Completeness of the Calculus of Equivalences

Let us continue our discussion of the calculus of (logical) equivalences. We first prove that the equivalence relation defined by the calculus possesses the standard properties of an equivalence relation.

Equivalences

(E1) $F \sim F$ reflexivity

(E2) $\dfrac{\mathscr{F}_1 \sim \mathscr{F}_2}{\mathscr{F}_2 \sim \mathscr{F}_1}$ symmetricity.

(E3) $\dfrac{\mathscr{F}_1 \sim \mathscr{F}_2, \mathscr{F}_2 \sim \mathscr{F}_3}{\mathscr{F}_1 \sim \mathscr{F}_3}$ transitivity.

The deduction trees for these properties are shown in Figure 6.2 (isolated occurrences of subformulas and variables are underscored). Note that the trees for the rules of inference (cases (b) and (c)) each constitute a *conditional inference* in which equivalences or formulas that form the premise of the rule we wish to prove (rather than the axioms) are the terminals. Figure 6.2(c) shows a condensed deduction in which the subtree for deriving $\mathscr{F}_2 \sim \mathscr{F}_1$ from $\mathscr{F}_1 \sim \mathscr{F}_2$ is replaced by its "metavertex." The properties of the equivalence relation we have proved may be used to derive whole chains of equivalence transformations.

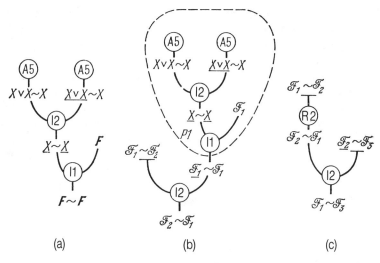

Figure 6.2. Deduction tree in calculus of equivalences. (a) E1: reflexivity; (b) E2: symmetricity; (c) E3: transitivity (isolated occurrences of formulas and variables are underscored).

Theorem 6.6. *Suppose that* F *is a logical formula whose variables belong to the set of logical variables* $\{X_1, \ldots, X_n\}$. *Then one or the other of the two equivalences*

$$F \sim K(X_1, \ldots, X_n)$$

or

$$F \sim f,$$

is deducible, where $K(X_1, \ldots, X_n)$ is a principal disjunctive normal form.

Before proving the theorem, we wish to note that since the calculus is well-formed, by virtue of Theorem 6.5 the formula $K(X_1, \ldots, X_n)$ may be found in a unique way. It is the principal disjunctive normal form of the function specified by F.

A complete proof of Theorem 6.6 is too cumbersome. Instead we will merely map out the stages in which F is transformed into K, accompanying these stages by an example. In the example, we will use more concise notation for the conjunction $(X_1 X_2$, without any operation sign) and for the negation $(\bar{X})$.

Suppose that $F = (\bar{X}_1 \equiv X_2 \lor \bar{X}_3)$. We first reduce F to a form containing only variables, disjunctions, conjunctions, and negations. The equivalence is eliminated by means of A11, the implication by means of A10, and the constant f by means of A1 and A7.

$$\bar{X}_1 \equiv X_2 \lor \bar{X}_3 \sim (\bar{X}_1 \supset X_2 \lor \bar{X}_3)(X_2 \lor \bar{X}_3 \supset \bar{X}_1) \sim$$

$$\sim (\neg \bar{X}_1 \lor (X_2 \lor \bar{X}_3))(\neg (X_2 \lor \bar{X}_3) \lor \bar{X}_1) \sim .$$

By axiom A8, the negation preceding the parentheses may be distributed over the terms of the disjunction. If there is a conjunction within the parentheses, by axiom A8 it may also be replaced by a disjunction. The double negations may be eliminated by A2:

$$\sim (X_1 \vee X_2 \vee \bar{X}_3)(\bar{X}_2 X_3 \vee \bar{X}_1) \sim .$$

All the parentheses may then be removed by means of axiom A9. Here we have used the properties of the conjunction $XX \sim X$ and $\bar{X}X \sim \mathbf{f}$, which are obtained from A5 and A6 by means of A8 and A2. If all the conjunctions prove to be equal to $\mathbf{f}$, we obtain the equivalence $F \sim \mathbf{f}$:

$$\sim X_1 \bar{X}_2 X_3 \vee X_2 \bar{X}_2 X_3 \vee \bar{X}_3 X_2 X_3 \vee X_1 \bar{X}_1 \vee X_2 \bar{X}_1 \vee \bar{X}_3 \bar{X}_1 \sim$$
$$\sim X_1 \bar{X}_2 X_3 \vee \bar{X}_1 X_2 \vee \bar{X}_1 \bar{X}_3 \sim .$$

All the conjunctions of a principal form must consist of all the variables $X_1, \ldots, X_n$. Wherever necessary, additional variables may be introduced by multiplying conjunctions by an identically true disjunction $(X \vee \bar{X})$. Here we have used the property of the conjunction $X\mathbf{t} \sim X$ (from A7):

$$\sim X_1 \bar{X}_2 X_3 \vee \bar{X}_1 X_2 (X_3 \vee \bar{X}_3) \vee \bar{X}_1 (X_2 \vee \bar{X}_2) \bar{X}_3 \sim$$
$$\sim X_1 \bar{X}_2 X_3 \vee \bar{X}_1 X_2 X_3 \vee \bar{X}_1 X_2 \bar{X}_3 \vee \bar{X}_1 X_2 \bar{X}_3 \vee \bar{X}_1 \bar{X}_2 \bar{X}_3 \sim .$$

Proceeding in the same way via A5 and this time ordering the conjunctions lexicographically by means of A3, we obtain a principal disjunctive normal form,

$$\sim X_1 \bar{X}_2 X_3 \vee \bar{X}_1 X_2 X_3 \vee \bar{X}_1 X_2 \bar{X}_3 \vee \bar{X}_1 \bar{X}_2 \bar{X}_3. \qquad \square$$

Theorem 6.7. *The calculus of equivalences is complete.*

In fact, suppose that F_1 and F_2 are two equivalent formulas. This means that they specify one and the same Boolean function f. In this case, by Theorem 6.6 there are two deducible equivalences

$$F_1 \sim K, \quad F_2 \sim K,$$

where K is either $\mathbf{f}$ or the principal normal form of f. By the symmetricity and transitivity of the equivalence relation, we at once find that

$$F_1 \sim F_2. \qquad \square$$

6.3. Propositional Calculus

Valid Formulas

Let us go back and discuss the underlying motives that have inspired the development of mathematical logic. A logical formula is a symbolic, condensed, and exact expression of some judgment, or proposition, about certain initial assertions, or logical variables understood in a definite interdependence as represented by means of connectives, or logical operations. We explained that the truth or falsity of a proposition is a single-valued function of the truth values of the initial assertions. Algebraic logic consists in methods of transforming logical formulas without changing their logical content, i.e., the truth function (Boolean function) specified by them.

It is natural to distinguish those logical formulas that specify identically true Boolean functions. These formuals are called *valid formulas, tautologies,* or *laws of logic.* Let us write down several such formulas, accompanying their symbolic expression by their verbal description.

$A \lor \neg A$: Whatever the proposition A asserts, it is valid to say that A is either true or false;

$A \supset A \lor B$: Given any assertion A, either the assertion itself or some arbitrary additional assertion B follows;

$(A \supset B) \supset (C \lor A \supset C \lor B)$: Whatever rule of inference we use, it is preserved whenever we consider both the premise and the conclusion combined in disjunction with any additional assertion C.

The concept of valid formulas emphasizes the fact that a Boolean function specified by formulas preserves its truth value over all the truth values of its arguments. The concept of a tautology emphasizes that an identically true assertion is in some sense trivial, and does not provide us with any information about the interdependence of the propositions occurring in it. In fact, if we know that A & B is true, we also know that both A and B are true propositions. However, the truth of the assertion $A \supset A \lor B$ does not create any relationship between A and B. Thus, it is more proper to say that a valid formula characterizes some property of the logical connectives occurring in it, which manifests itself regardless of the semantic content and even the truth values of the logical variables occurring in this formula. This higher degree of generality is emphasized by the use of the term, "law of logic."

Now that the concept of valid formulas has been thoroughly studied, we may quickly review how it is related to equivalence transformations of logical formulas. In fact, from the above definitions we at once have the following assertion.

Theorem 6.8. *Suppose that* A *and* B *are logical formulas. The equivalence* $A \sim B$ *is an identity transformation if and only if the formula* $A \equiv B$ *is valid.*

This theorem leads us to the thought that the problem of finding equivalence transformations of logical formulas is only a special case of the more general problem of constructing a calculus by means of which it would be possible to deduce all the valid formulas (including those which describe the identity equivalence relations) starting with certain axioms and using the rules of inference.

We will approach this problem from our experience in constructing the calculus of equivalence relations of algebraic logic. We have already had occasion to remark in passing on the great variety and "multi-dimensionality" of the axiomatic structure of equivalence relations. Some axioms reflect more the properties of the method of constructing the formulas ("parenthesisology" of axioms A12–A14) than the properties of the logical operations. Other axioms merely express a single operation in terms of others (for example, A11) or one object in terms of another (for example, A1). In fact, $A \equiv B$ is valid if and only if the formula $(A \supset B)$ & $(B \supset A)$ is valid. Any conjunction is valid if and only if its terms, in this case $A \supset B$ and $B \supset A$, are valid. In other words, if we know how to derive valid formulas of the form $A \supset B$ and are given a rule of inference which states that "if A and B are deducible, so is A & B," all the valid formulas that may be interpreted as equivalent will be deducible. Thus, unlike the other logical operations, the sign $\equiv$ will be interpreted not as a fundamental logical operation whose meaning is made manifest through the medium of the independent axioms, but rather as denoting a more complex construction introduced for purposes of abbreviation.

We will continue further on with this in mind. Thus, as a synonym for **t** we may consider the formula $X \vee \neg X$. The synonym for **f** is then the formula X & $\neg X$. We may then attempt to deduce every conceivable valid formula that makes reference to these truth values in light of these synonyms. We may further simplify the syntax of the logical formulas by waiving the formalism of priority for the two-place operations:

$\langle$ variable $\rangle$:: = $A|B|C \ldots |X|Y|Z,$

$\langle$ atomic $\rangle$:: = $\langle$ atomic $\rangle | \neg \langle$ operand $\rangle,$

$\langle$ operand $\rangle$:: = $\langle$ atomic $\rangle|(\langle$ binomial $\rangle),$

$\langle$ two-place operation $\rangle$:: = $\vee |$&$| \supset,$

$\langle$ binomial $\rangle$:: = $\langle$ operand $\rangle \langle$ two-place operation $\rangle \langle$ operand $\rangle,$

$\langle$ formula $\rangle$ :: = $\langle$ atomic $\rangle | \langle$ binomial $\rangle.$

Once again, we may stipulate that parentheses may be omitted in formulas, though this will now be done as a matter of abbreviation for convenience in reading and writing, and not as a rule of the formal theory.

The universal use of axiom schemas makes it possible to avoid rules of inference, which would otherwise mandate interchanging variables and substitution.

Propositional Calculus

With these prefatory remarks in mind, we may now demonstrate a calculus of valid logical formulas (the calculus L) that resembles the calculus described by the American mathematician S. Kleene in 1952.

Propositional Calculus (Calculus L)

Axiom Schemas

(A1) $A \supset (B \supset A)$.

(A2) $(A \supset (B \supset C)) \supset ((A \supset B) \supset (A \supset C))$.

(A3) $(A \& B) \supset A$.

(A4) $(A \& B) \supset B$.

(A5) $A \supset (B \supset (A \& B))$.

(A6) $A \supset (A \lor B)$.

(A7) $B \supset (A \lor B)$.

(A8) $(A \supset C) \supset ((B \supset C) \supset ((A \lor B) \supset C))$.

(A9) $(\neg A \supset \neg B) \supset ((\neg A \supset B) \supset A)$.

Rule of Inference

(I1) $\dfrac{\mathcal{A}, (\mathcal{A}) \supset (\mathcal{B})}{\mathcal{B}}$.

A propositional calculus is well-formed if any deducible formula is valid. It is complete if any valid formula is deducible (in this calculus). There is one further important property of the propositions—what is known as *consistency*. This property asserts that there exists no formula A such that both A and $\neg$A would be deducible in the calculus. By means of the concept of consistency, it is possible to define the property of completeness in a second way: A propositional calculus is complete (in the narrow sense) if adding to the calculus as an axiom at least one formula not deducible from it makes the calculus inconsistent (contradictory). The above calculus L is well-formed and complete, as well as consistent and complete in the narrow sense. The properties of consistency and completeness in the narrow sense are interesting in that they are defined in terms of the calculus itself, and do not require an interpretation of formulas as constructions that specify truth functions. At the same time, these properties (at least for L) correspond precisely to the properties of well-formedness and completeness, which use the concept of valid formulas. The ability of a propositional calculus to describe its own useful properties without resorting to an interpretation based on concepts of truth and falsity, but relying exclusively on the concept of inconsistency, understood, moreover, purely formally, is a distinctive feature of the propositional logic, though not so frequent in formal theories.*

---

* We have allowed ourselves some freedom in drawing analogies, and we may now remark that this "nonessentialness" of the interpretation of logical propositions as bearers of truth and falsity reflects the commonly held belief that the most important element of a formal logical argument is precisely the consistency of its constituent judgments, and not so much the "correctness" of the ultimate conclusion.

Let us now elucidate the axiomatic structure of L. In these informal explanations, we will interpret propositions as events so that, for example, one event may "imply" another one.

Axiom A1 postulates that a current event may be made the consequent of any other event ("what is true follows from anything"). Axiom A2 asserts that if there exists a two-part chainwise dependence between events and if the first part of the chain occurs, we are then justified in assuming that the initial event implies the concluding event. Axioms A3 and A4 postulate that the occurrence of a compound event implies the occurrence of each of its constituent events. Axiom A5 postulates that the successive occurrence of two events implies the occurrence of the compound event. Axioms A6 and A7 show that the occurrence of any one of two events is due to either one or the other of these events. Axioms A8 asserts that if each of two events implies a third, to be sure that this third event occurs, we need only know that one or the other of the two original events has occurred. Axiom A9 postulates a method of proof by contradiction: If a premise implies both a conclusion and the negation of this conclusion, the premise is false. Finally, the rule of inference I1 is the well-known rule of detachment (*modus ponens*), which states that if it is known that (for example) night falls once the sun sets and if it is also known that the sun has indeed set, it is then valid to conclude that night has fallen.

Properties of the Propositional Calculus

That the calculus L is well-formed may be established quite simply by means of the truth tables. The proof of the remaining properties requires a whole series of intermediate assertions, most of which are of independent importance as rules of logical inference.

In our discussion of the calculus T (Section 6.2), we already had occasion to apply the concept of a "conditional inference," which we used as a proof of a derived rule of inference. A conditional inference is in the form of a deduction tree whose root is the construction we wish to deduce and whose terminals are either axioms or occurrences of arbitrary formulas that play the role of premises. We use the "deducibility symbol" $\vdash$ as a compact notation for assertions about the existence of a conditional inference of some formula (formula schema) B from a set of premises $\{A_1, \ldots, A_n\}$. By means of this symbol, an assertion of conditional inference may be wrftten in the form of a *production* $A_1, \ldots, A_n \vdash B$. The notation $\vdash B$ denotes an assertion about the (unconditional) deducibility of B. The conditional deducibility of B from the premises $A_1, \ldots, A_n$ is referred to simply as the *deducibility* of B from $A_1, \ldots, A_n$. It is also agreed that a true deduction tree for deducing B from the premises $A_1, \ldots, A_n$ should contain as terminal vertices occurrences from any subset of $\{A_1, \ldots, A_n\}$.

Rules of Logical Inference

(T1)   If $A_1, \ldots, A_{n-1}, A_n \vdash B$, then

$$A_1, \ldots, A_{n-1} \vdash A_n \supset B.$$

This may also be written as follows:

$$\frac{A_1, \ldots, A_{n-1}, A_n \vdash B}{A_1, \ldots, A_n \vdash A_n \supset B},$$

(T2) $A, A \supset B \vdash B.$

(T3) $A, B \vdash A \,\&\, B.$

(T4) $A \,\&\, B \vdash A.$

(T5) $A \,\&\, B \vdash B.$

(T6) $A \vdash A \vee B.$

(T7) $B \vdash A \vee B.$

(T8) $\dfrac{A_1, \ldots, A_n, B \vdash D, \; A_1, \ldots, A_n, C \vdash D}{A_1, \ldots, A_n, B \vee C \vdash D}.$

(T9) $\dfrac{A_1, \ldots, A_n, \neg B \vdash C, \; A_1, \ldots, A_n, \neg B \vdash \neg C}{A_1, \ldots, A_n \vdash B}.$

(T10) $\neg \neg A \vdash A.$

Rule T1 is called the *deduction theorem*. Together with T2, which is simply the rule of inference I1 which we have placed in this list for the sake of completeness, this theorem elucidates the exact logical sense of the implication as equivalent to deducibility: $\vdash A \supset B$ if and only if $A \vdash B$. With this equivalence in mind, the other rules are restatements and simple generalizations of the axioms of L.

Proof of Deduction Theorem

Lemma L1. $\vdash A \supset A.$

Proof.
1. $\vdash A \supset (A \supset A)$ by A1 with $B = A$.
2. $\vdash (A \supset ((A \supset A) \supset A)) \supset ((A \supset (A \supset A)) \supset (A \supset A))$ by A2 with $B = A \supset A$ and $C = A$.
3. $\vdash (A \supset (A \supset A)) \supset (A \supset A)$ by I1 with $\mathscr{A}$ from A1 with $B = A \supset A$ and $\mathscr{A} \supset \mathscr{B}$ from Step 2.
4. $\vdash A \supset A$ by I1 with $\mathscr{A}$ from Step 1 and $\mathscr{A} \supset \mathscr{B}$ from Step 3.   □

Suppose that some formula B may be deduced from the formulas $A_1, \ldots, A_n$. We distribute the formulas forming the tree for conditional inference into levels. All the terminal vertices are placed in the first level. In the *i*th level are placed vertices that have as their predecessors at least one vertex in the $(i-1)$th level. The theorem is proved by induction on the number of levels in the deduction tree.

In the first level we find either the deducible formulas (axioms) or formulas from the list $A_1, \ldots, A_n$. Let us prove that any formula B from the first level satisfies the theorem. If B is a deducible formula, using B and B $\supset (A_n \supset B)$ as the premises in I1 yields as conclusion $\vdash A_n \supset B$. If $B = A_n$, by Lemma L1 we find that $\vdash A_n \supset A_n$. If $B = A_i$ $(i < n)$, using (by axiom A1) the deducible formula $A_i \supset (A_n \supset A_i)$ and A_i as the premises of I1 yields $A_i \vdash A_n \supset A_i$. By the definition of conditional deducibility, we find that it is valid that $A_1, \ldots, A_{n-1} \vdash A_n \supset B$ for formulas B of the first level.

Let us consider an arbitrary formula B from the ith level and assume the theorem is valid for any formula from levels with lesser ordinal number. Formula B is obtained by applying I1 to the two premises A and A $\supset$ B, for which (by the induction hypothesis) both $A_n \supset$ A and $A_n \supset (A \supset B)$ are deducible from $A_1, \ldots, A_{n-1}$. Setting $A_n = A$, $A = B$, and $B = C$ in axiom A2 yields the deducible formula $(A_n \supset (A \supset B)) \supset ((A_n \supset A) \supset (A_n \supset B))$. Letting this formula be our $\mathscr{A} \supset \mathscr{B}$ and letting $A_n \supset (A \supset (A \supset B)$ be our $\mathscr{A}$ in I1 yields

$$A_1, \ldots, A_{n-1} \vdash (A_n \supset A) \supset (A_n \supset B).$$

Again taking formula $(A_n \supset A) \supset (A_n \supset B)$ as our $\mathscr{A} \supset \mathscr{B}$ in I1 and $A_n \supset A$ as our $\mathscr{A}$ yields the conclusion $A_1, \ldots, A_{n-1} \vdash A_n \supset B$. The deduction theorem is proved. □

The deduction theorem, likewise rules T8 and T9, are example of assertions about deducibility that may be proved not only by writing out a formal deduction in the calculus, but also by means of some general and informal process of reasoning about a particular deducibility without having to actually represent it. It is with this "second" layer of logical reasoning in mind that such assertions are called *metatheorems*. Figure 6.3 depicts the deduction tree of the conditional inference of metatheorem T8 (principle of proof by analysis of instances) and the production T10 (elimination of double negation).

By means of these rules of inference, the axiomatic structure of the propositional calculus may be brought closer to the rules of equivalence transformations of logical formulas. Understanding the condensed notation $(A) \equiv (B)$ as denoting the formula schema $((A) \supset (B)) \& ((B) \supset (A))$, we may formulate in the calculus certain well-known properties of the identity operation, as well as the relationship between deducibility and validity:

(T11) $\vdash A \equiv A$.

(T12) $A \equiv B \vdash B \equiv A$.

(T13) $A \equiv B, B \equiv C \vdash A \equiv C$.

(T14) $A, A \equiv B \vdash B$.

(T15) $\vdash A \vee \neg A$.

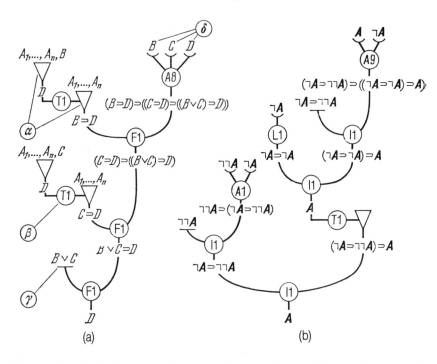

Figure 6.3. Deduction tree in propositional calculus: (a) metatheorem T8:

$$\frac{A_1, \ldots, A_n, B \vdash D, \ A_1, \ldots, A_n, C \vdash D}{A_1, \ldots, A_n, B \lor C \vdash D}; \text{(b) production T10: } \neg\,A \vdash A: (\alpha) \text{ notation of}$$

conditional inference; (β) application of metatheorem; (γ) premise of conditional inference; (δ) substitution in axiom schema.

The following obvious lemma asserting the transitivity of the implication is required for T13:

(L2) $A \supset B, B \supset C \vdash A \supset C$.

which, though it is contained implicitly in axiom A2, is obtained not directly from it, but rather by means of the deduction theorem. That is, we derive C from the three premises A, $A \supset B$, and $B \supset C$ by means of a double application of I1, after which the conditional inference $A \supset C$ is obtained by means of the deduction theorem. Figure 6.4 shows the deduction of T15 (law of excluded middle).

Unlike the calculus of equivalences of logical functions, the rule of substitution in the propositional calculus is not axiomatized (rule I2 in T), but instead proved in the form of a "replacement theorem."

Theorem 6.9. *Suppose that* C(A) *is a formula in which an occurrence of some formula* A *is isolated, and let* C(B) *be the formula that may be obtained from*

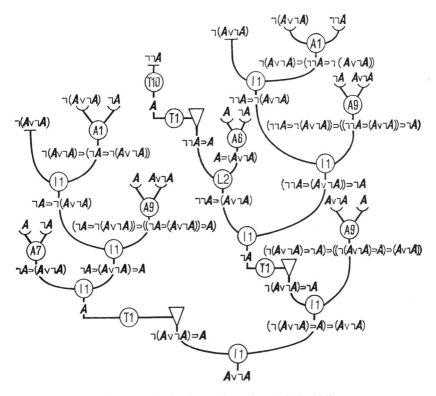

Figure 6.4. Deduction of law of excluded middle.

C(A) *by replacing the occurrence of* A *by* B. *Then*

$$A \equiv B \vdash C(A) \equiv C(B).$$

Proof. Let us consider the parsing tree for the formula C(A) in the language of logical formulas of L. The *depth of occurrence d* of a formula A in C refers to the number of arcs in the path from a vertex of A to the root of the parsing tree of C. We then carry out the reasoning by induction on *d*.

Basis of induction. If $d = 0$, C(A) = A and C(B) = B, so that the assertion of the theorem has the form

$$A \equiv B \vdash A \equiv B,$$

which is valid by the properties of a conditional inference.

Induction step. Suppose that A has depth of occurrence $d + 1$ in C. In accordance with the syntax of the language of logical formulas, C(A) has one of the following forms:

$$C(A) = (M(A)) \supset (N),$$

$$(N) \supset (M(A)),$$

$$(M(A)) \& (N),$$

$$(N) \& (M (A)),$$

$$(M (A)) \lor (N),$$

$$(N) V (M (A)),$$

$$\neg M (A),$$

where the depth of occurrence of A in M(A) is equal to d, and therefore, by the induction hypothesis, we have the production

$$A \equiv B \vdash M (A) \equiv M (B).$$

We now formulate the following lemmas.

(L3) $A \equiv B \vdash A \supset C \equiv B \supset C.$

(L4) $A \equiv B \vdash C \supset A \equiv C \supset B.$

(L5) $A \equiv B \vdash A \& C \equiv B \& C.$

(L6) $A \equiv B \vdash C \& A \equiv C \& B.$

(L7) $A \equiv B \vdash A \lor C \equiv B \lor C.$

(L8) $A \equiv B \vdash C \lor A \equiv C \lor B.$

(L9) $A \equiv B \vdash \neg A \equiv \neg B.$

Proofs of several of these lemmas are given as examples in Figure 6.5. For each of the syntactic forms for C(A), we conduct our reasoning in accordance with the following schema. Suppose

$$C(A) = M(A)\rho N.$$

By the inductive hypothesis,

$$A \equiv B \vdash M(A) \equiv M(B).$$

By the corresponding lemma, we have

$$M (A) \equiv M(B) \vdash M(A)\rho N \equiv M (B)\rho N,$$

which by the transitivity of the deducibility property yields $A \equiv B \vdash C(A) \equiv C(B).$ □

By including the identity sign in the calculus and evaluating its properties, we are able to prove (in the calculus) all the identity equalities of the Boolean functions (1)–(39) in the form of deducible formula schemas (using formulas of the form $B \lor \neg B$ and $B \& \neg (B)$ in place of **t** and **f**, respectively). Most of the deductions may be obtained by direct application of the appropriate axioms and rules of inference from among T1–T10, though some of then are rather lengthy. As an example, in Figure 6.6 we present the proof of the distributive property of conjunction relative to disjunction.

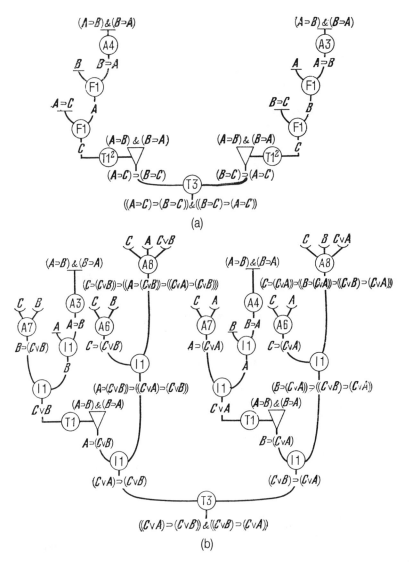

Figure 6.5. Derivation of lemmas from replacement theorem: (a) $A \equiv B \vdash A \supset C \equiv B \supset C$; (b) $A \equiv B \vdash C \lor A \equiv C \lor B$.

Completeness, Consistency, and Independence

Our study of the propositional calculus approaches an end. Let us outline a proof of the completeness of L.

Suppose we are given a valid formula A. By means of a chain of identity transformations and the replacement theorem, we obtain the deduction

$$\vdash A \equiv K_A,$$

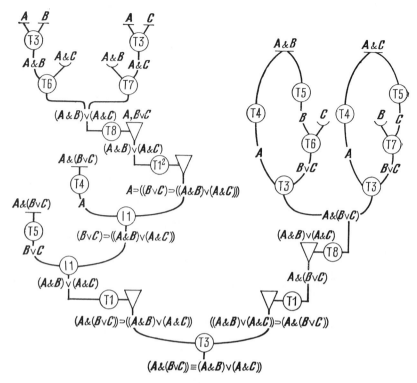

Figure 6.6. Deduction of distributivity of conjunction relative to disjunction.

where K_A is a principal disjunctive normal form. Since A is a valid formula, K_A must contain a complete set of elementary conjunctions which, by means of identity transformations, may be represented quite simply in the form

$$(X_1 \lor \neg X_1) \& \ldots \& (X_n \lor \neg X_n)$$

which, in turn, may be transformed into a deducible formula of the form $B \lor \neg B$. By T15, $\vdash B \lor \neg B$, whence by T14, A is deducible.

Consistency follows from the property of well-formedness and the fact that the negation of any valid formula is a valid formula.

Completeness in the narrow sense may be established by the following line of reasoning. Suppose that A is a formula in L. By the completeness of L, A is not valid. Suppose that $X_1, \ldots, X_n$ are the variables in A and let $\sigma_1, \ldots, \sigma_n$ be a set of values on which an interpretation of A has value **f**. In A we replace all occurrences of X_i by the formula $X \lor \neg X$ if $\sigma_i = \mathbf{t}$, and by $\neg (X \lor \neg X)$ if $\sigma_i = \mathbf{f}$. As a result, we obtain the formula A′ which is not only still not deducible in L,[*] but also has an identically false interpretation. But then $\neg$ A′ is

---

*Were A′ deducible, by the reverse substitution we would find that A is deducible.

deducible in L. We now include B as an axiom schema in L, replacing its variables by metavariables, yielding a calculus L' in which A is deducible. Since the rules for substituting formulas in place of variables in L' remain valid, A' is also a deducible formula in L', which contradicts the deducibility of ⌐ A' in L'. A rigorous proof of completeness in the narrow sense requires the following theorem.

Theorem 6.10. (*substitution theorem*). *Suppose that* $A(X)$ *is a formula with only unbound occurrences of the variable X and let* $A(B)$ *be the formula obtained by substituting the formula B for all occurrences of X. Then if* $\vdash A(X)$, $\vdash A(B)$.

Proof. Let us consider the deduction tree D of $A(X)$ and free all occurrences of X in all terminal formulas. Each of these formulas constitutes an axiom containing metavariables $M_1, \ldots, M_k$ replaced by some of their bound values $C_1(X), \ldots, C_k(X)$. If all occurrences of X are replaced by B, as before we obtain a correct application of the axiom with the metavariables $M_1, \ldots, M_k$ replaced by the values $C_1(B), \ldots, C_k(B)$. Performing the same substitutions in all nonterminal formulas of D yields a correct deduction tree D with the concluding formula $A(B)$.   □

In any particular calculus, the proof of the independence of the axioms and rules of inference, though usually in accordance with the general schema, nevertheless requires a considerable degree of inventiveness and a good understanding of axiomatic structure, in both its semantic sense and in its formal (textual) representation. With each axiom (or rule of inference) we associate some particular property of the formulas or interpretation of the formulas. On the one hand, this property must be nontrivial, i.e., there must exist deducible formulas some of which possess this property and some of which do not. On the other hand, the subset M of formulas deducible without the use of this axiom must be closed relative to the property, i.e., formulas in M must all either possess or not possess this property. Thus we find that the calculus is incomplete without this axiom.

Let us present two typical examples illustrating the proof of the independence of the axioms of L.

Independence of axiom A9:

$$(\urcorner A \supset \urcorner B) \supset ((\urcorner A \supset B) \supset A).$$

If A is a formula, $h(A)$ is the formula obtained from A by eliminating all occurrences of the sign $\urcorner$. For example,

$$h((\urcorner X \vee \urcorner Y) \supset \urcorner \urcorner X) = (X \vee Y) \supset X.$$

We claim that if A is any formula that may be obtained by replacing metavariables by their values in any of the axiom schemas A1–A8, $h(A)$ is a valid formula. For this purpose, it is sufficient to verify that $h(A)$ may be obtained from any one of these schemas in the same way as A. For example, for A5 we have

$$h((A \lor \neg B) \supset (\neg C \supset ((A \lor \neg B) \& \neg C))) = (A \lor B) \supset (C \supset ((A \lor B) \& C))$$

We say that a deducible formula A is *conservative* if its associated formula $h(A)$ is valid. Obviously, if A and A $\supset$ B are conservative formulas, B is also a conservative formula. Thus, we have found that the set of formulas deducible in L without axiom A9 possesses the property of conservativity. At the same time (setting $A = B = A$ in A9), the formula

$$h((\neg A \supset \neg A) \supset ((\neg A \supset A) \supset A)) = (A \supset A) \supset ((A \supset A) \supset A)$$

is not valid (it is equal to **f** whenever A = **f**) and, therefore, the formula

$$(\neg A \supset \neg A) \supset ((\neg A \supset A) \supset A)$$

is not deducible in L without A9.

Independence of axiom A3:

$$A \& B \supset A.$$

We vary the definition of the conjunction in our interpretation of the logical formulas, starting by assuming that

$$x \& y = y.$$

The conjunction then has the following truth table:

x	y	$x \& y$
f	f	f
f	t	t
t	f	f
t	t	t

Let us consider L without axiom A3. By direct verification using the truth tables, we find that the calculus is well-formed in this new interpretation. At the same time, the formula

$$(X \& Y) \supset X$$

is not valid in this interpretation (if X = **f** and Y = **t**, the value of the function is **f**). Thus, this formula, which is obtained from axiom schema A3, is not deducible in L without axiom A3.

Conclusion

Let us now summarize what we have set forth in this chapter.

We have presented a number of assertions from algebraic logic and the propositional calculus which we will require in subsequent chapters. In addition, using mathematical logic as an example, we have considered a method of constructing a formal theory as a means for the constructive study of abstract objects and properties of abstract objects. That the approach is indeed constructive is clear from the fact that we have associated with any abstract object (Boolean function) some construction (formula) that has the form of some text in a language (the language of logical formulas) specified by its own formal grammar (syntactic rules). The relationship between formal, but constructive objects and semantic, but abstract objects is established by means of an interpretation. A whole set of interpretations may be associated with a single formal object (for example, different Boolean functions may differ in terms of how many independent variables each has or how many operations may be defined in different ways, as in a proof of independence).

Language usually creates a redundant store of constructions, and it is for this reason that a calculus is created—to identify those constructions it is worth studying. A calculus is a method for the effective generation of formal objects that possess certain useful properties (for example, the ability to specify some function in the algebra of logical formulas or the property of being a valid formula in the propositional calculus).

A calculus is specified by means of axioms that play a dual role. Together, they specify an initial set of objects that possess some desired property, and each axiom is in and of itself the bearer (postulate) of some special property of an abstract object. The rules of inference play the role of inductive definitions by means of which new formal constructions are created (deduced) from given constructions without affecting the desired properties.

In constructing a calculus, special emphasis is placed on the possibility of formalizing general assertions into a formal theory, i.e., a theory related directly to the set of constructions. For this purpose, we usually introduce either special rules of substitution and replacement, or axiom schemas and reasonings involving the use of metavariables.

The ordinary problems discussed in the context of a calculus are those having to do with well-formedness (whether the calculus is closed relative to some property we wish to study), the completeness of the formal theory, and the independence of the axiomatic structure.

For some readers this chapter may be their first encounter with mathematical logic. For these readers, the author feels especially at fault for the incompleteness and somewhat superficial presentation of the chapter. Formally speaking, the material in this chapter is sufficient for further study in which the reader may hope to gain a full understanding. For those readers for whom the material presented in this chapter does not suffice, we would like to recommend a number of books on mathematical logic which, incidentally, served as the source of most of the definitions and proofs in the present chapter.

1. A. Lavrov and L. L. Maksimova. *Problem Book of Set Theory, Mathematical Logic, and Theory of Algorithms.* Moscow, Nauka, 1975. A condensed summary of the basic concepts of mathematical logic with a good assortment of thought-provoking and practice problems.
2. P.S. Novikov. *Elements of Mathematical Logic.* Moscow, Nauka, 1973. An introductory course, written with great care for the beginning reader.
3. E. Mendelson. *Introduction to Mathematical Logic.* Princeton, N.J. Van Nostrand, 1970. (Russian Translation: Moscow, Nauka, 1976). Modern and well-organized introductory textbook in a highly condensed presentation.
4. S.C. Kleene. *Introduction to Metamathematics.* New York, Toronto, van Nostrand, 1952. Advanced textbook unsurpassed in terms of completeness and outstanding in rigor, but entirely accessible for gaining a detailed understanding of the basic concepts.

CHAPTER 7

Yanov Schemas

7.1. Initial Observations

Logical Operators in Programs

A program is a construction that causes an automatic machine to begin operation. The command segment of a program indicates the content of the operation, and its object part, the data or objects on which the operation is to be performed. In the first part of the book we studied the problem of packing data in the memory of a computer within the context of an overly simplified formulation. If we think a bit about the command segment of a program, the first thing we notice is that there are two types of operations, those in which data are transformed (computations) and those in which properties of the data are tested (control operations). The properties of the data in a program specify conditions that govern the selection of a further direction for the computations. When a programmer begins to solve a problem, he encounters these conditions in meaningful expressions, such as "Is x a prime number?" "Is the matrix symmetric?" "What district is this city the center of?" "Are the connectivity components of the data graph linked?" "Will the bridge break under this load?" "Is this chess position a good one?"

The goal of our studies in the second part of the book is to construct a general theory for the programming of conditions. In glancing over the list presented above, it is clear that the first thing to do is narrow down the problem in some reasonable way. The conditions are far too diverse, but even more important, they conceal within themselves the solution of problems which, though special cases of the general program, are nevertheless rather complicated. One approach to making the formulation more rigorous is to separate methods of formulation and testing of conditions from methods of applying the result of some test for selecting a direction for the computations. In any rigorous definition of a program, this may be accomplished by introducing a special type of operator, called a *logical operator*. Each such operator A consists of two parts:

(1) some arbitrary function f defined on the objects of the program that takes one of n admissible and previously known values $c_1, \ldots, c_n$, and

(2) some set of n possible successors $s_1, \ldots, s_n$ of A.

The function f is called an *n-valued predicate*. By the rules of programming languages,* the mapping of the valuation domain of the predicate $\{c_1, \ldots, c_n\}$ is assumed known (i.e., when writing out the program). A logical operator is intended for the computation of the values of the predicate and for transferring control to one of the operators $\{s_1, \ldots, s_n\}$ corresponding to the computed value.

The next step is to select the most important special case of a binary selection to which an n-valued selection may be reduced, as shown in Figure 7.1. (Let us remark parenthetically that the extreme cases of sequential and cascaded implementations of an n-valued selection require the same number of logical operators in a program, though the mean number of binary selections is on the order of $n/2$ in the first case, but on the order of $\log_2 n$ in the second case.)

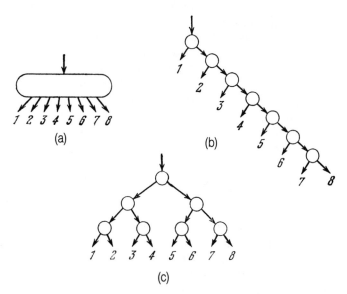

Figure 7.1. Binary implementations of n-valued parsing: (a) n-valued parsing; (b) sequential implementation; (c) cascaded implementation.

---

* Strictly speaking, the number of successors is at most equal to the number of values of the predicate, since there is no contradiction if the full "switching force" of a predicate is not used, i.e., if a single successor is associated with more than one value of the predicate.

Logical operators with binary predicates are useful not only because of their simplicity, but also because they may be written out in the language of logical formulas. In such an approach, the expressions of the predicates have a sort of two-level structure. The first level is formed by what are known as elementary logical predicates, while the second level consists of an arbitrary logical formula in which the expressions of the elementary predicates play the role of independent variables whose truth values are computed using some method external to the logical operator. It is because of this application of predicates in the first level that they are referred to as elementary. In actuality, particularly in languages that admit arbitrary functional notation, an elementary predicate may be a computational procedure of arbitrary complexity.

The structure of the logical predicates is highly developed in ALGOL 60. Below, in Backus–Naur form, we present the syntax of a ⟨simple Boolean⟩ in ALGOL 60.* Such concepts as ⟨variable⟩, ⟨function designator⟩ (i.e., notation for computing a function for given values of its arguments), and ⟨simple arithmetic expression⟩ (i.e., an expression not containing any if clauses) are assumed known:

⟨relational operator⟩ ::= ⟨ | ≤ | = | ≥ | ⟩ | ≠ ,

⟨relation⟩ ::= ⟨simple arithmetic expression⟩ ⟨relational operator⟩ ⟨simple arithmetic expression⟩,

⟨logical value⟩ ::= **true** | **false**,

⟨Boolean primary⟩ ::= ⟨logical value⟩ | ⟨variable⟩ | ⟨function designator⟩ | ⟨relation⟩ | (⟨Boolean expression⟩),

⟨Boolean secondary⟩ ::= ⟨Boolean primary⟩ | ¬ ⟨Boolean primary⟩

⟨Boolean factor⟩ ::= ⟨Boolean secondary⟩ | ⟨Boolean factor⟩ & ⟨Boolean secondary⟩

⟨Boolean term⟩ ::= ⟨Boolean factor⟩ | ⟨Boolean term⟩ ∨ ⟨Boolean factor⟩,

⟨implication⟩ ::= ⟨Boolean term⟩ | ⟨implication⟩ ⊃ ⟨Boolean term⟩,

⟨simple Boolean⟩ ::= ⟨implication⟩ | ⟨simple Boolean⟩ ≡ ⟨implication⟩.

Here are several examples of predicates.

(a) if clause: X belongs to the closed interval $[0, 1]$:

$$(x \le 1) \,\&\, (x \ge 0).$$

(b) if clause: y is outside the half-open intervals $[a, b)$ and $[2a, 3b)$:

$$\neg(a \le y \,\&\, y < b \lor 2 \times a \le y \,\&\, y < 3 \times b).$$

---

* Borrowed from Revised Report on *the Algorithmic Language ALGOL 60*. International Federation for Information Processing, 1962, with replaced by &.

(c) if clause: the point (X, Y) is inside a trigonometric circle, in particular is in its first or third quadrants:

$$(X{\uparrow}2 + Y{\uparrow}2 \leq 1)\,\&\,(X \times Y \geq 0).$$

(d) A "polling machine", a Boolean function which is true if at least two of its three logical arguments are true. It is simplest to find its expression by constructing its truth table:

x_1	x_2	x_3	F	x_1	x_2	x_3	F
f	f	f	f	t	f	f	f
f	f	t	f	t	f	t	t
f	t	f	f	t	t	f	t
f	t	t	t	t	t	t	t

From the table, we at once find its principal normal form:

$$\neg x_1\,\&\,x_2\,\&\,x_3 \vee x_1\,\&\,\neg x_2\,\&\,x_3 \vee x_1\,\&\,x_2\,\&\,\neg x_3 \vee x_1\,\&\,x_2\,\&\,x_3.$$

The rules for constructing a logical operator always presume two possible directions to the computations, called the *plus direction* and the *minus direction*. The plus direction is associated with a true value of the predicate condition, and the minus direction with a false value.

In some algorithmic languages, the positive direction is indicated by a label while the negative direction denotes the next printed statement; in other languages, both directions are indicated by labels, the first label being the positive label and the second the negative label. In ALGOL 60, the positive direction indicates the statement (which, naturally, may be a compound statement) that occurs between the word **then** and the word **else** or the semicolon. In the latter case (semicolon), the negative direction does not require any operations, and control passes to the next printed statement. In the former case (**else**), the negative direction indicates the statement that immediately follows the **else**. In ALGOL 60, a logical operator is called a *conditional statement* and is defined by means of the following syntax:*

$\langle$if clause$\rangle ::= $ **if** $\langle$Boolean expression$\rangle$ **then,**

$\langle$unconditional statement$\rangle ::= \langle$basic statement$\rangle | \langle$compound statement$\rangle |$ $|\langle$block$\rangle$,

$\langle$if statement$\rangle ::= \langle$if clause$\rangle | \langle$unconditional statement$\rangle$,

$\langle$conditional statement$\rangle \quad ::= \langle$if statement$\rangle | \langle$if statement$\rangle$ **else** $\langle$statement$\rangle | \langle$if clause$\rangle \langle$for statement$\rangle | \langle$label$\rangle :$ $\langle$conditional statement$\rangle$.

---

* It might be a good idea for the reader to try to figure out why the designers of ALGOL 60 did not count the $\langle$for statement$\rangle$ as one of the $\langle$unconditional statements$\rangle$. Of course, the $\langle$for statement$\rangle$ may be combined with $\langle$if clause$\rangle$ in the same way as an $\langle$unconditional statement$\rangle$.

If we recall that the basic statements include the sequential operator **goto** M, it becomes clear that the syntax of ALGOL 60 provides other methods of specifying positive and negative directions.

Next we give several fragments of ALGOL programs containing logical operators using the Boolean expressions presented above as conditions:

(1) **if** $(x \le 1) \& (x \ge 0)$ **then** $y := x$ **else** $y := \ln(x)$;

(2) **if** $(X \uparrow 2 + Y \uparrow 2 \le 1) \& (X * Y \ge 0)$ **then begin:**
   if $X \ne 0$ **then begin** $A := \arctan(Y/X)$; **goto** COMPUTE **end end**;
   ERROR: print (X, Y);

(3) **if** $\neg x_1 \& x_2 \& x_3 \vee x_1 \& \neg x_2 \& x_3 \vee x_1 \& x_2 \& \neg x_3 \vee x_1 \& x_2 \& x_3$
   then goto YES **else goto** NO;

As in the first part of the book, it will be best in our presentation to represent the program graphically. Since control transfers in a control flow graph are indicated by arcs whose orientation is specified by arrows, it is natural to call the positive and negative directions the *plus* and *minus arrows*, respectively. We will distinguish the plus arrow from the minus arrow by affixing a small circle to the base of the former. Figure 7.2 presents in graphic form several examples of logical operators.

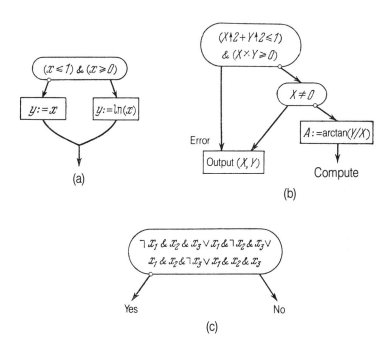

Figure 7.2. Examples of logical operators: (a) exclusive or branches with common successor; (b) chain of if clauses exiting from a branch; (c) compound if clause.

Polling Problem

Now that we've gone through a review chapter on mathematical logic, it is natural to focus our attention on the example of a polling machine. On the one hand, its condition constitutes a rather cumbersome expression, but on the other hand its actual computation presents no major problems; we only have to have a little more patience and program the principal normal form:

$$r_1 := \neg x_1;$$
$$r_2 := r_1 \& x_2;$$
$$r_2 := r_2 \& x_3;$$
$$r_1 := \neg x_2;$$
$$r_1 := r_1 \& x_1;$$
$$r_1 := r_1 \& x_3;$$
$$r_2 := r_2 \vee r_1;$$
$$r_1 := \neg x_3;$$
$$r_1 := r_1 \& x_1;$$
$$r_1 := r_1 \& x_2;$$
$$r_2 := r_2 \vee r_1;$$
$$r_1 := x_1 \& x_2;$$
$$r_1 := x_1 \& x_2;$$
$$r_1 := r_1 \vee r_3;$$

if r_1 then goto YES else goto NO.

I am certain that at this point even the most scrupulous reader would be troubled if we were to waste any more paper demonstrating so feeble an approach to programming this problem. In asking the reader's forbearance, we would also like to say that the example is presented not just for the sake of comparison, but also as a warning that such programs do appear in real life and, unfortunately, not so rarely.

Without any mathematical logic at all and without any general theory of programming, the three given variables x_1, x_2, and x_3 may be arranged quite simply in the following way.

Suppose that $x_1 = \mathbf{t}$.
Test x_2: If $x_2 = \mathbf{t}$, we have two votes and may write YES;
if $x_2 = \mathbf{f}$, when $x_3 = \mathbf{t}$ we obtain YES again, and when $x_3 = \mathbf{f}$, NO.
Suppose that $x_1 = \mathbf{f}$.
Test x_2. If $x_2 = \mathbf{t}$, everything again depends on x_3: when $x_3 = \mathbf{t}$, we have YES, and when $x_3 = \mathbf{f}$, NO;
if $x_2 = \mathbf{f}$, we already have two against, hence NO.

This selection procedure may easily be represented graphically (Figure 7.3(a)). Glancing at the figure, we can at once see how meaningless it would be

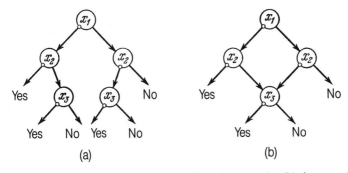

Figure 7.3. Polling machine: (a) unbiased direct approach; (b) improved direct approach.

to write out the test for x_3 twice; it suffices to draw the arrows from the two tests for x_2 to the single vertex of the graph (Figure 7.3(b)). It is apparent that expanding a compound logical condition into a series of tests of elementary predicates can greatly simplify a program.

Just this once, I would be a bit surprised if the reader was not at least a little skeptical, as such direct reasoning assuming, say, ten voters, might possibly be far more complicated and even fraught with error. It is therefore natural to consider methods of expanding compound predicates into elementary predicates in a more systematic fashion.

In this way we may at once achieve a reasonable narrowing of the problem (methodologically, in precisely the same way as in the introduction of the concept of a logical formula). We abstract from the methods of computing the elementary predicates, assuming them to be independent logical variables whose values are specified by other (previously computed) statements of the program. The predicate itself then becomes simply a logical formula.

Since a formula is created from variables by means of logical operations, a natural way of analyzing the process of expanding a conditional predicate is to analyze the principal logical operations. The corresponding rules may be exhibited without further ado:

(1) *Negation.* If an if clause is in the form of a negation $\neg x$, test x by interchanging the positive and negative directions in the statement (Figure 7.4(a)).

(2) *Disjunction.* If an if clause is in the form of disjunction $x \vee y$, test x and then exit in the positive direction if $x = \mathbf{t}$, or then test y if $x = \mathbf{f}$. The exits from the test of y are the same as for $x \vee y$ (Figure 7.4(b)). Note that this rule relies directly on the following well-known properties of the disjunction:

$$\mathbf{t} \vee y = \mathbf{t},$$

$$\mathbf{f} \vee y = y.$$

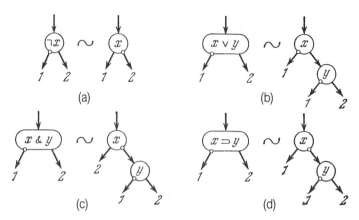

Figure 7.4. Rules for expanding if clauses: (a) negation; (b) disjunction; (c) conjunction; (d) implication.

(3) *Conjuction.* If an if clause is in the form of a conjunction x & y, test x and then exit in the negative direction if $x = \mathbf{f}$, or then test y if $x = \mathbf{t}$. The exits from the test of y are the same as for x & y (Figure 7.4(c)). Note that this rule relies on the following analogous properties of the conjunction:

$$\mathbf{f} \& y = \mathbf{f},$$
$$\mathbf{t} \& y = y.$$

(4) *Implication.* If an if clause is in the form of an implication $x \supset y$, test x and then exit in the positive direction if $x = \mathbf{f}$, and then test y if $x = \mathbf{t}$. The exits from the tests of y are the same as for $x \supset y$ (Figure 7.4(d)). Here we are using the following properties of the implication:

$$\mathbf{f} \supset y = \mathbf{t}, \qquad \mathbf{t} \supset y = y.$$

Once these rules have been formulated, we may easily find that they are interdependent. That is, we may start with the rules for negation and disjunction and derive from them the rule for conjunction, using the relation

$$x \& y = \neg(\neg x \lor \neg y),$$

and similarly derive the rule for implication, using the identity

$$x \supset y = \neg x \lor y.$$

This derivation is shown in Figure 7.5.

Obviously, in applying these rules we may expand an arbitrary logical operator in an entirely formal manner by using the parsing tree of the logical formula that forms the condition. We recommend that the reader undertake this process for the condition in the polling machine and compare the result with the program illustrated in Figure 7.6(a).

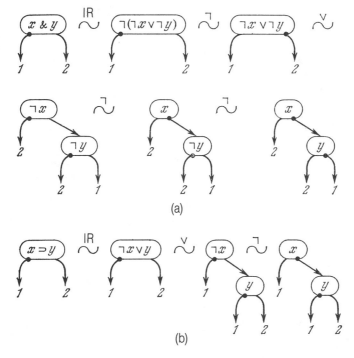

Figure 7.5. Obtaining deducible rules: (a) rule for conjunction; (b) rule for implication. (IR—identity replacement of condition; ρ, application of rule for operation ρ).

Let us carefully review what we have obtained. Naturally, the program is far from the elegant polling machine of Figure 7.3(b). However, it is precisely the ill-contrived nature of the program, which literally leaps before our eyes (each condition is tested a total of four times!), which suggests that there is more for us to do here.

Let us undertake an exhaustive analysis of the program in Figure 7.6(a). It consists of four "levels," in each of which there is a kind of "corridor" exiting to the terminal vertex with four "ladders" leading to the initial vertex of the lower level. By moving through the corridor from the initial vertex, we are in fact testing the values of the elementary predicates one after the other and, depending on the combination of values of these predicates, ending up at the terminal output to declare YES or dropping down the ladder to the initial vertex of the corridor in the lower level. There is an opportunity to improve the program, in that once we have ended up at some level P by moving up the ladder, we will already know the values of some of the predicates and could then select, at level P, indeed at once, the necessary direction without wondering which way to go.

Let us implement this notion a bit more carefully, beginning with the lower levels of the program. So as not to overly complicate the drawing, let us make

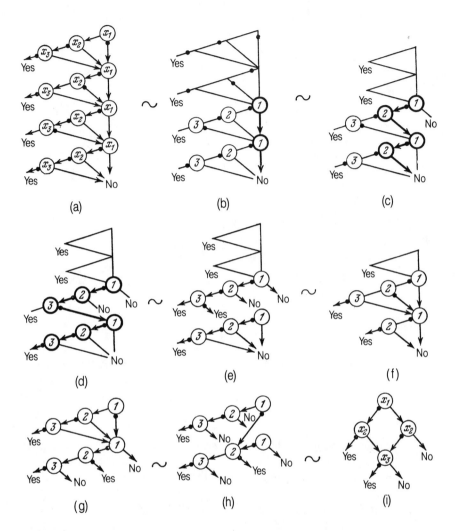

Figure 7.6. Systematic simplification of polling machine.

our representation of the program even more schematic by replacing the variables by their ordinal numbers, abbreviating YES and NO by Y and N, and not bothering to draw in detail whatever parts of the program we are not considering at the particular moment (e.g., Figure 7.6(b)).

If x_1 is false as we enter the second level, then once we have reached the first level moving from x_1 along the minus arrow, we find that condition x_1 from the first level forces us to change direction to N. But if so, we may change the minus arrow emanating from the second level x_1 to point to H in our program, thereby eliminating the repeated test of this condition (Figure 7.6(c)).

For the second-level condition x_2 to put us on the first level, we would have to have $x_1 = t$ and $x_2 = f$. However, once we have traversed the second level, this combination of values forces us to change direction to N. To explain this result, we may once again redirect the minus arrow from the second-level x_2 to point to N (Figure 7.6(d)).

Reasoning analogously for the case in which we end up on the first level starting from the second level x_3, we redirect the plus arrow from x_3 to point to N and obtain the program shown in Figure 7.6(e). There are two points worth noting here. First, there is no longer any ladder leading to the first level. Thus, there is no point from which we could end up in this part of the program and, consequently, it may be simply eliminated from the program. In the logical operator with condition x_3 on the second level, the positive and negative directions coincide and for that reason no test is needed. The positive arrow pointing to the entry x_3 may thus be changed to point to Y, and the operator with x_3 eliminated (Figure 7.6(f)). Repeating analogous reasoning for the next pair of levels leads to the program shown in Figure 7.6(g).

After the next series of changes of directions of the arrows, we obtain the program depicted in Figure 7.6(h). Removing the logical operator with x_1 to which no control transfer now leads, linking together the two identical copies of the operator with condition x_3, and returning to the earlier notation yields the desired result (compare Figure 7.6(i) with Figure 7.3(b)).

Initial Statement of the Problem

With this example in mind, we may make a number of important observations, and thereby lay the foundations for our investigation. We are considering a program that contains conditions which may be computed as Boolean functions of elementary predicates and which may be represented in the form of logical formulas containing the basic logical operations. In these programs, it is possible to implement equivalence transformations that vary the structure of the logical operators, but not the content of the program itself. The rules of these transformations have the form of identity relations between program fragments in their diagrammatic representations. These include rules for expanding (and combining together, if read from right to left) conditions (Figure 7.4), and rules for redirecting arrows (except for repeated tests) and eliminating inapplicable operators and "ungluing" (or gluing) operators with the same effect (Figure 7.7). In part, these relations rely on the properties of Boolean functions, and in part on the rules of execution of logical operators. Transforming a program that relies on these relations may lead to an improvement of various of its characteristics (simplicity, a more graphic structure, reduced run time). It is therefore natural to try to construct a calculus of program transformations that preserve equivalence and the logical operators associated with program execution.

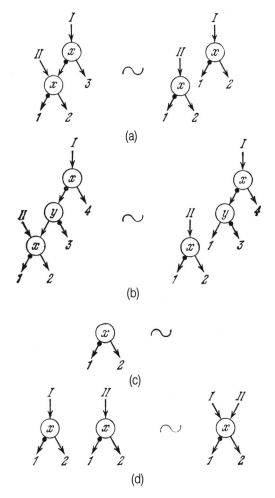

Figure 7.7. Additional rules of transformations: (a) local redirection of plus arrow; (b) "remote" redirection of plus arrow; (c) elimination of inapplicable logical operator; (d) gluing together logical operators that have the same effect.

Now that we know something about the propositional calculus, we may immediately decide which parts of the calculus would be useful in the solution of this problem.

1. A language must be constructed in which the formal objects corresponding to actual programs may be described constructively. These formal objects are called *Yanov schemas*.
2. A mechanism of interpretation must be described by means of which Yanov schemas may be associated with actual programs and an equivalence relation between programs must be introduced.

3. A definition of equivalence of Yanov schemas must be given in terms of the notion of equivalence of programs, and then investigated.
4. A metalanguage must be introduced in which the calculus of equipotent (i.e., equivalence-preserving) transformations of Yanov schemas may be described, and this calculus itself has to be devised.
5. This calculus must be studied in terms of well-formedness and completeness of axioms and rules of inference.

7.2. Search for Basic Definitions

Analysis of Constraints

The first thing we have to do is delimit the scope of our formalism. We have already remarked on a number of important constraints. The most important one is that our study will be limited to properties of programs that are associated with conditional statements—and only with the "second level" of these statements, i.e., Boolean functions of elementary predicates. In other words, we are not interested in any of the other statements of a program in and of themselves. For us, the only important thing is the sequence (specified by the logical operators themselves) in which these statements may be executed without interfering with the various operations in which the conditions are applied. Such an approach is rather self-evident in the example of the polling machine. Here we investigated a way of testing conditions in a part of a program that contains only conditions and that has a single input and two outputs, YES and NO. Our concern was focused solely on whether we had selected the exit properly in accordance with the values of the logical operators arriving at the input. We could have stopped here once we had constructed an "algebra of logical operators" through the introduction of a desired output as an interpretation of the function used to select the desired exit and then ensuring that this function was preserved under any transformation of the logical operators.

However, even simple examples demonstrate that it is natural for us to want more. We have seen that "storage" of the result of a test of the value of some condition is one way of simplifying compound logical operators; it was in this way that we were able to avoid repeated tests and eliminate any unnecessary logical operators that had cropped up. The influence of the choice of direction, i.e., the computed value of a condition, extends not only to the immediate successor (Figure 7.7(a)), but, under certain conditions, has certain "long-range" consequences (Figure 7.7(b)). That is, the chain of conditions along which information about previously made choices seems to be passed may be rather lengthy. We might, however, ask how to proceed if an arithmetic operator is inserted in the path of such a chain (Figure 7.8). Obviously, the answer depends only on whether or not A recomputes the variable x. In fact, if

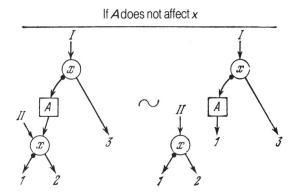

Figure 7.8. Redirecting an arrow for an arithmetic operator.

we know with some degree of reliability that A may not alter the value of x, the arc emanating from A may be directed at once to point to the result 1. Such a transformation may otherwise turn out to be against the rules. Thus, we may conclude that the statements should be included in the formalism, further, because of the "reach" of the logical dependencies, we are forced to extend our formalism to the concept of a program as a whole. There is, however, one simplifying circumstance worth nothing. The formal concept of an arithmetic operator also requires such things as the ability to distinguish one statement in a program from another statement and, for each statement, to know which logical variable it may affect.

To achieve a reasonable definition of a program, we must introduce the concept of memory for storage of processed data. We already have one type of memory, i.e., logical variables that store the values of the elementary predicates computed by some statement or specified prior to the start of a program run. As regards storage for other data processed by the program, the situation is both simpler and more complicated. We have already remarked that the only information needed from the arithmetic operators are the conditions this or that operator may compute more times than is necessary As for any other data the statement reads in or processes—this we are not interested in. This attitude of ignoring the details of how a statement works may be expressed in a hypothesis, i.e., we assume that both the argument and the result of a statement constitutes the entire memory as a whole. In such an approach, the memory for the data seems like a monolithic unit that does not have to be partitioned into locations. This type of memory may only be assumed as a working hypothesis in the statements without any need for explicit notation and, therefore, simply does not appear in the formal definition of Yanov schemas.

There is a negative side to this assumption: impoverishment of the theory. The "overall" effect of the application of any arithmetic operator—applied from the entire memory to the entire memory—is, naturally, an overly strong assumption not justified for the majority of actual programs. On the other hand (running ahead of ourselves a bit), bear in mind that it is precisely by means of such "blurring" of the initial suppositions that we may impart to Yanov theory a classical sense of completeness.

As in the case of the storage packing problem, it is natural to combine statements in a program by means of a control flow graph. And here we confront our first roadblock: How are we to select a method of representing the graph and what should be its level of generality? Since we have already limited ourselves to logical operators with binary predicates on which we have conferred all responsibility for selecting the direction of computation, we now confront the natural requirement that any vertex of the control flow graph have no more than two successors. As it will be necessary to describe the computational process specified by a program in the course of interpreting Yanov schemas, we will have to specify the entry and exit statements in the control flow graph. If we admit several initial statements, we will be forced to infer the existence of some event in which the entry statement is selected "for the very first time." We don't see any special need for creating such additional entities and instead suppose that there has to be a single entry statement, which we will label by a special entry arrow. The exit statement may be interpreted in a natural way as a halt instruction, i.e., it does not implement any transformation of data and does not designate any successor. It is reasonable to require that the corresponding vertex in the control flow graph not have any arc existing from it. Also, we may readily agree that whether there are several exit statements or just one makes no real difference; for the sake of greater simplicity, we will limit ourselves to a single exit statement.

The next choice we face is that between a simply connected or multiply connected control flow graph. The reader may recall that we imposed connectivity as a requirement in the storage packing problem. There this requirement was sufficient, since the storage packing procedure for each connectivity component was applied independently, and the graph itself remained invariant. In our present case, we already know that the control flow graph changes in the course of transforming Yanov schemas; in particular, vertices may be multiplied and arcs moved from certain vertices to other vertices. The polling machine example alone was sufficient grounds for conjecturing that even if the initial graph has to be connected, connectivity may be violated in the course of the transformations. This result suggests not imposing any additional requirements on the control flow graph.

In discussing the language for describing Yanov schemas, it may become necessary to use some textual representation of the control flow graph. However, at this point we would like to show the reader that the concept of a language doesn't have to be applied all that literally. Instead, wherever possible, constructive objects may be interpreted as abstract objects, and wherever necessary, other graphic forms for representing objects besides textual representations may be used.

In particular, we will give a definition of Yanov schemas that uses the abstract concept of a directed graph without, for the time being, introducing any special symbols for such characteristics of a directed graph as the entry arrow, plus and minus arrows, and exit statement. So as to better combine the abstract interpretation of a graph and the symbolic language that specifies the statements and the logical conditions, we will assume that a control flow graph consists of abstract vertices with which concrete statements and logical conditions are associated.

Definition of Yanov Schema

Suppose we are given a countable set of *predicate symbols*

$$\mathscr{P} = \{P_1, P_2, \ldots\}$$

and *operator symbols*

$$\mathscr{A} = \{A_1, A_2, \ldots\}.$$

By a *condition* we understand any logical formula with predicate symbols from $\mathscr{P}$ as the logical variables. An *operator* $A = A(P)$ is understood to refer to a pair consisting of the operator symbol A and some set (possibly empty) P of predicate symbols. The set $P = P(A)$ is called the *shift* of A. A *control flow graph* is a directed graph whose set of vertices consists of a nonnegative number of *transformers*, a nonnegative number of *recognizers*, and a single *halt instruction*. Each transformer has a single successor, and each recognizer two successors. There are two types of arcs emanating from a recognizer, called the

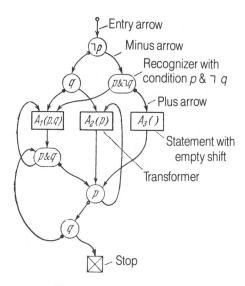

Figure 7.9. Yanov schema.

plus arrow and the *minus arrow*. A halt instruction does not have any successors. There is a single vertex in the control flow graph called the *entry vertex* and labelled by an *entry arrow*.

Suppose that $\{P_1, \ldots, P_k\}$ is an arbitrary nonempty set of predicate symbols. A *Yanov schema* $G(P_1, \ldots, P_k)$ is an arbitrary control flow graph with whose recognizers we associate conditions, and with whose transformers, operators. The logical variables of each condition and each shift of the operators belong to the set $\{P_1, \ldots, P_k\}$; all the symbols of the operators in a schema are pairwise distinct.

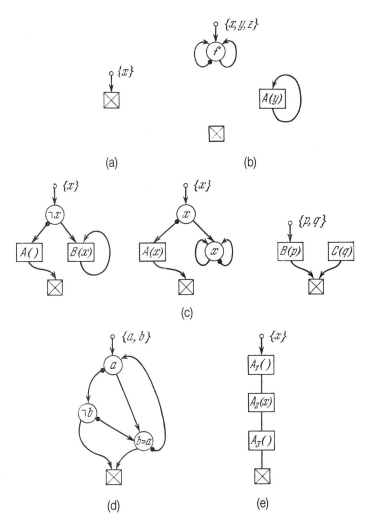

Figure 7.10. Examples of degenerative Yanov schemas: (a) maximally empty schema; (b) multiply connected schema; (c) incompletely connected schemas; (d) schema without statements; (e) schema without conditions.

As an example, Figure 7.9 presents a Yanov schema that also illustrates a graphical notation for all the elements of the formal definition. In Figure 7.10 we give examples of different types of degenerative schemas by means of which we may verify that the theory is correct for different "extreme cases."

Figure 7.11 presents the Yanov schema for the three-experts problem. The figure needs some explanation. Three experts E_1, E_2, and E_3 are responsible for approving or rejecting some document. To review the documents, the experts first arrive at some sort of preliminary opinion about the document by hearing each other out. Here $x_i = \mathbf{t}$ denotes that E_i approves the document. E_1 and E_3 are "skeptics" in the sense that if they have a negative view of a

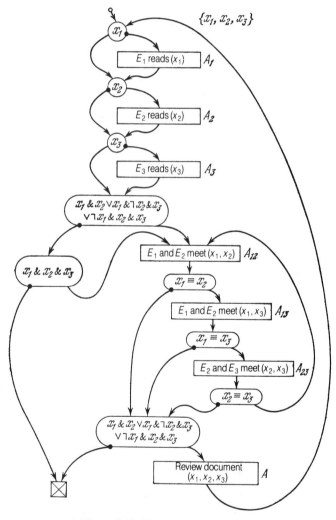

Figure 7.11. Three-experts problem.

document, they will be all for submitting it to a vote without first reading it. But if they think highly of a document, after hearing each other out they will undertake to read it ($A_1(x_1)$ for E_1 and $A_3(x_3)$ for E_3), which, naturally, may influence their evaluation. E_2 is a volunteer and takes the opposite position. If the document is reputed to be a good document, he is willing to submit it to a vote without reading it, and in the opposite case undertakes to study it (operator $A_2(x_2)$).

A test vote then follows (produced by the formula of the polling machine considered earlier). If the test vote turns out to be unanimous and in the affirmative, the document is considered approved. Otherwise, it is made the subject of a series of lobbying efforts. These conversations occur as the experts meet in pairs (the operator $A_{ij}(x_i, x_j)$ denotes a conversation in which E_i and E_j are in accord). If the experts are deadlocked, the result is assumed to be a foregone conclusion and is sent back for another vote. The series of lobbying efforts is repeated if none of the three paired conversations lead to a deadlock up until this point.

A repeated vote in the affirmative means that the document has been approved. In the case of a negative decision, the document is reviewed (operator $A(x_1, x_2, x_3)$), after which the document passes through the process once again.

7.3. Equivalence of Yanov Schemas

Functional Equivalence

Suppose we are given a Yanov schema $G(p_1, \ldots, p_k)$ with operator symbols $A_1, \ldots, A_n$. To transform the schema into a program ready to run, we must find an *interpretation* of its operator and predicate symbols, and then describe an algorithm for executing the *interpreted schema*.

Let us first specify some set D of *memory states* $d: D = \{d\}$. Since we are studying properties of schemas that are valid in any interpretation, the particular nature of this set is of no interest to us.

Further, we associate with each predicate symbol p_i ($i = 1, \ldots, k$) some predicate function $\pi_i(d)$ that maps D onto the set of logical values $\{\mathbf{f}, \mathbf{t}\}$:

$$\pi_i: D \to \{\mathbf{f}, \mathbf{t}\}.$$

The symbol p_i will be interpreted as a *predicate variable*.

Finally, with each operator symbol A_j ($j = 1, \ldots, n$) we associate some (possibly partial) function $\varphi_j(d)$ that maps D into itself:

$$\varphi_j: D \to D.$$

With this set of correspondences in mind, the algorithm for the interpreted schema has the following form.

Initial Step. Select an arbitrary $d \in D$ as the initial memory state, and then assign values to all the predicate variables thus:

$$p_i := \pi_i(d) \qquad (i = 1, \ldots, k),$$

then transfer control to the entry vertex of the control flow graph.

Execution Step. Suppose d is the current memory state, and let $\Delta = (\sigma_1, \ldots, \sigma_k)$ be an ordered tuple of the current values of the predicate variables. We assume control has been transferred to vertex S.

(a) Suppose S is a halt instruction. Then d is declared the result of executing the schema in the given interpretation, and the execution itself is complete.
(b) Suppose S is a recognizer with condition $F(p_1, \ldots, p_k)$. We compute $\sigma = F(\Delta)$, transferring control to the recognizer's successor in the direction of the plus arrow if $\sigma = \mathbf{t}$ or the minus arrow if $\sigma = \mathbf{f}$.
(c) Suppose S is the operator $A_j(P_j)$. We compute the current memory state $d' = \varphi_j(d)$, and assign to each predicate variable $p_i \in P_j$ a new value:

$$p_i := \pi_i(d'),$$

as a result of which a new sequence Δ' of current values of the predicate variables is formed. Control is then transferred to the unique successor of A_j.

Since each step in the execution of G with interpretation I is uniquely determined by the current memory state, the final memory state d thereby becomes a function $F_{G,I}$ of the initial state d_0:

$$d = F_{G,I}(d_0).$$

Obviously, in the general case this function is partially defined. There are two other reasons why a result may be indefinite, besides the fact that the functions that interpret the formal symbols of the schema are partially defined:

(a) infinite execution, in that in executing one operator after another we never arrive at a stop;
(b) empty loop, i.e., in moving from one recognizer to another and bypassing the operators, we arrive at a previously encountered recognizer. Since each recognizer functions independently, and since the values of the predicate variables do not change, the control transfer loop is again executed and this occurs an unlimited number of times.

We say that two Yanov schemas G_1 and G_2 are *comparable* if they are each defined on the same set of predicate symbols, further, if the operator symbols in the operators $A_1 \in G_1$ and $A_2 \in G_2$ are the same, then $p(A_1) = p(A_2)$.

If two schemas are comparable, we may then give them a consistent interpretation in which the same functions are associated with all the predicate symbols and the common operator symbols. If the shifts are identical, this means that identical operators also function identically in identical memory states.

Definition. Two comparable schemas G_1 and G_2 are *equivalent* in a consistent interpretation I if

$$F_{G_1, I}(d) = F_{G_2, I}(d).$$

An equality between two partially defined functions asserts that if for some d one function is defined, then so is the other, further, the values of the two functions coincide.

Definition. Two comparable schemas G_1 and G_2 are *functionally equivalent* if they are equivalent in any consistent interpretation.

In some sense this is the most natural definition of an equivalence between schemas. However, in and of itself it does not yield a good "stratagem" for establishing an equivalence between schemas nor for constructing a system of equivalence-preserving transformations.

Operational Equivalence

Experience gained in debugging actual programs suggests it would be far easier to establish that a program will run correctly if not only the result of a computation, but also a sort of "history" of how it was obtained, was available. It's a simple matter to agree that the complete sequence of executed operators and sequences of values of predicate variables would provide an extremely detailed history of a program run. By means of the sequence of operators, it would be possible to establish the sequence of memory states, while the sequence of values of the predicate variables would serve to create a path from one operator to the next. This dual sequence we call the *operational history* of the execution of an interpreted Yanov schema. Let us now give a more rigorous definition.

Suppose we are given an interpretation I of a schema G. We call the sequence of values of the predicate variables an *upper sequence*, and the sequence of operators, the *lower sequence*.

Initial Step. The upper and lower sequences are empty. Suppose we are given some initial memory state d. We compute the current tuple Δ of values of the predicate variables and place it in the upper sequence, and then move on to the entry vertex.

Execution Step. Control is transferred to the vertex S by means of the current tuple Δ of values of the predicate variables.

(a) If S is a recognizer with condition F, we check to see whether or not it is labeled. If not, we label it and move on to the desired successor depending on the computed condition F(Δ). If S is labeled, this means we have entered an empty loop. Execution of the schema is halted at once, and the operational history and result of the execution of the schema are not determined.

(b) If S is a halt instruction, the symbol of the halt instruction ($\boxed{\times}$) is written in the lower sequence, execution of the schema is completed, the operational history is constructed, and the current memory state declared the result of the program run.

(c) If S is an operator, it is executed, thereby forming a new memory state, its operator symbol is written in the lower sequence, the tuple of values of the predicate variables recomputed as necessary, the entire labeling of recognizers is eliminated, and control is transferred to the unique successor of S.

For a schema G in an interpretation I, the operational history thus defined becomes a single-valued function $H_{G,I}(d)$ of the initial memory state d. Analogously, we say that two comparable schemas G_1 and G_2 operate identically in a consistent interpretation I if

$$H_{G_1,I}(d) = H_{G_2,I}(d).$$

Definition. Two comparable schemas G_1 and G_2 are *operationally equivalent* if they operate identically in any consistent interpretation.

Inter-Relation Between Different Types of Equivalence

Since we have two independent definitions of equivalence of Yanov schemas, we have to study them together. The interdependence of the functional and operational equivalence is fully explicated by the following assertion.

Theorem 7.1. *Two comparable Yanov schemas are functionally equivalent if and only if they are operationally equivalent.*

The proof from operational equivalence to functional equivalence follows directly from the definitions. Since the sequence of operators in an operational history is precisely the same thing as the order of application of these operators to the memory in an execution of an interpreted schema in which the initial state remains the same, at any step of application of the operators of two operationally equivalent schemas we will be dealing with identical memory states, even after transfers to halt instructions.

The proof in the opposite direction is more complicated and relies essentially on the fact that the schemas are equivalent in any interpretation. The basic idea of the proof is to search for a special interpretation V that would store the operational history of execution of the schema in memory. A different computational history is created for each initial state selected. The variety of initial states suffices for creating every possible operational history of the schema in the process of executing the schema. It turns out that if one schema generates some operational history, the other schema has to generate this history too, since in this case equivalence in V would be violated.

Memory states are represented by two words, h and w, where h is a word in the alphabet of logical values and operator symbols that stores the operational history of execution of an interpreted schema. In turn, w is an infinite sequence of logical values, serving as the source of the tuples of current values of the predicate variables in the next step of execution of the program.

We will say that a pair of tuples of logical values (Δ, Δ') is *admissible* for an operator $A(P)$ if the set of ordinal numbers of the components in which Δ and Δ' differ is a subset of the ordinal numbers of predicate symbols belonging to the shift P. By definition, in the course of being executed, $A(P)$ may recompute only those predicate variables that occur in P. Thus, an admissible pair consists of Δ and Δ' such that Δ may be "shifted" to Δ' by means of $A(P)$.

Let us now give a rigorous definition of an interpretation V. Suppose we are given two functionally equivalent schemas G_1 and G_2 defined on the predicate symbols $p_1, \ldots, p_k$ which together contain the operators $A_1(P_1), \ldots,$ $A_n(P_n)$; $\varphi_j(h, w)$ is defined and equal to (h', w') if and only if $w = \Delta \Delta' \Omega$, where (Δ, Δ') is any admissible pair for $A_j(P_j)$, and Ω is the "remainder" of the word w. In this cases,

$$h' = h\Delta A_j,$$

$$w' = \Delta' \Omega.$$

φ_j ($j = 1, \ldots, n$) is not defined for the other memory states; $\pi_i(h, w)$ is always defined and equal to the ith letter of w ($i = 1, \ldots, k$).

Lemma 1. *If in an interpretation V of the schema $G(p_1, \ldots, p_k)$*

$$F_{G, V}(\varnothing, w) = (h', w'),$$

then*

$$h'\Delta \boxed{\times} = H_{G, V}(\varnothing, w),$$

where Δ are the first k letters of the word w'. (Recall that $\varnothing$ denotes the empty word.)

A rigorous proof of this lemma, which we leave as an exercise for the reader, requires induction on the number of steps in the execution of G on the initial memory states $(\varnothing, w)$ in the interpretation V.

Thus, let us consider an arbitrary interpretation I and arbitrary initial memory state d for which the execution of at least one of the two schemas G_1 and G_2 is defined, hence

$$F_{G_1, I}(d) = F_{C_2, I}(d).$$

---

* In order for the constructions to be formally comparable, we suppose that the upper and lower sequences in H merge into a single sequence; $\Delta_0 A_{i_1} \Delta_1 A_{i_2}$ and so on.

Consider the operational history of the given computation of either of these schemas, say G_1:

$$H_{G_1, I}(d) = \begin{matrix} \Delta_0 & & \Delta_1 & \cdots & & \Delta_k \\ & A_{i_1} & & & \cdots & A_{i_k} & \boxed{\times} \end{matrix}.$$

We now look at the initial memory state (h_0, w_0) in V, where

$$h_0 = \varnothing,$$

$$w_0 = \Delta_0 \Delta_1 \ldots \Delta_k \Omega,$$

and where Ω is an arbitrary infinite tuple of logical values.

We claim that in this case,

$$F_{G_1, V}(h_0, w_0) = (\Delta_0 A_{i_1}, \Delta_1 \ldots A_{i_k}, \Delta_k \Omega).$$

The proof of this assertion is virtually identical to the proof of the lemma, with the sole difference that in the latter we proved that in V the schema in the word h establishes a history of its own operation, whatever that might be. In the present assertion, by contrast, we find that the execution reproduces precisely the history we are interested in, that is $H_{G_1, I}(d)$.

Since G_1 and G_2 are equivalent in any interpretation, including V, we find that

$$F_{G_2, V}(h_0, w_0) = (\Delta_0 A_{i_1} \Delta_1 \ldots A_{i_k}, \Delta_k \Omega).$$

By the lemma, we conclude that

$$H_{G_2, V}(h_0, w_0) = \Delta_0 A_{i_1} \Delta_1 \ldots A_{i_k} \Delta_k.$$

Now it remains for us to prove that the computational history $F_{G_2, I}$ will be the same.

Since we have considered a consistent interpretation of G_1 and G_2, the initial values of the predicate variables $p_1, \ldots, p_k$ for G_2 are the same in the initial memory state d as for G_1, i.e., Δ_0. The run history of G_2 in V shows us that A_{i_1} is the first executed operator in G_2 of the input tuple Δ_0, i.e., the same as in the history $H_{G_1, I}(d)$. Once again, by the consistency of the interpretation once the operator A_{i_1} in G_2 has been processed, we obtain the same memory state $d' = \varphi_{i_1}(d)$ and the same tuple of values of predicate variables Δ_1 as in $H_{G_1, I}(d)$.

Repeating the reasoning just conducted step by step, we find that

$$H_{G_2, I}(d) = H_{G_2, V}(h_0, w_0) = H_{G_1, I}(d). \qquad \square$$

Corollary. *If two schemas G_1 and G_2 are equivalent in an interpretation V, they are equivalent in any interpretation.*

Proof. In fact, suppose we have defined $F_{G_1, I}(d)$ and a corresponding operational history $H_{G_1, I}(d)$ for some interpretation I and initial memory state d. In V there exists an initial memory state (h_0, w_0) that computes this history. Since G_1 and G_2 are equivalent in V, this memory state also creates a history for G_2. Repeating the concluding discussion of the theorem, we see that the same history will be obtained in a computation according to the schema in the interpretation I for the initial memory state.   □

Let us now consider more carefully something rather remarkable about V. The set of values $(h, w) = F_{G, V}(\varnothing, w_0)$ yields the set $\{h\}$ of all the operational histories of G which, as we have just explained, fully characterizes the computational capabilities of the schema. The corollary just proved may be reformulated in yet another way.

Lemma 2. *Two schemas G_1 and G_2 are functionally equivalent if and only if the sets of their operational histories coincide.*

Formal Equivalence

The most interesting thing about Yanov schemas is that the set of operational histories may be extracted from such a schema without our having to resort to the concept of an interpretation. Let us describe a procedure for creating certain constructions, which we will call *configurations*, for an arbitrary Yanov schema $G(p_1, \ldots, p_k)$. In outward appearance, configurations are indistinguishable from operational histories, though we will construct them using an essentially different method.

Initial Step. The upper and lower sequences are empty. We consider any k-tuple $\Delta_0 = (\sigma_1, \ldots, \sigma_k)$ as the values of the variables $p_1, \ldots, p_k$, and enter it in the upper sequence, moving on to the initial vertex.

Next Step. Suppose we have arrived at vertex S via the tuple Δ:

(a) if S is a labeled recognizer, we have arrived at an empty loop, and the construction of the configuration is halted at once without producing any result;

(b) if S is an unlabeled recognizer of R with condition $F(p_1, \ldots, p_k)$, we label R, compute $F(\Delta)$, and, via the same tuple, move on to the successor of R in accordance with the value of $F(\Delta)$;

(c) if S is a halt instruction, we enter the halt symbol $\boxed{\times}$ in the lower sequence; the construction of the configuration is complete;

(d) if S is the operator $A_i(P_i)$, we enter A_i in the lower sequence, and in the upper sequence enter an *arbitrary* tuple Δ' which forms with Δ an admissible pair (Δ, Δ') for $A_i(P_i)$. We remove the labeling of the recognizers and move on to the unique successor of A_i via tuple Δ'.

The procedure just described is a special case of a type of construction of importance throughout mathematics, called a *generating process*. The description of a generating process is very similar to the description of an algorithm, in fact a generating process itself resembles a computational process. One critical difference is that at certain places in a generating process there are points of indeterminacy (uncertainty) at which a single-valued computational event is supplanted by an arbitrary selection from some, admittedly rigorously described (and in our case, even finite) set. Because of these points of indeterminancy, a generating process creates ("generates") an entire set of possible outcomes.

The set specified by a generating process is considered an effectively defined set, since by agreement it is understood that any selection may be made at the points of indeterminacy. In addition, it is easily seen that an algorithm is a special case of a generating process in which the only point of indeterminacy occurs in the arbitrary selection of the initial data for the algorithm.

Let us now turn to the set $K(G)$ of configurations of the Yanov schema G.

Lemma 3. *The set of configurations of an arbitrary Yanov schema coincides with the set of its operational histories.*

Proof. The inclusion on one side follows from the definition of an operational history, and on the other side is implied by the interpretation V and the Lemma 1 related to it.   □

Definition. Two Yanov schemas $G_1(p_1, \ldots, p_k)$ and $G_2(p_1, \ldots, p_k)$ are formally equivalent if

$$K(G_1) = K(G_2).$$

From Lemma 3, we have the following assertion.

Theorem 2. *Two Yanov schemas are functionally equivalent if and only if they are formally equivalent.*

A remarkable property of Yanov schemas is that all three types of equivalence (functional, i.e., in terms of results; operational, i.e., in terms of computational history; and formal, i.e., in terms of the set of all possible chains of operators generated by the schema) are extensionally equal, i.e., describe one and the same class of Yanov schemas. The true significance of this circumstance, of course, can be realized only by comparison with other branches of theoretical programming. For the time being, however, we will use this circumstance only for the purpose of retaining the same notation ($\simeq$) for all three equivalences. We will employ the notion of formal equivalence associated with the concept of a configuration as a basis for the construction of a system of equivalence-preserving transormations.

CHAPTER 8

Calculus of Equivalence Transformations

8.1. Construction of Calculus

Initial Analogies and Conjectures

Comparing Yanov schemas with their progenitors—the formulas of the propositional calculus—does not disclose any major complication of the constructions. Therefore, although we will try to continue along the lines of the broad canvas indicated in our construction of the formal axiomatic theory, with only rare exceptions we cannot just repeat in a literal fashion the reasonings we were guided by in the introductory chapter on mathematical logic.

We will try and introduce the calculus of equivalence-preserving transformations of Yanov schemas in what we believe is a natural way so as to show the reader how to make conjectures about these sorts of objects in any way whatsoever. However, as we have already remarked, a shortage of space and the demands of an introductory presentation preclude any attempt at "resurrecting" the original ideas of the creators of the theory, even if we were to ask them the most detailed sorts of questions. The secret of any discovery remains for each individual concealed, locked up as if "under seven seals" that only the individual can lift up, and only on his or her own.

We will introduce rules of transformation as axioms or rules of inference, postulating elementary and intuitively independent properties of Yanov schemas. Some of these properties have been known to us from the very beginning in the form of rules of transformation, for example, redirecting plus arrows (Figure 7.7(a)) or expanding a disjunction (Figure 7.4(b)), while others (for example, the concept of admissible tuples) are again best represented in the form of convenient rules, and, finally, a third group reveal themselves only when we take a more detailed inventory of properties.

However, let us try to create some order in our universe. We must construct a system of transformations that would preserve our principal invariant—the set of (well-formed) configurations created by the generating process described at the end of the preceding section—for all mutually transformable schemas. We have not inserted the term, "well-formed," by chance. In fact, in its natural evolution our generating process creates a substantially more extensive set of objects, consisting not only of finite chains of operators that lead up to an empty loop, but also infinite chains.

On the other hand, even given this "extra" degree of freedom of operation the generating process cannot affect everything introduced into an actual schema. The most obvious examples are the isolated vertices, i.e., parts of the control flow graph that are not reachable from the entry or from which there is no path to the halt instruction, or which suffer from both drawbacks simultaneously (Figure 7.10).

We could conceive of schemas constructed and operating with "maximal economy" in some sense, i.e., schemas that contain only "executable" operators and that do not implement any sort of "useless" operations, such as those leading to infinite motion relative to its transformers and recognizers. If we really mean to construct a complete calculus, we have to be sure that any schema could be transformed into any other schema equivalent to it, in particular, a schema that possesses this type of economy of operation. Our calculus therefore requires particular types of rules by means of which it would be possible to find, eliminate, and, when necessary, add such redundant fragments of a schema.

In the simplest cases the redundant fragments reveal themselves quite suddenly. Here is one such self-evident rule: A transformer with operator without entry arcs is unreachable and may be eliminated. Another obvious case occurs when there is a plus arrow entering a vertex from a recognizer with identically false condition. However, this instance may be restated in the form of a more elementary, independent rule, as follows: A recognizer R with identically false condition may be replaced by an arc emanating from a predecessor of R to a successor of R, moving in the direction of a minus arrow. The plus arrow from R then vanishes together with R itself.

In the general case, the property of an element of a schema to be "unnecessary" is not a characteristic of the element itself, but rather a property of the entire schema as a whole. An inapplicable operator may be a vertex in an isolated component of the control flow graph, while the fact that a condition is an identity condition may be concealed by a chain of preceding or succeeding tests of other conditions.

Two sufficiency conditions may be easily formulated. A vertex V of the control flow graph of a Yanov schema is said to be *quasi-reachable* if there exists a path in the schema from the entry arrow to V. Analogously, a vertex V is said to be *quasi-productive* if there exists a path in the schema from V to a halt instruction.*

---

* We suggest the reader reconstruct the logical relationship between these definitions and the statement of sufficiency conditions of unreachability and nonproductivity of vertices.

The results of the first part of the book suggest that the properties of reachability and productivity so stated may be readily described in terms of direct and inverse transitive closures. Thus, a reachable vertex belongs to the direct transitive closure of an entry vertex of the control flow graph, while a productive vertex belongs to the inverse transitive closure of a halt instruction. An important feature of Yanov schemas, however, is that in recognizers the successors are not selected arbitrarily, but by means of some method stipulated by the condition. Thus, the fact that a vertex is unreachable in the construction of a configuration may be concealed by the existence of a path from the entry vertex that does not contain a recognizer with opposite conditions. Thus, we must now introduce a number of corrections in the inductive procedures given earlier for the construction of transitive closures.

Reachability and Admissibility

Let us first study reachability, and as a start suppose that none of the operators affects any of the predicate variables. This is known as the case of an *empty shift distribution*.

Initial Step. We consider some tuple Δ of values of the predicate variables and label it the entry arrow.

Inductive Step. Suppose that the tuple Δ labels the entry arc of some vertex V of the control flow graph.

(a) If V is an operator and if its exit arc does not contain Δ as label, we label it the tuple Δ.
(b) If V is a recognizer with condition* F and if none of its exit arcs has Δ as label, we label the plus arrow of V with the tuple Δ if $F(\Delta) = \mathbf{t}$, and with the minus arrow otherwise.
(c) If V is a halt instruction, we do nothing.

The *labeling* so described is complete whenever there is nothing left to do on any of the inductive steps.

Once we have performed such a labeling process for each tuple Δ that may be applied to the entry arrow, we find that each arc of the control flow graph is labeled by some set (possibly empty) of tuples of values of predicate variables. Recall from Chapter 6 that any Boolean function may be represented by its truth set and, conversely, any set of tuples of values of logical variables may be thought of as the truth set of some Boolean function. Then we may assert that a vertex V of a control flow graph is *reachable* if and only if at least one of the entry arcs of the Boolean function that labels it is not identically false.

---

*In speaking of a recognizer with condition F, we are allowing ourselves a certain degree of freedom in that we are not introducing any special notation for the Boolean function corresponding to some formula F.

As we have just said, it is clear that this property remains true if we do away with the constraint of an empty shift distribution. The general case differs from the one we have considered only by the fact that if there is a tuple Δ at the entry arc of operator $A(P)$, there will be an entire family of tuples $\{\Delta'\}$ each of which forms with Δ an admissible pair (Δ, Δ').

The second obvious observation is that this inductive process of labeling with sets of tuples (or, what is the same thing, sets of logical formulas) does not have to be done for every entry tuple separately. A "universal" process could be implemented, in which a complete set of tuples, i.e., an identically true function, is fed to the entry arrow, and an identically false function is fed to all the other arcs, as their initial value. Each recognizer R with condition F could then be interpreted as a sorting process such that if a set of tuples Φ is fed through some entry vertex, the set on which F is true, i.e., $\Phi \& F$, is added disjunctively to the function that labels the plus arrow at R, while the set of tuples from Φ on which F is false, i.e., $\neg F \& \Phi$, is added disjunctively to the function that labels the minus arrow at R.

To complete this generalization, we must try to understand how to express (in terms of Boolean functions) the role of operators that constitute the sources of output tuples that form admissible pairs with entry tuples. Suppose that F is the set of tuples that arrive at the entry of operator $A(P)$. Recall that $P \subseteq \{p_1, \ldots, p_k\}$ and that F is the function $F(p_1, \ldots, p_k)$. Let Φ be the set of all tuples Δ' that form with some tuple Δ from F an admissible pair. We consider any tuple $\delta = \sigma_1, \ldots, \sigma_k$ and the set $\text{Var}(\delta)$ of tuples obtained from δ by renaming the variables from P. Then, by definition, if $\delta \subseteq F$ or, what is the same thing, $F(\delta) = \mathbf{t}$, then $\text{Var}(\delta) \subseteq \Phi$. Further, if $F(\delta) = \mathbf{f}$, but there is in $\text{Var}(\delta)$ a δ' such that $F(\delta') = \mathbf{t}$, as before $\text{Var}(\delta) \subseteq \Phi$. This is also self-evident, since for any $\delta' \subseteq \text{Var}(\delta)$, it is true that $\text{Var}(\delta') = \text{Var}(\delta)$. But if for any $\delta' \subseteq \text{Var}(\delta)$, it is the case that $F(\delta') = \mathbf{f}$, then certainly $\text{Var}(\delta) \cap \Phi = \phi$. Hence we find that $\max(\mathbf{f}, \mathbf{t}) = \mathbf{t}$:

$$\Phi = \max_{p_i \in P} F(p_1, \ldots, p_k).$$

It remains for us to figure out how to arrange information about the labeling of the arcs of a schema by means of Boolean functions that represent sets of tuples in such a way as to make it possible to traverse a given arc when producing a configuration. As in any inductive process, we may use information about the labeling only after it is complete. The point at which the labeling is "saturated" may be taken as the completion condition, i.e., the point at which any further transferring of logical tuples from entries to exits would not affect any of the Boolean functions already there. Since only disjunctive build-up may occur in the labeling process, i.e., a process that is strictly monotone, saturation has to happen. We say that a saturated labeling is *stationary* and suppose that in such a labeling some recognizer R with condition F has a function Φ on a plus arrow. From the labeling rules, it follows that:

(a) $\Phi \subseteq F$,

(b) the condition of the recognizer R is to transfer control via the plus arrow only to tuples that belong to Φ. Hence it follows that in R condition F may be replaced by Φ.

The meaning of this transformation is that all inadmissible tuples, i.e., those on which this condition is obviously not computed, are "truncated" from the truth sets of the conditions of the schema. For this reason, for example, any condition that converts a positive control to an unreachable operator is replaced by an identically false condition.

In applying the rule of elimination of identically false conditions, we remove the operator's entry arc after which we may remove the operator as well.

Thus, we see that it is more correct to think of the property of a vertex in a Yanov schema to participate in the process of generating configurations in conjunction with sets of tuples of predicate variables. That is, a vertex V is said to be *reachable* if there exists a nonempty set of tuples Φ that are *admissible* for V, i.e., tuples such that V is encountered when generating the configurations.

Productivity

Using analogous concepts, let us try to describe the productive vertices in Yanov schemas. We will define the process of generating *residual configurations* for an arbitrary vertex V in a schema and an arbitrary tuple Δ of predicate variables. The process of generating residual configurations differs from the general case of ordinary configurations only in the initial step, which in this case consists in moving to V via the tuple Δ.

We say that a tuple Δ is *productive* for a vertex V if there exists for this pair a residual configuration. Correspondingly, a vertex in a schema is said to be *productive* if the set Ψ of its productive tuples is nonempty.

We have already guessed that the concepts of admissibility and productivity exhaust the problem of residual constructions in a schema. That is, a vertex that is simultaneously admissible and productive is precisely the sort of entity made use of in the set of configurations of a schema.

Let us consider the inductive process of labeling the arcs of a Yanov schema with Boolean functions, which we select in such a way that for each vertex these functions gather together the set of its productive tuples.

Initial Step. Obviously, in the case of a halt instruction any tuple is productive ($\Psi \boxed{\times} \equiv t$). That is, this function labels all arcs leading to a halt instruction.

Inductive Step. (Recognizer). Suppose that the plus and minus arrows of some recognizer $R(F)$ are labeled Ψ_+ and Ψ_-, respectively, which by hypothesis are assumed to be productive tuples of the successors of the recognizer. Naturally, for any set of tuples M the recognizer may "transmit" only F & M via the plus arrow, and only $\neg$ F & M via the minus arrow. Hence we find that $\Psi_R = $ F & $\Psi_+ \cup \neg$ F & Ψ_-. In this case—and only in this case—does F correctly distribute the set of its own productivity tuples among its successors. All arcs leading to R are labeled Ψ_R.

Inductive Step (Operator). Suppose the exit arc of some operator $A(P)$ is labeled by the function Ψ. Obviously, any tuple Δ such that $\Psi(\Delta) = $ t is productive not only for a successor of $A(P)$, but also for $A(P)$ itself. But then any other tuple $\Delta' \in \max_P \Delta$ will also be productive for $A(P)$, since the two tuples (Δ', Δ) form an admissible pair. Hence, we conclude that

$$\Psi_{A(P)} = \max_P \Psi$$

and all arcs leading to $A(P)$ are labeled with this function.

Obviously, everywhere a labeling is understood to refer to the disjunctive addition of labeling functions to those which label arcs as a result of preceding steps.

Just as in the case of reachability, we may consider how to arrange the information obtained after the arcs of a schema have been labeled to the saturation point. Let us consider an arbitrary operator A of a schema with its set Δ of productive tuples. If a nonproductive tuple is fed to its entry, i.e., from $\neg\Psi$, in this case we will know in advance that the process of constructing residual configurations for any further development will not lead to any results; the process quite simply terminates in an infinite loop. Thus, any manipulation with any $\Delta \in \neg\Psi$ will be useless. Such useless manipulation may be forestalled if we place in front of A a recognizer $R(\Psi)$ with plus arrow leading to A, and minus arrow ending in a *suppressor*, which is the simplest empty loop (i.e., recognizer with condition f and both exit arcs leading back to it). From now on we will represent a suppressor (Figure 7.10(b)) by the symbol $\otimes$. Note that by blocking movement from nonproductive tuples we are not only preventing "unnecessary" computations, but are also making the nonproductive tuples unreachable from corresponding fragments of the schema, which may result in their possible removal from the schema. Obviously, such blocking must also be applied to the entry arrow.

Figures 8.1 and 8.2 depict certain pairs of equivalent Yanov schemas. That these schemas are transformable is a result of the concepts of reachability and admissibility (Figure 8.1) and productivity (Figure 8.2).

List of Rules

Let us now draw some conclusions. Our rules for equivalence-preserving transformations may be grouped into five categories: logical rules; topological rules; rules of upper labeling; rules of lower labeling; and rules of replacement.

The logical rules postulate a relation between the basic Boolean functions of falsity, negation, and disjunction and the rules for the selection of plus and minus directions when testing conditions in recognizers. These rules are as

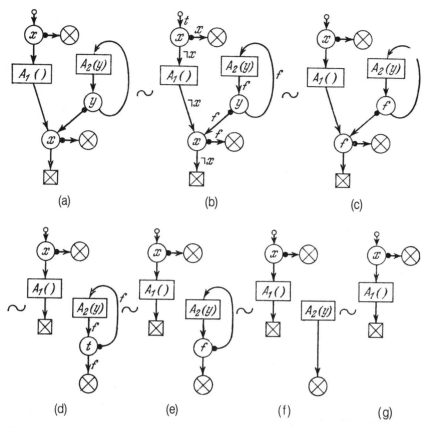

Figure 8.1. Transformation using the concept of admissibility: (a) initial schema; (b) stationary upper labeling; (c) truncation of inadmissible tuples; (d) elimination of a single identity condition, replacement of another condition by its negation, stationary upper labeling; (e) truncation of inadmissible tuples; (f) elimination of identity conditions; (g) elimination of operator without entry.

follows: (A1) elimination of recognizer with false condition; (A2) negation rule (Figure 7.4(a)); and (A3) expanding a disjunction (Figure 7.4(b)).

The topological rules postulate possible changes in the control flow graph, and consist of: (A4) rule for elimination of transformer without entry arcs; (A5) redirection of plus arrows (Figure 7.7(a)); and (A6) rule for matching any two suppressors. We have not spoken of these rules, though the fact that they are indeed necessary becomes clear after a little reflection.

The rules of *upper labeling* postulate: (A7) the absence of tuples prior to the start of the labeling; (A8) the admissibility of any tuple of values of predicate variables prior to the start of the construction of the configurations; (A9) rules for distributing tuples between plus and minus arrows when at a recognizer, and (A10) shift properties of operators as a source of admissible tuples. By

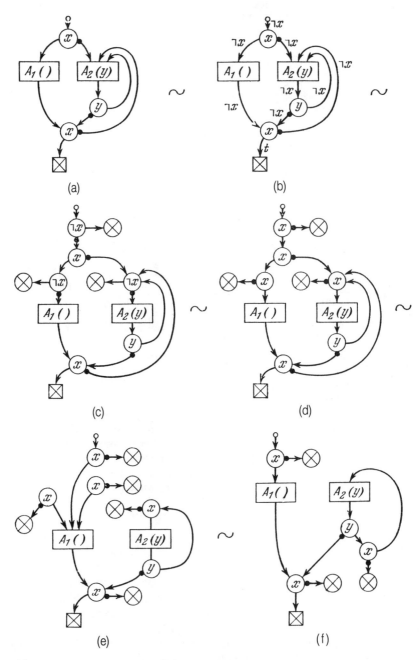

Figure 8.2. Transformation using the concept of productivity: (a) initial schema; (b) stationary lower labeling; (c) blocking of nonproductive tuples; (d) replacement of conditions by their negation; (e) redirecting arrows; (f) elimination of inapplicable recognizers.

means of rule (I1), which serves to "truncate" inadmissible tuples from the truth sets of conditions in recognizers, it is possible to gain information about admissible tuples in the conditions of a stationary upper labeling.

The rules of *lower labeling* postulate: (A11) the absence of tuples prior to the start of the labeling; (A12) initiation of the labeling, starting with a halt instruction, and transfer of label from exit arcs to entry arcs whenever a recognizer is encountered (A13) and whenever a transformer is encountered (A14). Rule (I2) in the stationarity conditions for a lower labeling blocks computations for nonproductive tuples.

By means of the replacement rule (I3), the occurrence of a logical formula in a schema may be replaced by any equivalent logical formula. The substitution rule (I4) postulates the preservation of equivalence when some segment of a schema is replaced by another equipotent segment.

It remains for us to introduce a meta-language for representing the calculus we have created. The calculus consists of axiom schemas (A1)–(A13) and rules of inference (I1)–(I5). The axioms and assertions of the rules of inference are represented in the form

$$\mathscr{F}_1 \sim \mathscr{F}_2,$$

where $\sim$ is the equivalence-preserving sign, and $\mathscr{F}_1$ and $\mathscr{F}_2$ are certain fragments of Yanov schemas. By a *fragment* of a schema G we understand some part (subgraph) of G that specifies how this part is related to the vertices of G. The exits of a fragment are the labeled arcs that show which vertices of the fragment are connected to the other vertices of the schema. The entries to the fragment consist of labeled arrows that show which vertices of the fragment the arcs from the other vertices of the schema lead to. The fragments may be either *actual* or *generalized*. In generalized fragments, rather than actual conditions and operators we are dealing with meta-variables whose values are arbitrary (or with specified constraints) logical formulas, operator symbols, and their shifts. Moreover, generalized fragments may contain *generalized entries* that specify which vertex an arbitrary (including empty) set of arcs emanating either from the other vertices of the schema or (if this is not expressly forbidden) from the exits of this fragments may lead to. The generalized inputs are shown by thick arrows, and (any) inputs are labeled with roman numerals, and the outputs by arabic figures. The conditions and labeling Boolean functions are written in the form of logical formulas. These definitions also serve to explain the sample fragment depicted in Figure 8.3. Here we have indicated that some arc must lead to the upper recognizer. Any arcs may enter A from the outside. Any arcs may lead to the lower recognizer, in addition to the input arrow, but none of these arcs may be an output arc of the fragment labeled by the numeral 2. If two output arcs are labeled by the same numeral, this means that both of them must lead to the same vertex of the schema.

The calculus of equipotent transformations of Yanov schemas is depicted in Figures 8.4 and 8.5. In the premises of rules (I1) and (I2) the symbol $\forall$ denotes

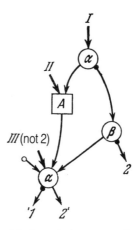

Figure 8.3. Sample fragment of a schema.

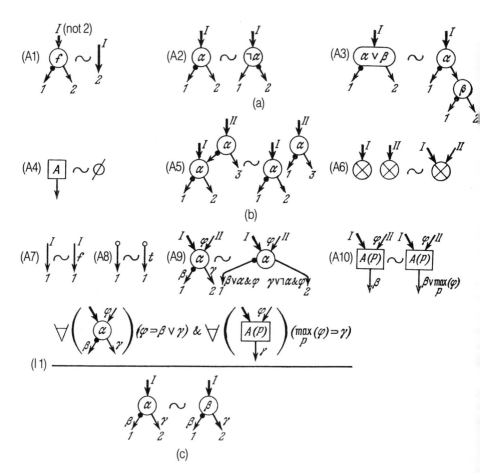

Figure 8.4. Calculus of equivalence-preserving transformations: (a) logical rules; (b) topological rules; (c) rules of upper labeling

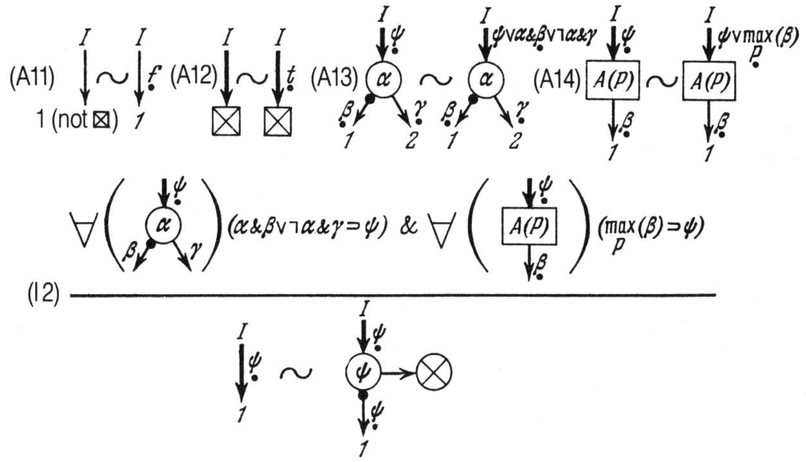

(c)

$$(13)\quad \frac{\alpha \equiv \beta}{F(\alpha) \sim F(\beta)} \qquad (14)\quad \frac{F_1 \sim F_2,\ F_3(F_1) \sim F_4}{F_3(F_2) \sim F_4}$$

(d)

Figure 8.5. Calculus of equivalence-preserving transformations (conclusion): (a) rules of lower labeling; (b) substitution rules.

the *universal quantifier* by means of which assertions of the form

$$\forall(T)(P)$$

may be formulated; an assertion such as the above is read as follows: "any object of the form T that may be found in a transformed Yanov schema satisfies property P."

8.2. Well-Formedness of the Calculus

Now that we have completed an exhaustive discussion of the axioms (Section 8.1), the validity of the logical and topological axioms is self-evident and requires no further discussion.

Upper Labelling

Let us consider the rules for an upper labeling. From the axioms, it is clear that in an upper labeling of the arcs of a schema, an entry arrow is the only unconditional source of sequences of values of the predicate variables. By

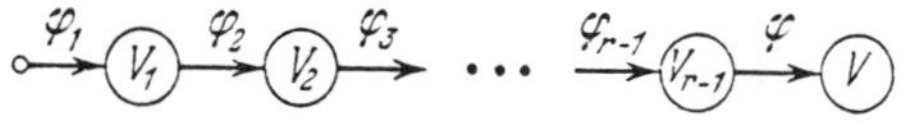

Figure 8.6. Path of upper labeling.

Axiom A9 only those tuples that are input to the entry of a recognizer are moved to the recognizer's exit arcs. Axiom A10 generates only tuples that may be obtained from tuples that are input to the entry of an operator, by the application of the operation of taking a maximum (note that $\max_P (\mathbf{f}) = \mathbf{f}$ for any P). Thus, if a set of tuples φ appears in an arc s leading to some vertex V of a schema, as a result of the application of Axioms A7–A10, this will mean that each of these tuples could arise in the arc only as a result of the application of Axioms A7–A10 to a chain of fragments of the schema forming a path from the entry arrow to V (Figure 8.6). This may be stated more precisely as follows. For any Δ such that $\varphi(\Delta) = \mathbf{t}$, there exists a path in the schema from the entry arrow to a vertex V formed by the vertices $V_1, \ldots, V_r$ and arcs labeled by the functions $\varphi_1, \ldots, \varphi_r$, where $V_r = V$, $\varphi_1 \equiv \mathbf{t}$, and $\varphi_r \equiv \varphi$, further there exists a sequence of tuples $\Delta_1, \ldots, \Delta_r = \Delta$ that satisfies the following constraints:

(1) $\varphi_i(\Delta_i) = \mathbf{t}$;
(2) if V_i $(1 \leq i \leq r-1)$ is a recognizer with condition F, then $\Delta_{i+1} = \Delta_i$ and $F(\Delta_i) = \mathbf{t}$ if V_i is connected to V_{i+1} by a plus arrow, else $F(\Delta_i) = \mathbf{f}$;
(3) if V_i $(1 \leq i \leq r-1)$ is a recognizer with operator $A(P)$, Δ_{i+1} differs from Δ_i by at most the values of variables that belong to P.

We have already called a tuple Δ *admissible* for some vertex V of a schema if it is possible to move to V via Δ in the process of generating a configuration (Section 7.3). The reasoning just given proves that any tuple that belongs to a function φ labeling some entry of V is admissible for V.

Let us say that the set Φ_V of all admissible tuples for a vertex V is the *complete condition* for the operation of this vertex. We have proved the assertion

Lemma 1. *If an arc labeled φ leads to some vertex V,*

$$\varphi \supset \Phi_V.$$

The next lemmas follow directly from the form of Axioms A9 and A10.

Lemma 2. *If the plus and minus arrows of a recognizer with condition F are labeled by the functions β_+ and β_-, respectively,*

$$\beta_+ \supset F, \qquad \beta_+ \& \beta_- \equiv \mathbf{f} \qquad and \qquad F \& \beta_- \equiv \mathbf{f}.$$

Lemma 3. *If m arcs labeled by the functions $\varphi_1, \ldots, \varphi_m$ lead to a recognizer (using the notation of Lemma 2),*

$$\beta_+ \vee \beta_- \supset \varphi_1 \vee \ldots \vee \varphi_m.$$

Lemma 4. *If m arcs labeled by the functions $\varphi_1, \ldots, \varphi_m$ lead to the operator $A(P)$ and if the exit of the operator is labeled by the function β,*

$$\beta \supset \max_P (\varphi_1 \vee \ldots \vee \varphi_m).$$

The state of a Yanov schema in which the premise of the rule of inference I1 holds is called the *stationary* upper labeling. This name, which we have already used informally in the preceding section, is justified by the fact that under the conditions of a stationary labeling no further application of Axioms A9 and A10 would change the upper labeling of the arcs of the schema. The next assertion is self-evident.

Lemma 5. *Under the conditions of a stationary upper labeling and in the notation of Lemmas 3 and 4, for any recognizer,*

$$\beta_+ \vee \beta_- \equiv \varphi_1 \vee \ldots \vee \varphi_m$$

and for any operator $A(\mathrm{P})$,

$$\beta = \max_P (\varphi_1 \wedge \ldots \wedge \varphi_m).$$

The underlying meaning of rule (I1) establishes the next assertion.

Lemma 6. *Under the conditions of a stationary upper labeling, for any recognizer R whose exit arcs are labeled β_+ and β_-,*

$$\beta_+ \vee \beta_- \equiv \Phi_R.$$

Proof. The implication $\beta_+ \vee \beta_- \supset \Phi_R$ follows from Lemmas 1 and 5. Let us prove the implication $\Phi_R \supset \beta_+ \vee \beta_-$. Suppose that the tuple Δ is admissible for some recognizer R. This will mean that there exists a path from the entry arrow to the vertex V that passes through the vertices $V_1, \ldots, V_r = R$ and a series of tuples $\Delta_1, \ldots, \Delta_r = \Delta$ such that in traversing the schema we approach V_i by means of the tuple Δ_i ($i = 1, \ldots, r$). Now suppose that the entry arrow and arcs encountered as we move along the path passing through $V_1, \ldots, V_r$ are labeled (in accordance with the stationary labeling) by the functions $\varphi_1, \ldots, \varphi_r$. We will prove by induction that $\varphi_i(\Delta_i) = \mathbf{t}$ ($i = 1, \ldots, r$). For $i = 1$ this is self-evident, since $\varphi_1 \equiv \mathbf{t}$.
    Let

$$\varphi_{i-1}(\Delta_{i-1}) = \mathbf{t}. \tag{1}$$

Suppose that V_{i-1} is a recognizer with condition F and labels β_+ and β_- on its exit arcs. In this case,

$$\Delta_i = \Delta_{i-1}. \tag{2}$$

Since the labeling is stationary, $\varphi_{i-1} \supset \beta_+ \vee \beta_-$, which means (by (1)),

$$\beta_+(\Delta_{i-1}) \vee \beta_-(\Delta_{i-1}) = \mathbf{t}. \tag{3}$$

If $F(\Delta_{i-1}) = \mathbf{t}$,

$$\varphi_i = \beta_+ \tag{4}$$

which by Lemma 2 cannot happen, if $\beta_-(\Delta_{i-1}) = \mathbf{t}$. This means that, by (3), $\beta_+(\Delta_{i-1}) = \mathbf{t}$ and by (4) and (2), $\varphi_i(\Delta_i) = \mathbf{t}$. If $F(\Delta_{i-1}) = \mathbf{f}$, then $\varphi_i = \beta_-$ and, reasoning analogously, we find (by Lemma 2 and (2)) that $\varphi_i(\Delta_i) = \mathbf{t}$ as well.

Suppose that V_{i-1} is a transformer with operator $A(P)$ whose exit is labeled, and let f_Δ be a function for which Δ is its truth set. Since Δ_{i-1} and Δ_i differ by at most the values of variables from P,

$$\max_P f_{\Delta_{i-1}}(\Delta_i) = \mathbf{t}. \tag{5}$$

But by (1)

$$\max_P f_{\Delta_{i-1}} \supset \max_P \varphi_{i-1} \tag{6}$$

and by the stationarity property,

$$\max_P \varphi_{i-1} \supset \varphi_i,$$

whence by (5) and (6), $\varphi_i(\Delta_i) = \mathbf{t}$.

Applying the inductive assertion just proved for $i = r$, we find that $\varphi_r(\Delta) = \mathbf{t}$; hence by Lemma 5, we have proved the desired implication, and with it Lemma 6 as well. □

Lower Labeling

Let us now consider the rules of a lower labeling.

Lemma 7. *Under the conditions of a stationary lower labeling for any vertex V of a schema G, the function Ψ_V which labels the entries of V is identical to the function Π_V, which is true on the set of productive tuples for V.*

Proof. As to the implication

$$\Pi_V \supset \Psi_V$$

the assertion of the lemma is self-evident, since any sequence of vertices from V to $\boxed{\times}$ and the sequence of tuples through which these vertices pass in the construction of an arbitrary residual configuration created by the tuple Δ and vertex V taken together and read in reverse order specify a sequence of application of Axioms A11–A14 that creates a labeling at the entry of V which includes Δ. By the stationarity property, any sequence will be obviously realized.

Now suppose the contrary, i.e., suppose that it is known that $\Psi_V(\Delta) = t$. Then there exists a sequence S of vertices of the schema

$$V = V_1, V_2, \ldots V_r = \boxed{\times}$$

and a sequence of functions

$$\Psi_V \equiv \Psi_1, \Psi_2, \ldots, \Psi_r \equiv t,$$

which label arcs between these vertices and which possess the following property. For any segment Σ of the sequence formed by certain recognizers (and only recognizers) and bounded either by operators, or (on the left) a start section, or (on the right) a halt instruction,

there exists a realizing tuple Δ that belongs to all the labeling sets from the segment Σ and which (once it has been fed to the start section of Σ) passes through vertices forming Σ in the control flow graph. In this case:

(1) if a segment of recognizers Σ_0 is also the start section of some sequence S, Δ could be its realizing tuple;

(2) if the two segments Σ and Σ' are separated by an operator $A(P)$, the tuples Δ and Δ' that realize these segments form a pair (Δ, Δ') admissible for $A(P)$.

This assertion, which is a restatement of the rules of application of Axioms A11–A14, at once yields a construction of the residual configuration generated by the tuple Δ and vertex V. □

Lemma 8. *Under the conditions of a stationary lower labeling, any application of rule I2 is well-formed.*

An argument proving this assertion has already been carried out in the preceding section in our introduction of the concept of a lower labeling.

Equivalence-preserving Relation

Note that since a schema as a whole is a special case of the concept of a fragment, by means of rules I3 and I4 it is possible to deduce equivalence-preserving relations for schemas. The properties of an equivalence-preserving relation understood as a binary relation are expressed by the following lemma.

Lemma 9. *The equivalence-preserving is reflexive, symmetric, and transitive.*

Proof. Reflexivity follows from rule I3 (for identical α and β). Symmetricity follows from rule I4 if we use

$$\mathscr{F}_1 \sim \mathscr{F}_2, \qquad \mathscr{F}_1 \sim \mathscr{F}_1,$$

as the premise. The proof of transitivity requires the relations

$$\mathscr{F}_1 \sim \mathscr{F}_2, \qquad \mathscr{F}_2 \sim \mathscr{F}_3,$$

as premise. By symmetricity, this premise may be rewritten in the form

$$\mathscr{F}_2 \sim \mathscr{F}_1, \qquad \mathscr{F}_2 \sim \mathscr{F}_3,$$

whence by rule I4 it follows that $\mathscr{F}_1 \sim \mathscr{F}_3$.   □

The formal possibility of interpreting this axiomatic structure as rules for the transformation of schemas is provided by the following assertion.

Lemma 10. (Substitution Rule). If $\mathscr{F}_1 \sim \mathscr{F}_2$,

$$\mathscr{F}(\mathscr{F}_1) \sim \mathscr{F}(\mathscr{F}_2).$$

Proof. Using

$$\mathscr{F}_1 \sim \mathscr{F}_2, \qquad \mathscr{F}(\mathscr{F}_1) \sim \mathscr{F}(\mathscr{F}_1),$$

as the premise in rule I4 yields $\mathscr{F}(\mathscr{F}_2) \sim \mathscr{F}(\mathscr{F}_1)$, whence (by symmetricity) follows the assertion of the lemma.   □

Remark. In conjunction with the substitution rule, the property of symmetricity guarantees the invertibility of the system of transformations specified by the axiomatic structure. Note, too, that the validity of rule I4 was established in our informal evaluation of the axiomatic structure in the last chapter.

The above exhaustive study of the calculus of equivalence-preserving transformations is summarized in the next assertion.

Theorem 8.1. *Any two equivalence-preserving Yanov operator schemas are equivalent.*

8.3. Canonical Schemas and Technical Theorems

Canonical Schemas

A Yanov schema $G(p_1, \ldots, p_k)$ with operators $A_1, \ldots, A_n$ is called a *matrix schema* if it contains $(n+1)^2$ recognizers $R_{ij}(F_{ij})$ ($i = 0, \ldots, n; \; j = 1, \ldots, n$

+ 1), and a single suppressor-recognizer $\otimes$ all of which are connected in the following way.

1. Each recognizer R_{ij} has a single entry.
2. An entry arrow leads to the recognizer R_{01}, and the exit arc of operator A_i leads to recognizer R_{ij} $(i = 1, \ldots, n)$.
3. The plus arrow of recognizer R_{ij} $(i = 0, \ldots, n; j = 1, \ldots, n)$ leads to operator A_j, and the minus arrow, to recognizer $R_{i,j+1}$.
4. The plus arrow of recognizer $R_{i,n+1}$ $(i = 0, \ldots, n)$ leads to a halt instruction, and the minus arrow to a suppressor.
5. The conditions $F_{ij}(i = 0, \ldots, n; j = 1, \ldots, n+1)$ satisfy the relations

$$F_{ij_1} \& F_{ij_2} \equiv \begin{cases} F_{ij_1}, & \text{if } j_1 = j_2, \\ \mathbf{f}, & \text{if } j_1 \neq j_2. \end{cases}$$

6. Each condition is either $\mathbf{f}$ or has the form of a principal disjunctive normal form.

An operator A of a schema G is said to be *executable* if there exists a configuration of G containing it. A *canonical* Yanov schema is a matrix schema all of whose operators are executable and all of whose conditions are true only on its admissible and productive tuples. An example of a canonical Yanov schema (equivalent to the example given in Figure 7.9) is shown in Figure 8.7.

Two Yanov schemas are said to be *equal* if they are comparable, if their control flow graphs are isomorphic, if plus and minus arrows are distributed

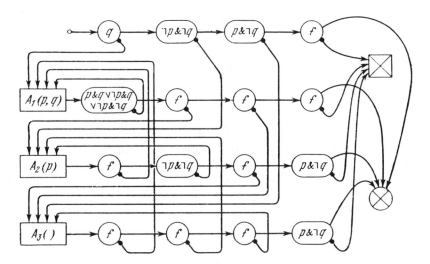

Figure 8.7. Canonical Yanov schema.

in them identically, and if the same operators and conditions are associated with corresponding vertices.

The next theorem establishes special properties of canonical schemas.

Theorem 8.2 *If two canonical Yanov schemas are not equal, they are not equivalent.*

Proof. If two unequal canonical schemas do not contain the same number of operators or contain different operators, the sets of configurations of these schemas will not coincide by virtue of the executability of each of the operators. Thus, it remains for us to consider only comparable schemas G_1 and G_2 containing the same set of operators $A_1, \ldots, A_n$.

If two such schemas are not equal, this will mean that there exist a tuple Δ and recognizer R_{ij} such that

$$F_{ij}^{(1)}(\Delta) = \mathbf{t} \tag{1}$$

and

$$F_{ij}^{(2)}(\Delta) = \mathbf{f}, \tag{2}$$

where $F_{ij}^{(1)}$ and $F_{ij}^{(2)}$ are the conditions correlated with R_{ij} in G_1 and G_2, respectively. By (1), Δ is admissible and productive for R_{ij}. That is, there exists a configuration for G_1 that begins as follows:*

$$\Delta_1 \ldots \Delta_r \quad \Delta$$

$$A_{i_1} \ldots A_{i_r} \tag{3}$$

If there are no configurations whose start section has the form (3), we have thereby proved that G_1 and G_2 are not equivalent.

Suppose that G_2 also has a configuration whose start section is equal to (3). Then, obviously, by (1) and the fifth property of matrix schemas, the symbol A_j (or a halt instruction if $j = n+1$) will occur in this configuration after the symbol A_i in G_1, while the symbol A_j will most certainly not occur in G_2. This assertion completes the proof of Theorem 8.2.   □

Technical Theorems

The proof that it is possible to construct for any Yanov schema some canonical schema equipotent to it is clearly the main application of the calculus we have constructed. For this purpose, we will require a whole series of additional rules of transformation, which we will refer to below as technical theorems (abbreviated TT). Each technical theorem has the form of a deducible equivalence-preserving relation between certain fragments $\mathscr{F}_1$ and $\mathscr{F}_2$; the statements of the 11 technical theorems are presented in Figure 8.8.

---

* Here A_i is the operator symbol of the operator A_i.

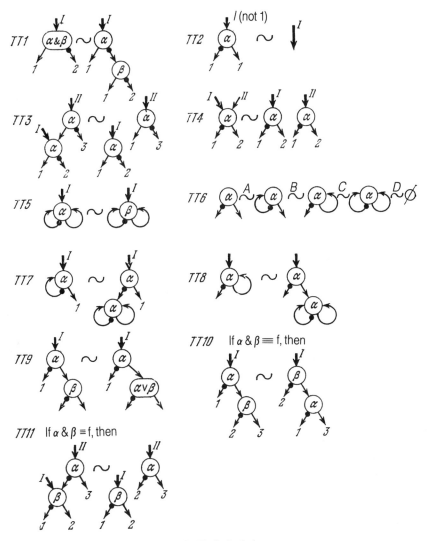

Figure 8.8. Technical theorems.

The proofs of these theorems, presented in Figures 8.9–8.11, have the form of chains of equivalence-preserving relations, beginning and ending with the fragments $\mathscr{F}_1$ and $\mathscr{F}_2$, respectively. Above each equivalence-preserving sign we have written the axiom, rule of inference, or previously proved technical theorem according to which the particular equivalence-preserving relation is valid. A starred reference denotes the application of an axiom or theorem in inverse form, i.e., where the right side of the equivalence-preserving relation forming the assertion is replaced by its left side.

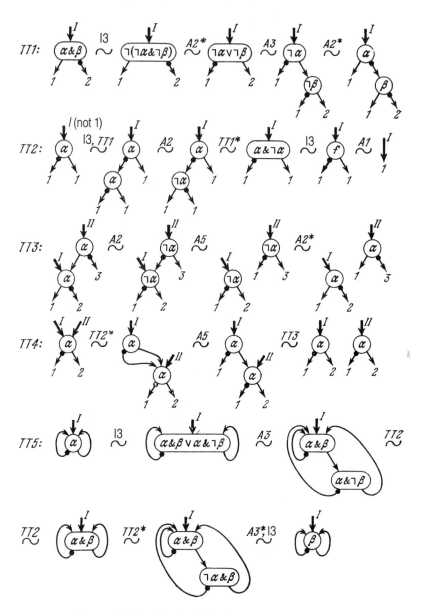

Figure 8.9. Proofs of technical theorems TT1–TT5.

The only proof that might require some additional remarks is that of Theorem TT6-B. Since the fragments which the theorem speaks about does not have any entries, its labeling, which we apply in accordance with Axiom A7, will be invariant relative to any occurrence of this fragment in an arbitrary schema. Therefore, it is permissible to apply rule I1.

Let us now give in advance several topological definitions. A sequence of

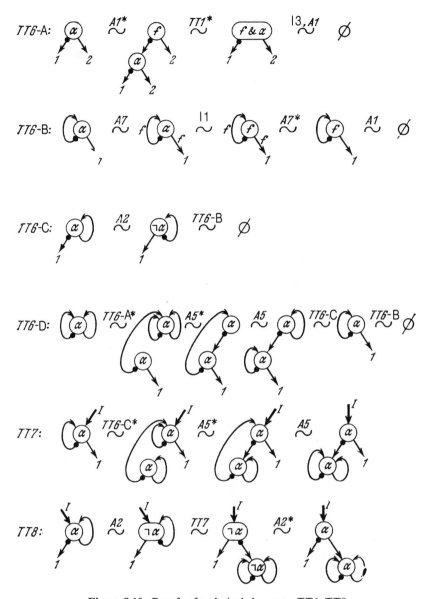

Figure 8.10. Proofs of technical theorems TT6–TT8.

recognizers $R_1, \ldots, R_t$ in a schema is called a *chain* if R_i has R_{i+1} as its successor $(i = 1, \ldots, t-1)$. A chain is said to be *regular* if each recognizer in the chain has a single entry only. A closed chain (R_t connected to R_1) is called a *loop*. A recognizer one of whose exits is simultaneously its entry is called a *semi-loop*.

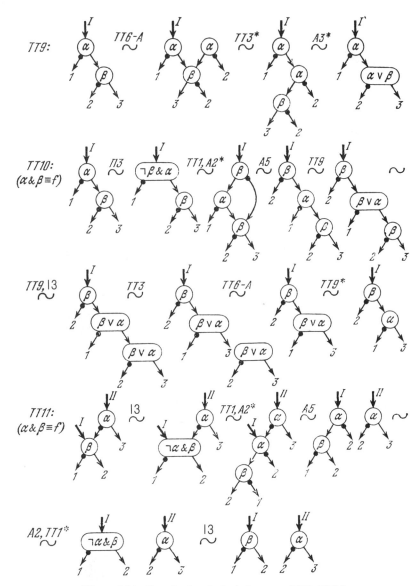

Figure 8.11. Proofs of technical theorems TT9–TT11.

8.4. Completeness of Calculus

The central theme of the current section is the following theorem.

Theorem 8.3. *For any Yanov schema G there exists a canonical schema G_C equipotent to it.*

The proof of the theorem will be given in the form of an algorithm that transforms G into G_C through the successive application of axioms, rules of inference, and the technical theorems considered above.

Creation of Chains

Step 1. Standardization of recognizer which is not identically false is written in principal disjunctive normal form. By Axiom A3, all the recognizers are then expanded in such a way that the condition in each assumes the form of an elementary conjunction (note that any two elementary conjunctions δ_1 and δ_2 are either equal or *orthogonal*, i.e., $\delta_1 \& \delta_2 \equiv \mathbf{f}$).

Step 2. Redirection of plus arrows. Let us define the process of redirecting the plus arrows of each recognizer R of a schema by the following rule:

(a) if R is a suppressor, no arrow is redirected;
(b) if R is a semi-loop, apply Theorem TT7;
(c) if a plus arrow from R leads to a transformer, halt instruction, or suppressor, no arrow is redirected;
(d) if a plus arrow from $R(\alpha)$ leads to the recognizer $R(\beta)$, apply Axiom A5 if $\alpha \equiv \beta$, or apply TT11 if $\alpha \& \beta \equiv \mathbf{f}$.

We will successively apply these rules to each recognizer in the schema. Moreover, if any of the recognizers ends up without any entry as a result of a redirection, it is at once eliminated by Theorem TT6. There are two cases when redirecting a plus arrow:

A. Redirecting an arrow is halted in a natural way in accordance with rules (a) and (c).
B. After a sequence of redirections through recognizers $R_1, \ldots, R_t$ $(t \geq 1)$, the arrow from $R(\alpha)$ again points to the entry R_1, so that $R_1, \ldots, R_t$ form a loop. In this case, we consider $R_1(\beta)$.

If $\beta \equiv \alpha$, the plus arrow from $R_1(\alpha)$ is most certainly directed along a loop. For the time being, we will forget about the plus arrow from $R(\alpha)$ and begin redirecting the plus arrow from $R_1(\alpha)$. Naturally, it will pass through the same sequence of redirections as did the arrow from $R(\alpha)$ initially, i.e., after a series of redirections the plus arrow from $R_1(\alpha)$ will point to the entry of $R_1(\alpha)$. Thus, $R_1(\alpha)$ becomes a semi-loop which, by Theorem TT7, is transformed into a suppressor. The plus arrow from $R(\alpha)$ turns toward this suppressor, which by Axiom A6* forks, after which the original form of $R_1(\alpha)$ is reestablished for the sake of order.

Suppose that $\beta \& \alpha \equiv \mathbf{f}$. Then $\alpha \& \neg \beta \equiv \alpha$ or $\neg \beta \equiv \alpha \vee \gamma$, where γ is some principal normal form. We apply Axiom A2 to $R_1(\beta)$. Obviously, the plus arrow from $R_1(\neg \beta) = R_1(\alpha \vee \beta)$ proceeds along the loop $R_1, \ldots, R_t$. Applying Axiom A3 to $R_1(\alpha \vee \gamma)$ reduces the present case to the preceding one, after which we again restore $R_1(\alpha \vee \gamma)$ to the form $R_1(\beta)$.

Thus, we have suceeded in directing the plus arrow of each recognizer that is not a suppressor either to a suppressor, a transformer, or a halt instruction.

Step 3. Elimination of loops along minus arrows. Obviously, after the second step the recognizers $R_1, \ldots, R_t$ forming these loops will be connected to each other by minus arrows exclusively (provided these are the only loops left in the schema). If $t = 1$, such a semi-loop may be eliminated by Theorem TT8.

Let us first consider a regular loop $R_1, \ldots, R_t$, i.e., a loop without any entries from outside. In this case, we apply Axiom A2 to $R_1(\alpha)$ and, using Axiom A3, expand $\neg \alpha$ into elementary conjunctions.

All the plus arrows that arise subsequently will lead to $R_2(\beta)$. These plus arrows are redirected by the rules of Step 2, and, as a result, it turns out that $R_2(\beta)$ lacks entry arcs and may be eliminated (Theorem TT6). Since $R_1, \ldots, R_t$ is a regular loop, all the recognizers in this loop that follow R_2 may be deleted one after the other in exactly the same way as the recognizers that arise when expanding R_1.

Let us now consider an arbitrary loop $R_1, \ldots, R_t$ having l entries from the outside, and study any one of these entries. If this entry emanates from a recognizer, after Step 2 of the proof it can only be a minus arrow from some recognizer $R(\alpha)$. If the entry emanates from a transformer, by Axiom A1* we may insert $R(\mathbf{f})$ between it and the loop. We apply Axiom A2 to $R(\alpha)$ and, using Axiom A3, expand it into elementary conjunctions. All the plus arrows which thereby arise will be in the same recognizer R_i ($1 \leq i \leq t$) in which the minus arrow from $R(\alpha)$ had previously occurred. By the rules of Step 2, we then redirect all the plus arrows from R_i. Naturally, at the conclusion of the redirection none of these plus arrows will be connected to any of the recognizers $R_1, \ldots, R_t$, and thus the loop $R_1, \ldots, R_t$ now has $(l-1)$ entries. Repeating this process of eliminating entries in the loop l times, we finally obtain a regular loop, which may be eliminated in accordance with the rules of the preceding paragraph.

Step 4. Elimination of multiple entries to a recognizer. Let us consider an arbitrary recognizer R. Since there are no loops in the schema, there is always a chain in it that leads from R either to a transformer, a halt instruction, or a suppressor. The length $h(R) \geq 0$ of the longest such chain is finite; we call $h(R)$ the *height* of R. Obviously, if there is an arc from R to some R', $h(R) > h(R')$. Let us now consider recognizers in the schema with more than one entry and with maximal height h_{max}, and apply Theorem TT4 to it. A schema with maximal height $h_{max} - 1$ is then obtained. Successively carrying out this procedure by multiplying recognizers in accordance with Theorem TT4, we ultimately obtain a schema in which all the recognizers that are not suppressors will have one entry only. Multiple entries to a suppressor (of course, disregarding entries emanating from the suppressors themselves) may be eliminated by means of Axiom A6*.

Final Canonization

Step 5. Standardization of chains. After the fourth step we may already see some similarity between the transformed schema and a canonical schema. Figure 8.12 gives the result of the fourth step for the initial schema of Figure 7.9. All the recognizers of the schema have been grouped into regular chains connected by minus arrows. An entry into a chain emanates either from an entry arrow or a transformer. A minus arrow from the last recognizer leads either to a transformer, a halt instruction, or a suppressor.

We first try to get the number of chains in the schema to equal $n + 1$ exactly, where n is the number of operators. For this purpose, if an entry arrow of the schema or an exit arc of a transformer leads directly to some transformer, we apply Axiom A1* to it, with the plus arrow of the inserted recognizer $R(\mathbf{f})$ leading, for the sake of definiteness, to a halt instruction.

Now let the minus arrow s of the last recognizer of each chain lead to a suppressor. If s leads to a transformer, by Axiom A1* we insert in its place a recognizer $R(\mathbf{f})$ with plus arrow leading to a suppressor. Applying Axiom A2, we replace $R(\mathbf{f})$ by $R(\mathbf{t})$ with a plus arrow leading to an operator and with minus arrow leading to a suppressor, and then, using Axiom A3, expand $R(\mathbf{t})$ into elementary conjunctions.

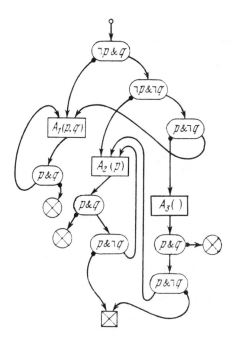

Figure 8.12. Schema prior to standardization of chains.

To ensure orthogonality, we use Theorem TT10, grouping together recognizers along each chain in such a way that all recognizers with the same elementary conjunctions are next to each other, forming a chain g. Applying Theorems TT3 and TT6, we eliminate all the recognizers in each g, other than the first one.

Now let us try to get each of the $n + 1$ chains to contain control transfers to each of the n operators and a halt instruction. For this purpose, we use Axiom A1*, inserting at any point in a chain a recognizer $R(\mathbf{f})$ with plus arrow leading to a missing transformer. Then, using Theorem TT10 we order the recognizers along the chain in accordance with the numbering of the operators, i.e., in the sequence $A_1, \ldots, A_n$, halt instruction, suppressors. As a result of this ordering, recognizers with plus arrows leading to suppressors are all grouped together at the end of the chain. By Theorem TT5, all the suppressors are made entirely identical with condition equal to $\mathbf{f}$, and by Axiom A6 all the suppressors are combined into a single suppressor. As a result, recognizers both of whose exit arcs lead to the same terminus can appear at the ends of the chains. By Theorem TT2, these recognizers are deleted. Finally, by Axiom A3* in each chain we group together all elementary conjunctions leading to the same operator into a single recognizer.

Steps 1–5 result in a matrix schema G_M equivalent to the initial schema G.

Step 6. Ensuring executability. Let us first try to get the conditions of all the recognizers equal to one only on admissible sets. For this purpose, we construct a stationary upper labeling of G_M using Axioms A7–A10 and then apply rule I1 to each recognizer. Since $F \supset \Phi_{R(F)}$ now holds for each $R(F)$, we have achieved the desired result. Applying Axioms A7–A10* eliminates the labeling from the schema.

Next, by Axiom A1 all recognizers of the form $R(\mathbf{f})$ are deleted from the schema. There could then be operators without entries in the schema. We delete these operators using Axiom A4 and then, using Theorem TT6, the chains of recognizers that follow them.

Now let us create a stationary lower labeling by means of Axioms A11–A14 and, by means of rule I2, block all movement in the schema that proceeds via nonproductive tuples. By Axiom A6 we bring together all the new suppressors.

Again we implement a stationary upper labeling and apply rule I1 to each recognizer. We remove recognizers with identically false conditions and any operators without entries that might be present. Since all the nonproductive sequences are now inadmissible as a result of the blocking, after this step all the recognizers will be true only on admissible and productive tuples.

As a result, any isolated fragments of the schema still remaining will be in the form of regular loops consisting of isolated operators. Let us consider any such loop and, using Axiom A1*, replace one of its arcs (A_i, A_j) by a recognizer $R(\mathbf{f})$ with minus arrow leading to A_j and plus arrow leading to a suppressor. By Axiom A2, we replace it by $R(\mathbf{t})$ such that a minus arrow again leads to a suppressor. We create a stationary upper labeling in this fragment, and apply rule I1 to $R(t)$, which causes the fragment to assume the form $R(f)$. Eliminating it by Axiom A1, we find that the exit from A_i leads to a suppressor, and that A_j is left without any entries. By "opening up" the loop in this way, we can delete the entire isolated fragment that begins with A_j by means of Axiom A4.

If necessary, once this procedure is complete we may again standardize chains of recognizers, thereby restoring the matrix form of the schema. Theorem 8.3 is proved.   □

Theorem 8.4 (*Completeness*). *Any two equivalent Yanov schemas are equivalence-preserving.*

Proof. Suppose that

$$G_1 \simeq G_2. \tag{1}$$

By Theorem 8.3, there exist canonical schemas $G_C^{(1)}$ and $G_C^{(2)}$ for G_1 and G_2, respectively, such that

$$G_1 \sim G_C^{(1)}, \qquad G_2 \sim G_C^{(2)}. \tag{2}$$

$$G_C^{(1)} = G_C^{(2)} = G_C, \tag{3}$$

since if we had $G_C^{(1)} \neq G_C^{(2)}$, by Theorems 8.3 and 8.2 we would have arrived at a contradiction with (1). Thus, (2) may be rewritten in the form $G_1 \sim G_C$ and $G_2 \sim G_C$, whence by the symmetricity and transitivity of the equivalence-preserving relation we find that $G_1 \sim G_2$.   □

8.5. A Final Historical Survey

Lyapunov Program Schemas

A.A. Lyapunov was responsible for major contributions to the effort to transform programming into a scientific discipline. In the early 1950s, he was among the first mathematicians to develop a symbolic system for programming, a system which, incidentally, retained the sense of the theoretical assumptions of the field at the time. An important concept introduced by Lyapunov was that of an operator, understood as both a unit of operation and a unit of program structure. As a unit of operation, an operator implements a transformation of the contents of the computer's memory, i.e., it maps one memory state into another; this is also the reason for the name "operator." As a unit of program structure, an operator is denoted in such a way as to show its type, location in the program, and its actual contents (description).

An important property of an operator is that its interpretation as a unit of operation is relative in nature. Two operators A and B executed one after the other implement some joint transformation of a memory state, i.e., they also form some operator C. In order for A and B to be executed in sequence, they must be placed one after the other in the program, thus: AB. Their relation to C then looks like this: $C = AB$, and any information, for example, that A and B could be executed in arbitrary order and yield the same result, may be expressed algebraically, e.g., by the equality $AB = BA$.

Expressed in the language of algebra, we may say that the operators of a program form a semigroup in which there may exist definite relations. The study of operator semigroups has assumed fundamental importance in theoretical programming.

The analogy between two operators AB occurring next to each other and the product of two numbers clarifies such notation as

$$\prod_{i=1}^{n} A(i)BC(i).$$

also introduced by Lyapunov. This expression denotes the n-fold iteration of the operators ABC, while the symbols $A(i)$ and $C(i)$ show that the description of these operators depends on the value of the iteration index i (for example, taking variables in turn from a sequence of locations forming a vector).

To express control transfers as a function of the conditions, Lyapunov introduced the concept of a logical operator. Logical operators serve to map a memory state into two selected values, say 0 and 1 or **true** and **false**, and two paired symbols, the transmitting arrow $\overset{i}{\uparrow}$ and the receiving $\overset{i}{\downarrow}$ arrow, which are both used in a program in the following way (p is the symbol of a logical operator):

$$\ldots \overset{i}{\downarrow} \ldots P \overset{i}{\uparrow} \ldots$$

The notation i (for example, a number) is used to distinguish pairs of corresponding receiving and transmitting arrows. For one value of P, control is transferred to the operator that follows right after the transmitting arrow $\overset{i}{\uparrow}$, while for the other value, control is transferred to the operator right after the receiving arrow $\overset{i}{\downarrow}$.

There are two parts to a program written out in Lyapunov notation. The first part, or *program scheme*, consists of operator symbols and shows both the order in which the operators are arranged in a program and the direction of the control transfers. In the second part, all the operators forming the program are specified. Here is how a program for the solution of 50 quadratic equations of the form $a_i x^2 + b_i x + c_i = 0$ ($i = 1, \ldots, 50$; cf. Example 9 in Section 1.3) would sort of look like in this notation:

Program schema:

$$A_1 \prod_{i-t}^{50} (A_2(i) A_3 A_4 P_5 \overset{1}{\uparrow} A_6 \overset{2}{\uparrow} \overset{1}{\downarrow} A_7 \overset{2}{\downarrow} A_8 A_9(i)) A_{10} \quad \text{HALT}$$

Description:

A_1 input of all coefficients a_i, b_i, and c_i ($i = 1, \ldots, 50$):

A_2 transfer of values of coefficients a_i, b_i, and c_i to locations a, b, and c;

A_3 computation of discriminant: $t_1 = 2a$, $t_2 = 2c$, discr $= b^2 - t_1 t_2$;

A_4 computation of intermediate values for the roots: $p = -b/t_1$, $q = \sqrt{|\text{discr}|}/t_1$;

P_5 test: discr < 0?

A_6 computation of modulus and argument of the complex pair of roots: $t = p^2 + q^2$, root1 $= \sqrt{t}$, root2 $= \arcsin(q/\text{root1})$;

A_7 computation of pair of real roots; root1 $= p + q$, root2 $= p - q$;

A_8 preservation of sign of discriminant: flag $= \text{sign}(\text{discr})$;

A_9 transfer of solutions of pair of roots of ith equation into array;

A_{10} printing of all solutions.

Lyapunov's original article, containing a detailed description of its symbols, was published in the first issue of *Problemy Kibernetiki* (Moscow, Fizmatgiz, 1958; translated in *Problems of Cybernetics*, Vol. 1, 1960, pp. 43–61) under the title, "The Logical Schemas of Programs." The technique, which has been given the name, "Lyapunov's operator method," first saw the light of day, however, much earlier, in 1950, right after Lyapunov had presented a series of lectures at Moscow University with the course description, Principles of Programming. The first algorithmic language and the first compilers of the pre-ALGOL period (1955–60) were designed on the basis of the operator method, as were the first formalisms of theoretical programming. This subject has been discussed in detail in an article by M.R. Shur–Bura and the present author, entitled "The Early Development of Computer Programming in the USSR," published in the journal, *Kibernetika* (No. 5, 1975; Kiev). (The original English text of the paper may be found in *A History of Computing in the Twentieth Century*, N. Mitropolis, J. Howlett, and G.-C. Rota (eds.), New York, Academic Press, 1980.)

Yanov's Logical Algorithm Schemas

In 1953 Lyapunov accepted a young mathematician, Yu.I. Yanov, as a postgraduate student and suggested that he investigate whether logical conditions in program schemas could be transformed in a systematic way.

Yanov completed this investigation in brilliant fashion, producing one of the first classical studies in theoretical programming. He considered a program model that consisted of some common data memory and k logical variables $p_1, \ldots, p_k$. Each of the n statements in a program $A_1, \ldots, A_n$ acts on the entire data memory and may vary some of the logical variables. Each of the logical operators (called *logical conditions* by Lyapunov) has the form of an arbitrary Boolean function of logical variables. In place of the *Lyapunov*

$arrows \uparrow$ and $\downarrow$, Yanov used a left half-bracket $\underset{i}{\llcorner}$ and a right half-bracket $\underset{i}{\lrcorner}$ with the same sense, selecting 0 (false) and 1 (true) as the values of the Boolean functions. A false condition transfers control to a right half-bracket, and a true condition, to the statement that follows the condition. Below is how the three-experts program (Section 7.2) might be written out in the form of such a logical algorithm schema:

$$\underset{14}{\lrcorner} x_1 \underset{1}{\llcorner} A_1(x_1) \underset{1}{\lrcorner} \bar{x}_2 \underset{2}{\llcorner} A_2(x_2) \underset{2}{\lrcorner} x_3 \underset{3}{\llcorner} A_3(x_3) \underset{3}{\lrcorner} x_1 x_2 \vee x_1 \bar{x}_2 x_3 \vee \bar{x}_1 x_2 x_3 \underset{4}{\llcorner}$$

$$x_1 x_2 x_3 \underset{5}{\llcorner} 0 \underset{6}{\llcorner} \underset{4}{\lrcorner} \underset{5}{\lrcorner} \underset{7}{\lrcorner} A_{12}(x_1, x_2) x_1 \equiv x_2 \underset{8}{\llcorner} 0 \underset{9}{\llcorner} \underset{8}{\lrcorner} A_{13}(x_1, x_3) x_1 \equiv x_3 \underset{10}{\llcorner}$$

$$0 \underset{11}{\llcorner} \underset{10}{\lrcorner} A_{23}(x_2, x_3) x_2 \equiv x_3 \underset{7}{\llcorner} \underset{9}{\lrcorner} \underset{11}{\lrcorner} x_1 x_2 \vee x_1 \bar{x}_2 x_3 \vee \bar{x}_1 x_2 x_3 \underset{12}{\llcorner} 0 \underset{13}{\llcorner} \underset{12}{\lrcorner}$$

$$A(x_1, x_2, x_3) 0 \underset{14}{\llcorner} \underset{6}{\lrcorner} \underset{13}{\lrcorner}$$

Yanov did not resort to the concept of an interpretation that would transform a schema into a program, and instead understood the process of implementation of a schema as one of generation of a set of values of the schema (sequence of operators) from a designated ("admissible" in our treatment) sequence of values of logical conditions ("configuration"). The set of values of the schema includes not only finite chains leading to a halt instruction, but also values that terminate in an empty loop, along with infinite sequences of statements. Two schemas are declared to be equivalence-preserving ("formally equivalent" as in Section 7.3) if they have identical sets of configurations. A relation of formal equivalence, which coincides with that presented here (Section 7.3), was also introduced by Yanov and called by him the *weak equivalence-preserving relation*.

Yanov described algorithms for recognizing equivalence for both types of formal equivalence (i.e., the equivalence-preserving and the weak equivalence-preserving relation). The algorithms did not rely on formal transformations nor did they make explicit use of canonical forms. For the case of the equivalence-preserving relation, though not for the weak equivalence-preserving relation, Yanov constructed a complete system of transformations or calculus consisting of 16 axiom schemas and four rules of inference. The property of a tuple to be productive was not axiomatized, as this was not needed in his definition of equivalence, nor was the property of reachability axiomatized, and instead of the upper labeling axiom Yanov provided an exhaustively described rule for "truncating" inadmissible sets. A complete presentation of Yanov's results may be found in his article, "The Logical Schemas of Algorithms" also published in *Problemy Kibernetiki* (No. 1, 1958) together with his teacher's fundamental work (Moscow, Fizmatgiz, 1958, pp. 75–127; translated in *Problems of Cybernetics*, 1960).

Rutledge's Work

The American mathematician John Rutledge made an important contribution to the development of the theory of program schemas, and, in fact, it was Rutledge who was the first to use the expression, "Yanov (program) schemas," in the literature. He gave an independent definition of the functional equivalence of Yanov schemes and proved that the concepts of functional and formal equivalence were equal extensionally. The presentation in Section 7.3 largely follows Rutledge's technique.

Rutledge considered Yanov schemas in abstract form, without relating them to any sort of printed or graphic representation of schemas. Instead of a control flow graph, he used the abstract mapping $f: \mathscr{A} \times P_k \to \mathscr{A} \cup \{\boxed{\times}\}$ ($\mathscr{A}$ is a set of operators and P_k a set of tuples of logical values of length k) which, for an operator $A_i \in \mathscr{A}$ and tuple $\Delta \in P_k$ prints out the operator symbol A_j or the halt instruction $\boxed{\times}$ or is not defined. Rutledge also introduced at this abstract level the concept of a canonical (matrix) form in which all nonequivalent schemas prove to be distinct. In general terms, Rutledge described the process of obtaining "all" equivalent schemas from a canonical form, moreover, he described processes analogous to upper and lower labeling in the form of direct and inverse transitive closures.

Rutledge made one further very important observation. The pair (A_i, Δ) is called a state, the pair $(\boxed{\times}, \Delta)$ a terminal state, and the pair $(\mathbf{o}, \Delta)$ the initial state ($\mathbf{o}$ is the "start" symbol). For any Yanov schema any state (A, Δ) ($A \in A \cup \{\mathbf{o}\}$) specifies a finite (possibly empty) tuple of "directly reachable" states $\{(A', \Delta')\}$, where A' is the only successor of the operator A ($A' \in \mathscr{A} \cup \boxed{\times}$), and where any Δ' forms with Δ an admissible pair for A'.

Let us construct a graph whose vertices are all the possible states in which the arc from vertex state V leads to all vertex states immediately reachable from V. To traverse the arcs of this graph, we move from one state to another. Any path from any initial vertex (infinite, interrupted, or exiting in a terminal state) corresponds to some configuration of the initial schema. Such an abstract device, capable of "passing" from one state into another, is called a *finite nondeterministic automation*.

It turns out that the graph just described, which represents a finite automation, fully characterizes a Yanov schema. In particular, the problem of equivalence of two Yanov schemas reduces to the direct comparison of the finite automata that characterize these schemas.

Automata theory constitutes an independent and rapidly growing field of mathematics. It is related to algebra, the theory of algorithms, and combinatorics. Rutledge's study, which was the first to take note of the relation between automata and program schemas, thereby enlarged the "technical foundations" of theoretical programming, a field which has since developed quite extensively (cf. V.A. Glushkov and A.A. Letichevskii, "Theory of Automata and Programming," *First All-Union Conference on Programming* (plenary reports), Kiev, 1968). Rutledge's paper was published in 1964 in the

Journal of the Association of Computing Machinery, Vol. 11, No. 1, pp. 1–9) under the title, "On Ianov's Program Schemata."

Novosibirsk Research

A paper by the present author, "Yanov Operator [Program] Schemas" introduced the concept of a representation of Yanov schemas in the form of graphs. By means of such a representation, it became possible to simplify the axiomatic structure, simultaneously making it more complete, in particular the concepts of reachability of operators and admissibility of sets were axiomatized by means of the upper labeling process. The presentation in Chapter 8 generally follows this article.

In 1968, while still a student at Novosibirsk University, E.L. Gorel' undertook an investigation of the axiomatic structure of Yanov schemas and proved the independence of the system of axioms presented in the latter article. Her study followed the methodology of proofs of the independence of axioms common in mathematical logic (cf. Section 6.3), though a search for the properties that characterize a particular axiom required considerable ingenuity, and the report by the rather young participant in the *First All-Union Conference on Programming* evoked the well-deserved admiration of specialists (E.L. Gorel', "Logical Independence of the Axiomatic Structure of Yanov Program Schemas," *First All-Union Conference on Programming. A. Questions in Programming Theory*, Kiev, 1968, pp. 3–26). Somewhat later, Gorel' constructed a complete axiom schema for formal equivalence which did not admit configurations of infinite length, but which could contain configurations ending in empty loops ("Yanov Operator Schemata with a Finite Equivalence Relation," *Kibernetika*, No. 5, 1971; translated in *Cybernetics*).

Conclusion

We have included in this brief survey only those studies that directly reduced the theory of Yanov schemas to the form in which it is presented in the present book. At the same time, the theory of Yanov schemas is, on the whole, far broader and has influenced a number of other branches of theoretical programming, indeed the set of problems peculiar to Yanov schemas is still far from exhausted. We propose to conclude this section, and our conversation with the reader, with a discussion of one such open problem for Yanov schemas which has been the focus of considerable efforts, but which has proven to be rather difficult. And we are inserting it in our book without worrying that at some point in the future our presentation might no longer be up-to-date.

In this theory, all the operators in the Yanov schemas are distinct and independent. Recalling the algebraic formulation presented "on the fly," we may say that in this theory Yanov schemas are defined on a free semigroup of operators. However, even in his original paper Yanov had remarked on the importance of program schemes in which there exist particular identity relations between operators and "products" of operators. A rather simple instance of these relations is presented by identity relations of the form $A_i = A_j$, i.e., relations in which by simply glancing at a schema we may "recognize" in it the same operators at different points in the program. Yanov, and following him, Rutledge, proved the solvability of formal equivalence and the fact that formal equivalence and functional equivalence were extensionally equal. Later on, V.E. Itkin constructed a complete system of transformations for schemas with identical operators.

The fact that there are identities between operators means that special defining relations may be introduced into a free semigroup of operators. It is this result that was directly responsible for an attempt to treat Yanov schemas as an arbitrary semigroup of operators. Two problems appeared at once, however. The shifts of the operators, i.e., the list of logical variables that are altered by the operators, bear important information about the operators. It is possible to consider arbitrarily general semigroups only for the "limiting" cases of empty or universal shift distributions. For the latter case, A.A. Letichevskii was able to describe a class of operator semigroups for which there exists an algorithm for recognition of formal equivalence between schemas. Yet another "pearl" is that the solvable cases of formal equivalence we have found are not well-formed, i.e., formal equivalence does not guarantee functional equivalence, and so we cannot apply the results of the theory to actual programs.

Special efforts have been devoted to the study of Yanov schemas with permuting operators, i.e., schemas in which identity relations of the form $AB = BA$ are possible. A number of solvable versions of formal equivalence have also been found, though in the general case the concept of formal equivalence is not well-defined. On the other hand, it has been proved that there are some definitions of equivalence for schemas with permuting operators such that no algorithm for recognition of equivalence may exist on theoretical grounds. Finally, some versions of equivalence rely on certain general types of problems that have long been known, though they have yet to be solved, problems that are of importance in other branches of mathematics as well. At the same time, advances in the construction of universal theorems for Yanov schemas with permuting operators would be not just of great theoretical importance, but would also provide a major impetus for the solution of a number of applied programming problems.

More detailed references and discussion may be found in an article by the present author, entitled "The Present-day Status of the theory of Program Schemas," published in *Problemy Kibernetiki*, No. 27, 1973.

I would hope that I have had some luck in finding readers who now read these final lines not just from the habit of peeking at the very end of a book, but rather only after having read through the book more or less from beginning to end. It is these readers who, I would hope, will understand my intention not just to set forth the solution of two problems of theoretical programming, but to try to also demonstrate the mathematical method at work. The reader may also notice some lack of balance between the two parts of the book. A presentation of the theory of Yanov schemas that would be as detailed as our discussion of Lavrov schemas might very well have made the book far too drawn out and too lengthy, however. And, as we said in the introduction, Parts 1 and 2 pursue different methodological goals.

Finally, those readers who are interested in questions of theoretical programming in their own right might wish to read a monograph by V.E. Kotov, entitled *Introduction to the Theory of Program Schemas* (Vvedenie v Teoriyu Skhem Program) (Novosibirsk, Nauka, 1978), published at around the same time as the present book.

Bibliography

Preface

P1. Rene Baire. Leçons sur la théorie des fonctions discontinues, A. Denjoy, ed. Paris: Collection Borel, 1905, 1930.

P2. Richard Courant and Herbert Robbins. *What is Mathematics?* London: Oxford, 1941.

P3. Aleksandr Ya. Khinchin. *Three Pear's of Number Theory* (translated from Russian). Baltimore: Graylock, 1952.

P4. George Polya. *Mathematics and Plausible Reasoning*. Princeton: Princeton University Press, 1954.

1. A.O. Buda, A.A. Granovskii, and A.P. Ershov. "Implementation of the ALPHA-6 programming system."—In: *Proc. Intern. Conf. Reliability of Software*. 1975. New York: IEEE/ACM, 1975, pp. 382–394.

2. E. Dijkstra. "Notes on structured programming." In: O.J. Dahl, E.W. Dijkstra, and C.A.R. Hoare (eds.). *Structured Programming* (APIC Studies in Data Processing, No. 8), New York: Academic Press, 1972.

3. R.A. Di Paola. *A Survey of Soviet Work in the Theory of Computer Programming*. Rand Memorandum RM-5424-PR, Rand Corp., Santa Monica, Cal., 1967.

4. A.P. Ershov. "On programming of arithmetic operators." *Dokl. Akad. Nauk SSSR* **118**:3 (1958) (translation: *Commun. A.C.M.* **1**:7 (1958), 3–6).

5. A.P.Ershov. *Programming Program for the BESM Computer* (translated by A. Nadler, translation edited by J.P. Cleaves). New York: Pergamon, 1959.

6. A.P. Ershov. "Reduction of the problem of memory allocation in programs to the problem of coloring the vertices of a graph." *Dokl. Akad. Nauk SSSR* **142**:4 (1962) (translation: *Soviet Math. Dokl.* **3**, (1962), 163–165.

7. A.P. Ershov. "Operator schemes on common and distributed memory." *Kibernetika* **4**:4 (1968) (translation: *Cybernetics* **4**:4 (1968), 55–61).

8. A.P. Ershov. "Operator algorithms. III. On Yanov operator schemas." *Problemy Kibernetiki* **20** (1968), 181–200.

9. A.P. Ershov. "Axiomatics of storage allocation." In: *Theory of Language and Methods of Constructing Programming Systems (Teoriya yazykov i metody postroeniya sistem orogrammirovaniya)*. Kiev–Alyushta, Press of the Institute of Cybernetics, Ukranian Academy of Sciences, 1972; see also: *Acta Informatika* **6**:1 (1976), 61–75.

10. A.P. Ershov. "The present-day status of the theory of programming schemas. "*Problemy Kibernetiki* **27** (1973), 87–110.

11. A.P. Ershov and G.I. Kozhukhin. "Estimate of the chromatic number of connected graphs." *Dokl. Akad. Nauk SSSR* **142**:2 (1962) (translation: *Soviet Math. Dokl.* **3** (1962), 50–53).

12. A.P. Ershov and M.R. Shura-Bura. "The early development of programming in the USSR." In: N. Mitropolos, J. Howlett, and G.-G. Rota (eds.). *A History of Computing in the Twentieth Century.* New York: Academic Press 1985, pp. 137–196.

13. A.P. Ershov, L.L. Zmievskaya, R.D. Mishkovich, and L.K. Trokhan. *Storage Economization and Allocation in the ALPHA Computer* (translation: *The ALPHA Automatic Programming System*) (APIC Studies in Data Processing). New York: Academic Press, 1971, 247 pp.

14. V.A. Glushkov and A.A. Letichevskii. "Theory of automatic programming." In: *First All-Union Conference on Programming*, Plenary Reports. Kiev, 1968.

15. E.L. Gorel'. "Logical independence of the axiomatic structure of Yanov operator schemas." In: *First All-Union Conference on Programming. A. Problems of the Theory of Programming.* Kiev, 1968, pp. 3–26.

16. E.L. Gorel'. "Yanov operator schemata with a finite equivalence relation." *Kibernetika* **5** (1971) (translation: *Cybernetics* **7**:5 (1971), 829–830).

17. S.C. Kleene. *Introduction to Metamathematics.* New York: van Nostrand, 1952.

18. V.E. Kotov. *Introduction to the Theory of Program Schemas.* Novosibirsk: Nauka, 1972.

19. I.A. Lavrov and L.L. Maksimova. *Problem Book on Set Theory.* Mathematical Logic, and Theory of Algorithms. Moscow: Nauka, 1975.

20. S.S. Lavrov. "Storage packing in closed program schemas." *Zh. Vvchis. Matem. i Matem. Fiz.* **1**:4 (1961) (translation: "Store economy in closed operator schemes." *USSR Comput. Math. Math. Phys.* **1** (1962), 810–828).

21. A.A. Lyapunov. "The logical schemas of programs." *Problemy Kibernetiki* (1960) (translation: *Problems of Cybernetics* **1** (1958), 48–81).

22. V.V. Martynyk. "Minimal storage allocation." *Zh. Vvchis. Matem. i Matem. Fiz.* **2**:3 (1962) (translation: "On the economical distribution of a store." *USSR Comput. Math. Math. Phys.* **2**:3 (1963), 469—481).

23. E. Mendelson. *Introduction to Mathematical Logic.* Princeton: van Nostrand, 1970.

24. P.S. Novikov. *Elements of Mathematical Logic.* Moscow: Nauka, 1973.

25. J. Rutledge. "On Ianov's program schemata." *J. A.C.M.* **11**:1 (1964), 1–9.

26. B.S. Shtarkman. "Minimization unit for working locations in the PP-2." *Problemy Kibernetiki* **1** (1958) (translation: *Problems of Cybernetics* **1** (1960), 208–213).

27. Yu. I Yanov (Ianov). "On the equivalence and transformation of program schemes." *Dokl. Akad. Nauk SSSR* **113**:1 (1957) (translation: *Commun. A.C.M.* **1**:7 (1958), 8–11).

28. Yu.I. Yanov (Ianov). "The logical schemas of algorithms." *Problemy Kibernetiki*, **1** (1960) (translation: *Problems of Cybernetics* **1**, 1960, 82–140).

29. Revised Report on the Algorithmic Language ALGOL 60. *International Federation for Information Processing*, 1962.

Subject Index